COPYING AND DUPLICATING

TABLE OF CONTENTS

© Eastman Kodak Company 1984
Library of Congress Number 83-82339

Copying and Duplicating

The practices of copying and duplicating permit making:

- Multiple copies of photographs when only a print exists.

- Duplicate black-and-white and color negatives to:

  Make old negatives printable.

  Obtain multiple copies of negatives for use in many places.

  Restore historical negatives that are deteriorating so that the images can be made long lasting.

  Make enlarged negatives so that they can be retouched.

  Make negatives where the image quality is enhanced so that quality prints can be made.

- Duplicate color transparencies so that the original transparency can be stored for long term keeping and the duplicates can be projected or displayed.

- Multiple black-and-white or color negatives or positives for use in many other applications.

The need for copies of photographs, paintings, documents, and other flat reflective originals and transparencies often arises. The commercial, professional, law enforcement, and industrial photographers as well as the advanced amateur, are often called upon to make copies or duplicates of such originals.

Of necessity, we have based the instructions on currently available photographic equipment and on current Kodak films, papers and chemicals. The reader will want to keep up-to-date on changes and improvements that may be made in these materials.

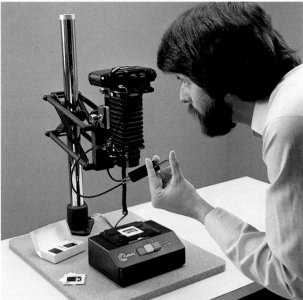

Photo by Tom Beelmann

Typical 35 mm duplicating equipment.

NOTE: A photographer does not have the unrestricted right to copy everything. Copyright laws restrict the right to make copies to the owners of a copyright. The copyright law as it pertains to the photographer is discussed early in the book.

There are fairly simple ways to make copies and duplicates. Other methods, while more complex, have the potential of making copies and duplicates with improved tone reproduction. Some sensitometry is included in this book to provide an understanding of what happens to tones in the photographic process, and why special copy films such as KODAK Professional Copy Films (black-and-white) and KODAK VERICOLOR Internegative Films (color) give improved tone reproduction when used to copy black-and-white and color originals. Densitometry is introduced as a method of controlling the photographic process.

One of the values of copying and duplicating is to retain the images of old photographs that have started to deteriorate. The copying techniques used in restoration are described in this book, but actual restoration is covered in more detail in KODAK Publication No. F-40, *Conservation of Photographs*. These two books are both needed by the museum workers and others involved with the restoration process.

W. Arthur Young

W. Arthur Young, *Co-author and Editor*

Thomas A. Benson

Thomas A. Benson, *Co-author and Assistant Editor*

George T. Eaton

George T. Eaton, *Co-author*

GLOSSARY

Explanation of Terms

In most trades or professions, common words are often used in a sense that may be unfamiliar to many lay people. Words that are synonyms in everyday language may be used to describe different products or procedures. Since these irregularities in the use of words often lead to misunderstandings, some terms peculiar to photographic copying and duplication are listed below with their generally accepted meanings.

Characteristic Curve: The graph that shows the relation between the logarithm of the exposure (in lux seconds) and the resultant density. Also called H&D or D-Log E Curve.

Continuous-tone Original: An original, such as a photograph, with a continuous range of tones from black to white and many in between. May be colored or monochrome.

Copy: This term is interchangeable with "original", used most often in the graphic arts industry. Also the photographic print or transparency that is made to replicate the original.

Copy (To Copy): To make copies by photographing two-dimensional, reflective objects, such as photographs, paintings, maps, printed matter, drawings etc.

Copyboard: An illuminated board, or easel to which the original is attached while being photographed. Copyboards are usually front lighted but transparent copyboards may also be lighted from behind for photographing transparent originals.

Copy Negative: The negative obtained by copying or photographing, two-dimensional designs, pictures or documents which are on an opaque base such as paper or canvas.

Copy Print: A positive print made from a copy negative, or by copying on a direct positive (reversal) paper.

Copyright: An exclusive right or privilege to publish, reproduce (copy), and distribute one's literary, dramatic, musical and artistic works, incuding photographs.

Densitometry: The practice of measuring photographic densities.

Diapositive: Same as an intermediate positive. A film positive made as the intermediate in the production of a duplicate of a film or glass plate negative.

Direct Positive: A positive photographic image that is made on reversal film or paper without the use of an intermediate copy negative. A reversal or direct chemical process may be used.

Document Copying: Photocopying of documents, line drawings, and text materials by electrophotographic or photographic means.

Dupe: Abbreviation for duplicate.

Duplicate: A photographic reproduction of a transparent original, usually a film negative or transparency.

Facsimile: An exact reproduction or copy of the original as far as this is possible within the limitations of the photographic process.

Halftone: A photomechanical reproduction of a continuous-tone original. The continuous tones of the original are represented by tiny dots of pure black and white (or color) called halftone dots.

Intermediate Positive: A film positive made as the intermediate step in the production of a duplicate of a film or glass plate negative—also called a diapositive or interpositive.

Internegative: A negative made from a transparency as the intermediate step in the production of duplicate transparency or a copy print.

Line Original: An original consisting of "lines" without any intermediate tones. The lines may be alpha-numeric (letters or numbers), broad areas of solid tones, colored, black or white on an appropriate background.

Lith: Abbreviation of the word "lithographic." Usually used to describe a film designed for reproducing line or halftone originals, or a developer for producing extremely high contrast.

Magnification: The ratio obtained by dividing image size by the object size. When the ratio is less than one, it is often called the reduction ratio. The ratio multipled by 100 is the percentage size.

Microfilm: Miniature copies on film of documents, checks, newspapers and such. Retrieval is simplified and storage space much reduced. Particularly suitable for keeping historical material and records, especially when the sheer bulk of paper makes it impossible to store the originals. The microfilm images are commonly 1/5 to 1/50 of the original size.

Original: The design, picture or document to be copied or duplicated.

Parallelism: The spatial relationship between the film plane and the copyboard. To reproduce a rectangular original as a rectangle it is essential that the film plane of the camera and the copyboard plane be equidistant at all points.

1

Photocopy: Generally means a reproduction of a document, or drawing made by a photographic or allied process.

Picture: As used in this book, a photograph or artwork representaiton.

Preservation: Copying or duplicating to preserve the image. The original is not changed.

Radiograph: An image made on a photographic film or plate by exposure to x-rays and from light fluoresced by special screens upon exposure to x-rays. The resultant image is negative. More commonly known as an x-ray.

Reciprocity: The reciprocity law states that exposure equals the illuminance on the emulsion surface times the exposure time. Reciprocity law failure occurs because emulsions change sensitivity with the length of the exposure time or with high or low values of illuminance.

Reflection Copy: Photographic prints, documents, line copy, paintings, and two-dimensional art which are copied by using light that is aimed at their surfaces and which reflects off of the surfaces to the camera.

Registration: The exact physical alignment of two photographic images, often accomplished by the use of pin register systems.

Reproduction: A duplicate of a photograph or similar original.

Restoration: In photography this term usually means to restore a torn, faded, stained or defaced photograph by a combination of copying, retouching or other handwork, on a copy negative and/or reproduction print. Technically, however, restoration means treating the original chemically or by some other means, to restore it, or to improve its condition.

Sensitometry: The science that involves the measurement of the response of photographic emulsions upon exposure to light.

Slide: A transparency made especially for projection. Today most slides are in color and the most common size is 24 x 36 mm contained in 2 x 2-inch mounts. Originally an abbreviation of "lantern slide."

Sub-surface Illumination: Location of a light source behind the copyboard or easel to provide transmitted light for copying transparent originals. The original is said to be trans-illuminated.

Transparency: A black-and-white or color positive photographic image on a film base which is viewed by transmitted light or projected.

Graphic Representation of Typical Photographic Tone Reproduction

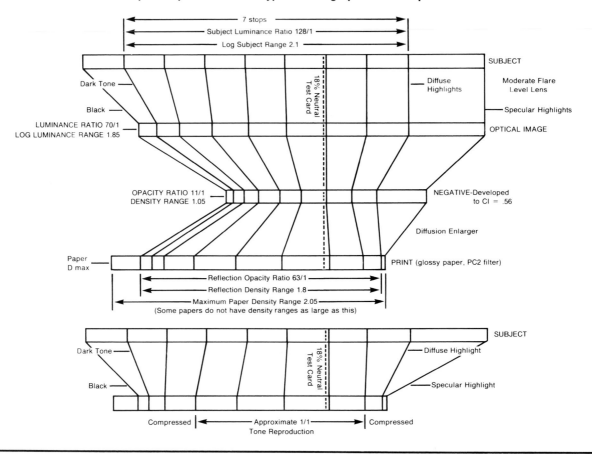

OVERVIEW OF COPYING & DUPLICATING PROCEDURES

Copying a Photograph

In a simple sense, copying is taking a photograph of a picture. However, if a normal film is used to make the copy negative and a regular process is given the film, the copy print made from the negative will show evidence that it is a copy print—and often may not give satisfactory tone rendition of the original photograph.

This is primarily the result of uneven compression and expansion of tones by photographic film and paper throughout the tonal scale.

Photographic Tone Reproduction

Photographic films generally compress the dark tones—that is, they show less visual distinction between dark tones than you could see in the original subject. Photographic papers compress both the dark tones and the light tones. Therefore, in a photographic print of an original subject, both the dark tones and the light tones are compressed.

The diagram on page 2 shows how the dark and light tones are compressed. It also shows that the middle tones have been expanded slightly. This type of tone reproduction of an original subject is normal. We are used to seeing this type of tone reproduction in photographs and we accept it as a reasonably accurate rendition of the original.

When we copy a photograph, we start with this type of unevenly compressed tonal rendition. If we take a normal photograph of the original photograph, the dark tones and the light tones get compressed again. When we look at the copy print, we see dark tones and highlights that have been compressed twice. The diagram on page 4 shows the tone reproduction of a copy print done by normal photographic means. Note that the middle tones have been expanded even more.

To the right, we reproduced an original print, a print from a copy negative on a camera film, and a print from a copy negative on KODAK Professional Copy Film. The compression of the highlight tones in the camera-film copy shows up especially in the lighter sky areas.

It is primarily to improve on this type of tone rendition that special copy films are made, and special techniques are used. The last photograph in the series shows a copy print made on a special copy film which gives an improved tone reproduction over that of the normal film.

Photo by Peter Gales

Reproduction of a print made from the original black-and-white negative. Most of the black-and-white reproductions in this book are printed by the two-black duotone process to maintain as much of the original print quality in the halftone reproductions as possible.

Copy by Phil Davola

Reproduction of a copy of the upper print made from a copy negative photographed on KODAK SUPER-XX Pan Film, a film made for regular camera use. It was developed in KODAK HC-110 Developer, which gives it a characteristic curve with an upsweep, making it suitable for copying. Some regular camera films cause a loss in copy highlight tone separation.

Copy by Phil Davola

Reproduction of a copy of the above print made from a copy negative photographed on KODAK Professional Copy Film. When properly done, the tone-reproduction quality of copy prints made this way can approach that of the original print.

Basic Requirements of a Copy Film

To make the best possible copy photograph, some method of reducing the compression in the highlights is required, and, at the same time, a method of reducing the mid-tone expansion is usually needed.

There are two photographic materials used in making a copy, the negative film and the paper. The tone reproduction characteristics of the paper are relatively fixed. The paper must go from white to black—all the way through the tonal range. Because of this requirement, there is no way to eliminate the shoulder and toe from a paper characteristic curve. It is the paper curve toe that compresses the highlight tones, and the shoulder that compresses the shadow tones. Since the paper cannot be used to improve the tone reproduction of the copy, it is the film that must do the job.

Kodak has designed a black-and-white film especially for copying that has an unusual characteristic curve. The portion of the curve used to record the dark and middle tones has a normal slope. The portion of the curve used to photograph the light tones has an upward sweep with a higher degree of contrast. A copy negative, properly exposed, records the dark and middle tones with normal contrast, but records the light tones with higher contrast. This expands the light tones that were previously compressed by the original film and paper. Kodak color copy films are available with the same characteristics. An ideal copy film would also expand the shadow tones, but this is not possible, photographically.

Graphic Representation of Copy Tone Reproductions

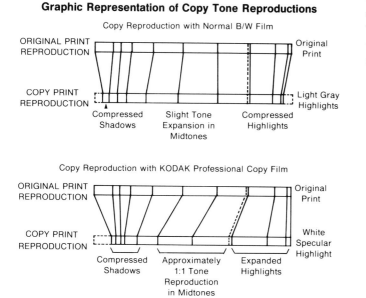

The upper drawing shows the severe highlight tone compression in a copy print made using a regular camera film as a copy film. The lower drawing shows the improvement in highlight tone reproduction achieved by using KODAK Professional Copy Film.

Special Copy Films that Improve Tone Reproduction

KODAK Professional Copy Film 4125 (ESTAR Thick Base) is the black-and-white sheet film especially designed for copying, while KODAK Ortho Copy Film 5125 is a long roll (70 mm, unperforated) film with a similar emulsion. The curves of this film on the next page show how the basic contrast of the dark and midtone range is slightly adjustable by changing the amount of development. In practice, once a satisfactory developing time has been determined, this time is used for each copy negative, while the negative contrast is controlled by increasing or decreasing the amount of exposure.

The lower left drawing shows two exposures on a copy film characteristic curve. The log exposure range is the same for each exposure. The upper exposure is 1 stop more than the first.

The density range of the negative resulting from the 14-second exposure is 1.05, while the 28 second negative has a density range of 1.25. Note that in the second exposure, much more of the lighter portion of the original has been exposed on the upsweep part of the curve—hence the medium-light tones have been expanded in addition to the normal expansion of the light tones. The 14 second exposure is the better one.

There are three Kodak color films that have similar characteristic curves to that of KODAK Professional Copy Film. The first two are KODAK VERICOLOR Internegative Film 4112 (ESTAR Thick Base) in sheet form, and KODAK VERICOLOR Internegative Film 6011 (Process C-41) in long-roll form. The third is a new film, KODAK VERICOLOR Internegative Film Type 2, 4114, made especially for copying transparencies. The illustrations show the characteristic curve of these films. The particular uses of these films are discussed later in this publication.

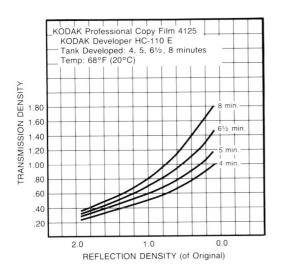

Characteristic curves of KODAK Professional Copy Film developed for different times. Five minutes is the recommended time for tank development in KODAK HC-110 Developer, Dilution E.

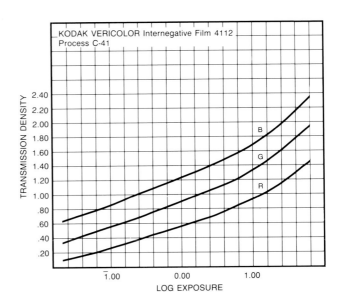

Characteristic curves of KODAK VERICOLOR Internegative Film 4112, showing the upsweep in the curves designed to enhance highlight tone separation when copying either color prints or transparencies. Negative density range (density difference) is controlled entirely by exposure.

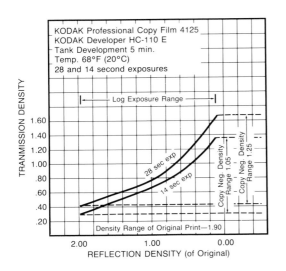

Characteristic curves of KODAK Professional Copy Film showing how contrast as measured by negative density range is controlled primarily by changing the copy exposure.

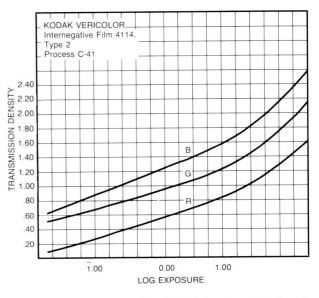

KODAK VERICOLOR Internegative Film 4114 is designed specifically for making color negatives from transparencies. The color sensitivity of each of the layers is designed to permit the interchangeable copying of transparencies made on KODACHROME and EKTACHROME Films.

COPYRIGHT AND RESTRICTIONS

Before you reproduce (copy or duplicate) a photograph or a transparency, it is advisable to determine who owns the rights to reproduce that photograph or transparency. For instance, a person who has purchased photographs or transparencies owns them, but the right to reproduce such photographs or transparencies is often retained by the original photographer.

Copyright

The Copyright Act of 1976 is a federal law enacted by Congress providing a form of monopoly for a limited time to encourage the production and publication of literary, dramatic, musical and artistic works. The Copyright Act of 1976 grants the owner of a copyright certain exclusive rights, including the right to publish and reproduce the copyrighted work and the right to distribute copies to the public by sale, rental, lease or lending. Certain works, for example, those for which the statutory monopoly period has expired and those which have been "published" (a term defined by statute) without a copyright notice are in the public domain and may be freely copied. However, to avoid potential copyright problems, it is always safer, as well as more courteous, to get written permission from the owner or the photographer, as the case may be, before copying a photograph or transparency.

Restrictions

Official Documents

Federal law forbids the copying of United States and foreign government obligations, such as paper currency (paper money), treasury notes, bonds, bills, checks, drafts and similar papers. Also, it is unlawful to copy postage stamps, internal revenue stamps—see below for philatelic exceptions—passports, drivers' licenses, immigration papers, U.S. government indentification cards, badges, or insignia, as well as military records or documents labeled "secret," "top secret," "confidential," or "restricted."

Exceptions to Copying Regulations

U.S. postage stamps and coins generally may be copied for identification or publication purposes. U.S. stamps, however, have the following copying restrictions: the reproductions must be in black-and-white only, and less than $3/4$ or more than $1^1/_2$ times the size of the stamp.

Cautionary Note

The foregoing brief commentary of conditions relating to photographic copying is for informational purposes only. It is not intended to be legal advice and Eastman Kodak Company assumes no responsiblity for actions based on the above statements. If you are unfamiliar with the law pertaining to copyright or have any doubt about the legality of copying anything, obtain legal advice before proceeding.

For general information regarding federal copyright law and procedures, write to the following address:

Registrar of Copyrights
Library of Congress
Washington, D. C. 20559

EQUIPMENT

Photographic copying requires the use of equipment that is basically similar to the equipment required for duplicating. Therefore, equipment will be considered first, and then its use in copying and in duplicating will be discussed.

Basic Requirements

A camera of some kind, a copyboard or easel, and light for illumination of the original and exposure of the photographic film or paper are the essential elements of any copying and duplicating equipment. There are at least four typical arrangements of these elements shown in the illustration.

Probably the most important requirements for any equipment include the following.

(1) **The camera must be mounted so that the lens axis is in line and perpendicular with the center of the copyboard.** This will help having the image centered in the image plane of the camera. Copyboards often have areas outlined with markings of some kind to aid in centering an original on the copyboard. This can be readily accomplished by drawing rectangles the size of the standard photographic paper sizes—4 x 5, 5 x 7, 8 x 10, 10 x 12, 14 x 17 inches—having the center of the rectangles coinciding with the center of the copyboard and therefore, the lens axis.

(2) **The copyboard and film plane must be parallel to each other to avoid image distortion.** This can be accomplished by using a spirit level on both the vertical and horizontal sides of the copyboard and the camera. Some commercial equipment has spirit levels mounted in both directions.

This procedure may not be considered precise enough in certain situations. A better technique is to have an accurate grid pattern on the focusing screen of the camera and then adjust either the copyboard or the camera, or both, until the grid pattern shows no distortion—vertically or horizontally.

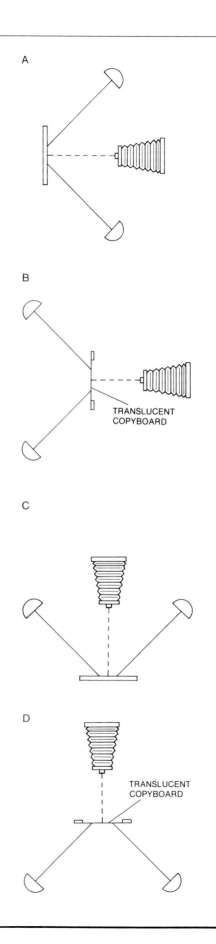

A. Top view of a horizontal arrangement for copying prints.   B. Top view of a horizontal arrangement for copying transparencies.   C. Front view of a vertical arrangement for copying prints.   D. Front view of a vertical arrangement for copying transparencies and slides.

Once the image of the copyboard center is centered on the ground glass, the perpendicularity of the copyboard to the lens axis can be checked with a flat mirror. A mirror is placed on the center of the copyboard, and the image of the camera lens will then be seen on the ground glass. If the image of the lens reflection is not centered on the ground glass, the copyboard is not perpendicular with the axis. Adjust the copyboard until the image of the lens is centered on the ground glass; it is then perpendicular to the axis.

A much refined version of these techniques is used when large master drawings are reduced 100X or more to produce master negatives for use in reticle or microcircuitry production. In some of these applications a travelling microscope mounted on a camera back is used to ensure parallelism and dimensional accuracy within 1/10,000 of an inch or better.

(3) **The lights used to illuminate the copyboard should be mounted to permit adjustment both vertically and horizontally.** (See Copyboard Illumination on page 27)

(4) **A ground-glass focusing screen is recommended.** Some cameras are equipped with such a screen on the back of the camera, for example, view cameras. Many cameras do not have them but can be so equipped by opening the back of the camera and placing a piece of ground-glass of the correct size in the film plane. Reflex cameras have screens for viewing and focusing.

These four requirements provide the basis upon which practically all copying and duplicating equipment is designed and anything else is a matter of refinement, for example, greater precision, multiple lamps for illumination, vacuum frames to hold original copy in place, camera backs that accept long rolls of film, bellows and extension tubes to permit focusing for close-up pictures, filter-pack holders, automatic exposure control, and others.

The range of equipment varies from simple adaptations of amateur and view cameras to elaborate graphic arts cameras called process cameras, to precise instruments for microfilming in quantity and for the production of printed circuit boards. The primary consideration here is with equipment for copying and duplicating flat originals where the end product is a photographic reproduction.

The best choice of equipment for any particular reproduction work is difficult to make without knowledge of all the circumstances, but the following considerations form a broad basis for making the choice.

(1) If a few copy negatives are needed only occasionally, a home-made stand, such as that illustrated by the drawing on the top of page 9, together with a view camera will serve the purpose.

(2) If the maximum size of the originals and the negatives required from them are both large, the installation will occupy a considerable amount of floor space. Process, or graphic arts, camera-and-copyboard units are suitable for such applications. See illustrations on page 15.

(3) If space is limited, consider a vertical copy camera, rather than the horizontal type.

(4) High-volume copying of small originals is routine work in photofinishing plants. Speed of operation is a main feature of equipment for this purpose. Consider exposing and processing material in long rolls for speed in handling.

(5) If the copying work is varied, look for the versatility of the equipment.

Simple Equipment

When expensive commercial equipment is not justified or available there are setups that can be built or assembled. An original can be attached to a wall or other solid flat vertical surface and a camera mounted on a tripod adjusted to have the center of the original coincide with the lens axis. Use a spirit level and careful measurement to be sure the original and film plane of the camera are parallel to avoid image distortion. Two or four studio floodlamps can be used for illumination.

A more permanent horizontal setup can be built having the copyboard, the camera and the lights mounted on a common base. The camera can be mounted on a box of sufficient height that the center of the copyboard coincides with the lens axis and in such a manner that the box moves backwards and forwards between two rails at right angles to the copyboard. (See illustration on page 9.)

A horizontal slide-copying device can be made consisting of a single-lens reflex camera, bellows focusing attachment, homemade bracket, diffuser, electronic flash unit, and rubber bands to hold the original slide and filters in position. The diffuser, required to scatter the light, can be translucent glass or translucent acrylic plastic such as DuPont Lucite® Type 4447 or 2447 Plexiglas. The horizontal track supporting the equipment parts is made extra long so that the unit can also be used for copying type, artwork, photos and other flat-plane subjects that are larger than 35 mm slides. (See illustrations.)

An all-purpose copystand as illustrated can be used for a small setup—one that is dependable and easy to operate.

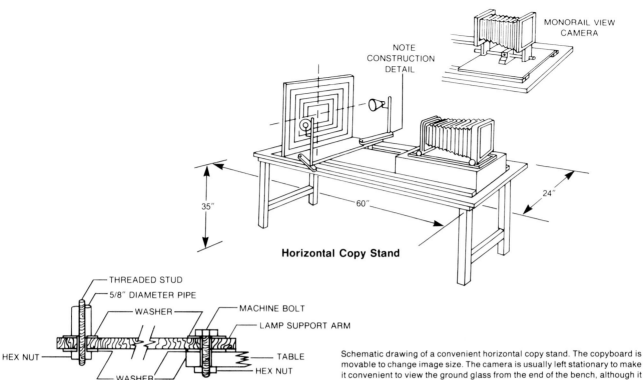

MONORAIL VIEW CAMERA

NOTE CONSTRUCTION DETAIL

35"

60"

24"

Horizontal Copy Stand

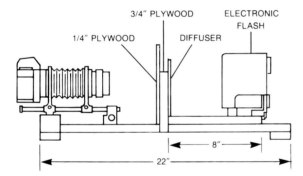

THREADED STUD

5/8" DIAMETER PIPE

WASHER

MACHINE BOLT

LAMP SUPPORT ARM

HEX NUT

TABLE

WASHER

HEX NUT

Adjustable Light Support Arm

Schematic drawing of a convenient horizontal copy stand. The copyboard is movable to change image size. The camera is usually left stationary to make it convenient to view the ground glass from the end of the bench, although it can also be moved. Dimensions are flexible to fit particular needs.

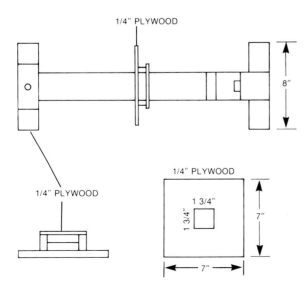

3/4" PLYWOOD

ELECTRONIC FLASH

1/4" PLYWOOD

DIFFUSER

8"

22"

1/4" PLYWOOD

8"

1/4" PLYWOOD

1/4" PLYWOOD

1 3/4"

1 3/4"

7"

7"

Horizontal Slide-Copy Stand

With a minimum of hardware, a few plywood scraps, and a diffusing sheet, you can construct your own slide-copying device. Purchase a 1-inch bolt (1/4 x 20), nut, and washer at your local hardware store to secure your camera/bellows/lens to the frame. For a diffuser you can use a piece of translucent glass or plastic, cut to fit. To cut out the square opening in the vertical easel, use a saber or keyhole saw. Adjust all of your vertical measurements to match the heights of your own bellows attachment and electronic flash.

The horizontal track supporting the slide/diffuser/flash assembly is extra long so that the unit can also be used for copying type, artwork, photos, and other flat-plane subjects that are larger than 35 mm slides.

Commercially Available Equipment

Photographic Enlargers: Some enlargers are designed so they can be converted for use as a camera in vertical copying and duplicating. This entails removing the lamphouse and substituting a camera back for the negative carrier. Lights to illuminate the original are attached either to the column or the baseboard.

This approach could be useful in very small photolabs where equipment must be reduced to a minimum or for amateurs who do their own laboratory work. Of course, such an enlarger could also be converted to a permanent setup.

35 mm Equipment and Accessories

Many copying and duplication jobs can be accomplished using a 35 mm camera. Copystands for use with those cameras are available from camera stores and photographic equipment suppliers. These stands usually consist of an upright column mounted on a baseboard.

The camera is attached to the column by means of its tripod socket and an arm-and-collar assembly, which slides up and down the column. Two or four lights to illuminate the original are also mounted on the column at a suitable distance from the baseboard. Some of the these stands can be disassembled and carried in a case when copying must be done on location, as might be necessary when working in a museum or an art gallery.

The 35 mm single-lens reflex is by far the most suitable camera for use on a copystand, because the image is clearly visible for focusing and centering the original on the film. Another advantage of the SLR is the ability to preview the depth of field at smaller apertures. Some SLRs have a simple attachment available that permits reversing the lens position for better resolution when very close focusing is required. It should be noted that the viewfinders in most 35 mm SLR cameras show only about 90% of the field covered by the camera lens on the film.

Special finder attachments are made for some 35 mm single-lens reflex cameras that permit viewing at right angles to the camera. These can be especially useful in some copying situations. Reflex finders also prevent light coming through the finder eye lens from reaching the photocells, thus helping to avoid false exposure measurements. This is illustrated on page 12.

It is very difficult to frame the image exactly on the film with range finder cameras because the camera lens and the viewfinder lens do not have the same field of view in close-up work. This condition is called parallax. However, the image can be focused and centered by opening the camera back and placing a small piece of fine ground glass or

A small copy stand is useful with 35 mm cameras for making copies from a limited size of originals. With the addition of an illuminator, the copy stand can be used to make transparency duplicates and copy negatives of transparencies.

A ground glass or piece of sheet acetate can be used for framing the image of copies with a 35 mm camera that does not have a reflex finder.

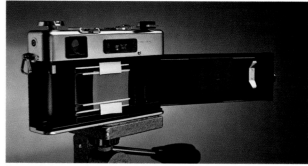

A focusing bellows can be used with single-lens reflex cameras for extending the lens-to-film distance for close focusing. Extension tubes are also shown.

A great range of cropping flexibility is provided by this more sophisticated bellows duplicating equipment.

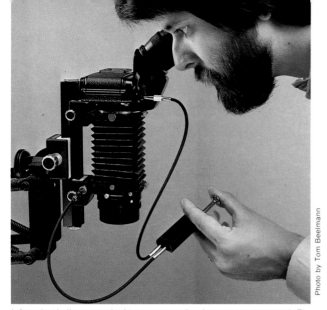

A focusing bellows attached to a camera in place on a copy stand. The original can usually be magnified several times on the film at maximum bellows extension.

A simple duplicator for copying slides mounts directly onto many 35-mm cameras. This device has an incorporated zoom lens for copying the slide image, and a built-in light diffuser. A small electronic flash unit can be used for illumination. The distance between the flash and the diffuser adjusts the exposure.

Four methods of close-focusing for copying and duplicating are represented by these lenses. On the left is a non-focusing lens for use with a bellows attachment. Top center is a macro lens which has extra long focusing threads. Macro lenses usually give up to a magnification of 0.5X (half-size) to 1.0X (full size) on the film without other attachments. On the right is a lens with a lens reversing ring. Regular camera lenses usually give sharper images at extreme close distances when placed "backwards" on the camera. At the bottom are close-up lenses which are attached to the camera lens like filters for close focusing.

matte acetate in the position normally occupied by the film. The ground side of the glass must face the camera lens in order to be located in the focal plane. Then, the shutter is set for a time exposure (T) or bulb (B) and triggered so that it remains open. To make the image more visible, darken the room or use a dark focusing cloth.

Accessories for 35 mm Cameras: The standard focal length of a lens for a 35 mm camera is about 50 mm. Usually these lenses have a minimum focusing distance of about 2 feet. As a practical matter, this means that the largest image of an 8 x 10-inch original, for example, is just about large enough to fill the negative.

For shorter distances than the 2 feet normally available, focusing cannot be done by the camera focusing mechanism. The camera back, the whole camera or the subject must be moved, and the distance between the lens and the film increased by use of a bellows unit or extension tube.

To make a same size copy (1:1 magnification) requires the image and the object each to be two focal lengths from the lens. A 2X magnification would have the size of the image in the film plane twice as large as the original object.

With a 35 mm camera equipped with a 50 mm lens the distance between the lens and film plane must be extended to achieve 1:1 or greater magnification. As indicated before, this can be done by using either a bellows-focusing attachment or a set of extension rings between the lens and the camera. (See illustration on page 10.) Most bellows devices will extend a normal lens to a distance great enough to produce focused images at a 3X or larger magnification. Both bellows focusing attachments and extension tubes reduce the amount of light reaching the film in proportion to their length and it is usually necessary to correct the exposure according to the instructions that come with the equipment. The effect on the amount of exposure is discussed on page 34. At these distances, the lens should be reversed to obtain better sharpness.

In the case of 35 mm slide duplication, specially designed units are commercially available. (See illustration.) Both types of close-focusing devices provide 1:1 magnification when used with an SLR camera equipped with a normal 50-55 mm lens. The illustration shows the adaptation of both the bellows-focusing and the extension tube accessories. These commercial units also have a built-in light source, filter drawer and a light diffuser.

In any case the light source should be consistent in color balance. Electronic flash, which is daylight balanced, is consistent and also allows the use of a small f-number for greater depth of field, although some correction may be needed with automatic flash at close distances. Photoflood lamps, balanced for Type A film, can be used, but require longer exposures and may result in poor exposures due to reciprocity failure of films not designed for long exposure times (see glossary for definition of reciprocity, and see reciprocity curves on Data Sheets).

Macro lenses, which have long focusing threads, permit close-focusing. When used alone the largest image produced is from about 1/2 life size to life

Photo by Tom Beelmann

A slide duplicating illuminator for use on a vertical copy stand has a modeling light for focusing and cropping, and an electronic flash to provide light for the exposure.

Photo by Tom Beelmann

A waist-level finder attachment mounted on a single-lens-reflex camera permits easier framing and focusing when doing vertical copying or duplicating.

Photo by Tom Beelmann

A magnifying, angled viewfinder gives an enlarged view of the image at an easy-to-use viewing angle.

Photo by Tom Beelmann

A rotating viewfinder is yet another type of accessory that makes copying and duplicating easier.

size, depending on the particular lens. When used in combination with extension tubes or bellows the range can be extended to reproduce subjects two, three or more times larger than life size on the film. Macro lenses have excellent optical performance at close distances, and are easy to use. They are available in normal to moderate-telephoto focal lengths and focus smoothly from infinity to just a few inches in front of the lens. There are also some zoom macro lenses available but the sharpness of copy negatives may not be as good as with single focal length lenses, and pin cushion distortion may occur. Most macro lenses are made for 35 mm cameras and a few for cameras that use 120 film. Process lenses and special copy lenses are also made for sheet-film cameras.

Another means of producing magnification is the use of supplementary close-up lenses which are placed in front of the regular lenses. They commonly come in sets of three rated +1, +2, and +3 diopter, but are also available in +5, +6 and +10 diopter powers; the greater the number, the greater is the magnifying power and the closer to the subject the camera must be placed. Two or more supplementary lenses can be used together to increase the power. The power is additive: +1, +2 = +3. The higher power lens should be placed closest to the camera lens for least effect on sharpness. Sharpness may be a problem and the use of small apertures is almost always required to obtain adequate definition. Supplementary lenses are not usually recommended for critical work because their use degrades the sharpness quality of the images, and tests should be made to determine if the image is sufficiently sharp for its intended purpose.

Many 35 mm cameras have interchangeable viewfinders and/or focusing screens. Some auxillary viewfinders that are useful in copying are illustrated.

The finder shown in the second picture is used with the pentaprism removed. It is a right angle viewfinder that has a flip-up magnifier. This is useful when the camera is used on a copy stand at eye level. Because a pentaprism is not used the image is reversed from left to right. This is the simplest and least expensive type of auxillary viewfinder.

The other two viewfinders must be mounted in a special pentaprism that is made for certain auxiliary viewfinders. The third illustration shows a magnification viewfinder. It enlarges the image of the frame and aids in critical focusing. The last type of viewfinder can be rotated to either the right angle position or to the normal position. Because it is used with a pentaprism the image is oriented correctly from left to right.

Interchangeable focusing screens may be helpful for improving ease of focusing with certain types of screens. Other screens are available with ruled lines that are useful when trying to square up a copy image in the camera.

Vertical Camera Equipment

Vertical Copy Stands: In addition to the small copy stands described earlier for use with 35 mm cameras, more elaborate stands can be obtained that can be used with almost any size camera including 35 mm. Long-roll backs are available for many 35 mm, 2 1/4 x 2 1/4 professional copy cameras. Although conventional picture-taking cameras are not necessarily the best for copying and duplicating, most can be of good service when it is not financially feasible or desirable to buy a special copy camera. The nature and volume of the copying work dictates the best kind of equipment to use. Cameras which permit ground glass focusing make framing and focusing much faster and more accurate.

Vertical Copy Cameras for General Work: If your copying and duplicating work is considerable in volume and if it is of a general nature, including originals up to 20 x 24 inches, consider a vertical copy camera similar to the ones shown here and on page 14.

Vertical cameras are generally easy to operate, but should be equipped with a reflex hood or other device to facilitate sizing and correct placement of the image on the film. Interchangeable camera backs allow various sizes of film to be used, and roll-film backs enable quantities of copy negatives to be processed continuously.

A vertical camera occupies less floor space than a horizontal model with the same capability. Some vertical cameras are constructed with high vertical columns and often require more head room than most other units.

Specialized Equipment for Microfilming: Microfilming is essentially a photographic document copying operation to produce reduced images on film of documents of all kinds and sizes. The objectives of microfilming include: (1) the reduction of storage space; (2) a more readily accessible file; (3) security of valuable records often by storage of a duplicate in a safe and environmentally controlled location; and (4) use of the negative to produce a smaller size print of the original for field use as with large engineering drawings.

Microfilming bound books and oversize documents require a sophisticated flat-bed machine or vertical copier such as the RECORDAK MICRO-FILE Machine, Model MRD-2. This unit takes either 16 mm or 35 mm film, has automatic film advance and easy manual focusing. Originals up to 26 x 36 inches can be photographed. The reduction range is 5:1 to 21:1. A column extension kit increases reduction ratio to 27:1. (See illustration.)

A complete copy stand with lights for 35-mm vertical copying. Fairly large originals can be copied with this equipment.

Larger copy stands are required for vertical copying with view cameras. Note the accessory finder that permits easy magnified viewing of the ground-glass image.

Microfilming very large originals such as engineering drawings, blue prints, maps and other large originals is accomplished on a vertical copier such as the RECORDAK MICRO-FILE Machine, Model MRG-1. The reduction range using 35 mm film is 12:1 to 36:1 and the largest document that can be photographed is 45 x 63 inches.

It should be mentioned here in passing that small documents like checks, tab cards, and papers up to letter size are copied continuously onto 16 mm roll film up to 2200 inches per minute on a machine such as the RECORDAK RELIANT 750 Microfilmer which provides reduction ratios from 24:1 to 50:1 in specific increments.

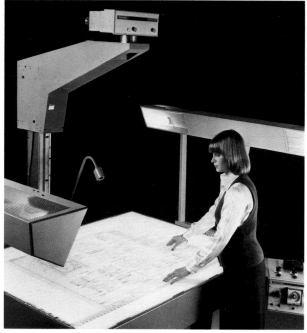

Volume copying of large-sized documents on high resolution unperforated 35-mm microfilm can be accomplished with this autofocus KODAK MICRO-FILE Micrographic Machine and copystand.

Photo courtesy KENRO Corp.

A large-format professional copy stand. The mirror back permits viewing the ground glass from the front.

Complete information about Kodak equipment and materials for microfilming can be obtained by writing to Eastman Kodak Business Systems Markets Division, Eastman Kodak Company, 343 State Street, Rochester, New York 14650.

Horizontal Camera Equipment

Horizontal Process Cameras: There are several makes of large horizontal cameras or process cameras like those used in the graphic arts. A typical camera is illustrated. The copyboard assembly travels on rails that may extend for 12 feet or more. The whole outfit, including the darkroom, often occupies a space of about 12 x 24 feet. The equipment is usually arranged so that the camera back can be fitted into an opening in the wall of a small darkroom. Thus, sizing, focusing and placing the image on the ground glass are done by remote control adjacent to the camera back within the darkroom. The copyboard usually consists of a board covered with a glass frame to hold the copy flat. For special jobs a vacuum copyboard is often used and some copyboards are designed to permit illumination of a transparency original from behind. Even though you may intend to use the equipment primarily for black-and-white work, it is important to make sure that the illumination is of a suitable type and balance for color work for the few jobs that may be done in color.

Not all process cameras are fitted to a darkroom. Some may be precision cameras that can be set up for both large and small originals. They may have a camera back designed for use with regular sheet-film holders.

Vertical Process Cameras: There are also some vertical process cameras of this type available that are very useful in limited space darkrooms.

These are all rigid, precision, versatile setups that can be used to copy originals of practically any size, but have a limited magnification range.

Photo by Tom Beelmann

Process cameras made for producing halftones for graphic arts purposes can also be used as copy cameras. The copyboard is in the foreground. The girl is adjusting the lens. The camera back is in a darkroom behind the wall at the back. Note the black walls to minimize reflections.

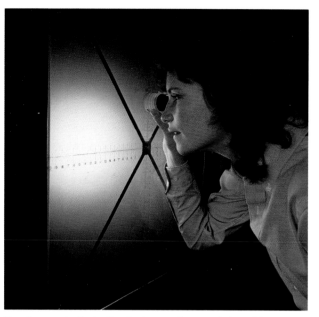

Here the operator is checking the focus on the ground glass of the process camera. She is in the darkroom behind the camera.

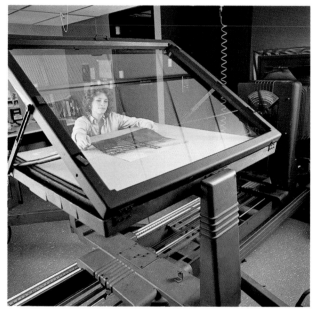

This is the copyboard of the process camera. The glass holds the copy flat. The copyboard is horizontal when the copy is being located, and is tilted to the vertical position for copying.

Still in the darkroom, the film is being placed on the process camera vacuum back. This is normally done in the dark, or in the light of an appropriate safelight. Note the control box in the lower right that controls the copyboard lights. The copyboard position and the lens standard are also controlled from behind the camera to permit sizing and focusing from the darkroom.

The operator is tilting the process-camera copyboard to the vertical position.

Lenses for Copying and Duplicating

Basic Requirements: A photographic lens can be designed to focus sharply across a flat plane at only one object distance. Most lenses for general work are designed to have a flat field at object distances greater than 8X the focal length. Most copying is done at close distances, and at close distances the sharp image field of such lenses is curved. This makes it difficult to obtain copy images that are sharp simultaneously both in the center and at the edges.

One way of compensating for this effect is to increase the depth of field by stopping the lens down to very small apertures (very large *f*-numbers). While this helps in most instances, it has several drawbacks. First, very small apertures introduce a high degree of diffraction which reduces the sharpness of the image. Second, it lengthens the exposure time. Not only does this require more time, it also frequently places exposure times where reciprocity-law failure becomes a sizable factor. With very long exposure times, the contrast of a negative copy film image is likely to change, requiring a change in development. In color films, long exposure times not only require a further adjustment in exposure, but usually also require filtration to help compensate for color shifts. Long exposure times also increase the possibility of sharpness loss due to equipment vibration.

A much better answer is to use a lens specifically designed to have a flat field when focused at close distances. For 35 mm and other small-format cameras, such lenses are known as macro lenses. For larger format cameras, lenses designed to have flat fields at the usual copy distances are called process lenses. Process lenses are available for film sizes of 4 x 5 inches up to very large sizes, such as 20 x 24 inches.

Another optical requirement is that the lenses used should produce *even* illumination across the focal plane. Critical examination of negatives reveals that most will be found more dense in the center than at the edges. This is due to the greater intensity of light at the center than at the perimeter of the circle of illumination projected by the lens. Wide-angle lenses for large formats have serious illumination falloff. This may not be too serious in the copying of continuous-tone originals on relatively low contrast films but the effect is normally accentuated to a serious degree on high-contrast negatives of line originals. This effect can be minimized by stopping the lens down and by using one that has a focal length slightly longer than normal for the film size being used. Some improvement can also be achieved by control of the copyboard illumination. See "Lighting" on page 26.

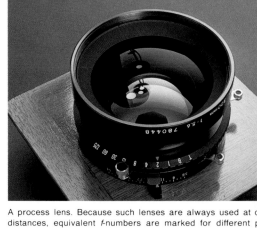

A process lens. Because such lenses are always used at close-working distances, equivalent *f*-numbers are marked for different percent sizes (magnifications). Most modern copy lenses are multicoated, which lowers the flare level.

Most process lenses available today are apochromatic lenses, that is, they are designed for full correction of chromatic aberrations. They are corrected so that images formed by light of three specific different colors all focus sharply in the same plane, which means that they are corrected for longitudinal chromatic aberration. They are also corrected for the difference in magnification of images in different colors—an aberration called lateral chromatic aberration which causes colored fringes at the edges of an image. Apochromatic lenses *must* be used for critical work in color copying and duplicating, and, of course, they perform well with any kind of original.

The correct focal length lens for use in copying and duplicating depends largely on the size of the negative to be covered with acceptable sharpness. As a general rule, the focal length should be, at least equal to the diagonal measurement of the negative format. The table below can be a useful guide.

Negative Diagonals

Size of Negative	Diagonal Measurement in Inches (approx.)	Diagonal Measurement in Millimetres (approx.)
35 mm	1³/₄	45
4.5 x 6 cm	3	75
2¹/₄ x 2¹/₄ in	3¹/₄	80
6 x 7 cm	3⁵/₈	92
2¹/₄ x 3¹/₄ in.	4	100
4 x 5 in.	6¹/₄	160
5 x 7 in.	8¹/₂	220
8 x 10 in.	12³/₄	325
11 x 14 in.	18	455

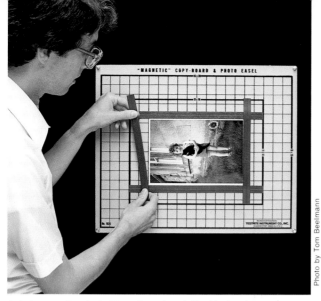

A dark-gray colored, steel-based copyboard. The black strips are magnets that hold the copy flat. The lines on the copyboard aid in orienting and centering the copy. Such a copyboard is quite suitable for the horizontal copy stand shown on page 9.

Photo by Tom Beelmann

Copyboards

A copyboard is essentially a flat, firm surface to which the original can be attached for copying. The board is illuminated with an arrangement of lights. The important features are that the board should be perfectly parallel to the camera back, or focal plane and be vibration free. Lack of parallelism results in a distorted image, makes it difficult to get all of the subject focused sharply, and, of course, vibrations cause unsharp negatives.

A simple copyboard can be made by attaching to a wall, or other firm support, a sheet of soft wood, cork or cardboard type building board. The board should be painted matte black to minimize flare and reflections. A white copyboard maximizes flare, a gray copyboard gives moderate flare, while a black copyboard minimizes flare. Flare causes a loss in contrast, extra compression of shadow tones, and lowers definition somewhat. It is useful to have concentric outlines of the most common paper sizes printed on the copyboard to aid in centering the originals on the copyboard.

Holding the Original in Place: Originals can be held down by pushpins, but it is not always desirable, or permissible, to make pinholes in the edges of a picture or a document. Alternatives are to use a steel copyboard and to hold the original with small bar magnets, or to hang a printing frame on the copyboard and put the original in that. Some manufactured copyboards have four jointed, spring-steel "fingers" to hold the four corners of the copy.

In copying with a vertical camera, holding the original in place is simplified. If the copy is free from curl, or quite flat, nothing is needed to hold it down. If the original does not lie flat, hold it down with a piece of glass, which must be clean and free from defects.

Many professional-type cameras are equipped with copyboards that can be rotated for easy copy orientation of the originals. A hinged glass frame clamps the copy to the board. The whole assembly is then rotated to the vertical position for focusing and exposing.

Vacuum Copyboards: Basically, a vacuum copyboard, or easel consists of a board perforated by many small holes. A vacuum pump sucks air through these holes and the resulting suction holds the original in place. Boards of this kind are used in process cameras to hold the film in place. (In making big enlargements similar boards are used for holding up big sheets of enlarging paper.)

The principal use for vacuum copyboards is for holding very large and flimsy originals, such as maps or engineering drawings. A great deal of time is saved by avoiding awkward manipulation of the material. A vacuum board and the pump that creates the suction are relatively expensive, but the cost is justified by a saving in time when the work is of sufficient volume or when precision copying is required. Tank-type vacuum cleaners can be used as a source of vacuum for smaller-sized, home-made vacuum copyboards.

Light Sources for Copyboard Illumination

Any source of light—including daylight—can be used for copying and duplicating on black-and-white films. In copying with color films, the color quality of the copyboard illumination must match that for which the film is designed.

Incandescent: Ordinary tungsten studio lamps (3200 K) are suitable for most applications, including color (when used with tungsten-balanced film). For small setups reflector-type bulbs can be used, but since the built-in reflector does not always mask the light, a lens hood should be used on the copy camera lens to reduce flare.

Photofloods (3400 K) can also be used for most copying, but due to their relatively short life they are not as economical as ordinary tungsten studio lamps.

Electronic Flash: Electronic flash is balanced for daylight and should be used with daylight-type color films. Filtration may be required for very close color balance. Pulsed-xenon lights are essentially daylight balance, but are usually not recommended for color because color contrast shifts may occur which cannot be corrected with filters.

Light Sources Used in Copying

Light Source	Color Temperature	Color Film Type	KODAK Light Balancing Filter
Tungsten Studio Lamp	3200 K	Tungsten (Type B)	No Filter
Photofloods	3400 K	Tungsten (Type A)	No Filter
		Tungsten (Type B)	81A
Blue Photofloods	4800 K	Daylight	82B
Quartz-Iodine (Tungsten-Halogen)	3200 K	Tungsten (Type B)	No Filter
100W General Service Incandescent	2900 K	Tungsten (Type B)	82B
Pulsed Xenon†	6000 K	Daylight	81A*
Electronic Flash	5600 - 6500 K	Daylight	81, 81A, 81B*

*Some light sources balanced for daylight may give an accurate color rendition on daylight balanced film without filtration.
†Not recommended for color. See text.

Note: Color copying with regular fluorescent light sources is not recommended because of the difficulties obtaining accurate color correction. If regular fluorescent illumination must be used a chart with suggested starting filter packs for some Kodak films used with fluorescent lamps is included in KODAK Publication AF-1, KODAK *Films-Color and Black-and-White*. The special fluorescent lamps with high color rendering index are suitable for color copying.

Safety Note: It is recommended that the manufacturer of the pulsed-xenon or quartz-iodine (tungsten-halogen) lamps be consulted for safety information pertaining to ultraviolet radiation and ventilation requirements due to ozone generation.

A reflector-flood lamp is shown at left. A tungsten bulb suitable for use in a reflector is at right. Above is an electronic flash unit suitable for copying.

Photo by Tom Beelmann

There are several advantages to using electronic flash as a light source. Flash duration is very short, preventing camera shake from introducing blur into the copy or duplicate. Also, color balance is very consistent provided the capacitor is always fully charged when shooting. The color temperature of the light that is emitted from electronic flash tubes is much more consistent than most tungsten sources. Electronic flash may still require filtration to achieve good color balance. An 81B filter often provides good color balance. Electronic flash is a cool light source. Unlike tungsten light sources, electronic flash does not generate much heat. Modeling lamps, which are tungsten lamps used in conjunction with electronic flash tubes to provide light for focusing, are generally low wattage and so do not generate excessive heat. However, modelling lights should be turned off during the exposure to avoid possible mixed balance illumination.

There are two disadvantages to using electronic flash. The first disadvantage is that exposure determination often must be accomplished with a test. Flash meters are a good way to determine exposure. For some duplicating procedures, exposures are determined using a through-the-lens light meter. In this case a flash meter could not be used. Once exposure has been determined by a test there is not much need for a light meter, providing that conditions remain the same.

The other disadvantage is related to expense. Inexpensive flash units, designed to be used on a camera can be used as copying light sources. Some manufacturers make inexpensive electronic flash units that can be screwed into a standard light socket. Flash units are sold that have tungsten light sources (modelling lights) built in to aid in lighting and focusing. These are usually more expensive than units without modeling lights. They are also more expensive than most tungsten lights. However, because photographic tungsten bulbs burn out after hours of usage, electronic flash may be less costly in the long run.

The table on the previous page shows what color film type and filter should be used for various light sources.

Daylight: While the use of daylight cannot be recommended as a commercial procedure, it is quite feasible as a temporary expedient. The work can be done either out-of-doors or in a well-lit room. A skylight is an advantage if available. Since daylight is variable in both color quality and intensity, expose the negatives as near to midday as possible. In

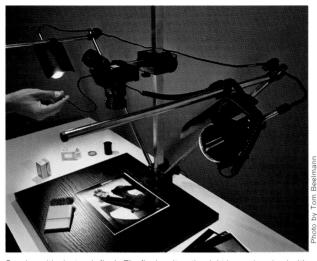

Copying with electronic flash. The flash unit on the right is synchronized with the camera. The unit on the left is equipped with a slave triggering device that flashes the slave unit when the synchronized unit is fired. Flash units courtesy of Rowe Photo, Inc., Rochester, NY.

Photo by Tom Beelmann

copying with color films, it is particularly important to avoid those times (two hours after sunrise, two hours before sunset) when the light has a yellowish cast. Use a combination of sun plus sky illumination. Open shade (skylight only) is bluish, as is the light on overcast days. Remember that light falling on the original may be affected by reflection from colored objects nearby.

Watch for variations in light caused by passing clouds. To assess correct exposure indoors and out, use a KODAK Gray Card at the copyboard in conjunction with an exposure meter.

The diffuse nature of fluorescent lighting makes it particularly useful when the grain in copies from textured-surface originals must be eliminated. Four tubes, in suitable reflectors, are arranged to form a square, the sides of which are parallel to the edges of the copyboard. The length of the tubes and their distance from the board depends largely on the size of the original being copied. Since this lighting set-up is not easy to adjust, it is most useful when originals do not vary much in size.

The color quality of fluorescent lighting is often unsuitable for use with color photographic materials. However, adequate results may be obtained by selecting tubes with a high CRI (Color Rendering Index). Fluorescent tubes have two advantages not possessed by most types of lighting; they generate very little heat and are relatively shadowless. Use exposure times of 1/30 second and longer to avoid variations in exposure caused by the pulsating nature of fluorescent lights. For a chart useful for balancing fluorescent lights to color film, write for *Current Information Summary* CIS-27 to the following address:

Dept. 412-L
Eastman Kodak Company
343 State Street
Rochester, NY 14650

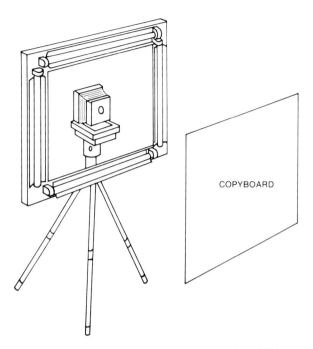

Four fluorescent lights mounted in a frame can be used to minimize the grain in a textured original.

Lamp Replacement

When one lamp, for example, in a set of four copying lights burns out, a new replacement will almost certainly be brighter than the remaining three lamps. To avoid adjusting a new lamp to get uniform illumination on the copyboard, replace all four lamps. In copying with color films it is especially important to follow this procedure, because new lamps are not only brighter, but have a higher color temperature than those that have been burning for some time. Variations such as these result in uneven color balance over the picture area.

NOTE: The darkening of lamps that have been burning for some time occurs with ordinary tungsten lamps, but it is not a problem with tungsten-halogen lighting.

Voltage Regulators: Fluctuations in the voltage of electrical current are generally not serious in copying with black-and-white films, but because even modest fluctuation causes a change in the color quality and intensity of the copying lights, such changes can be troublesome with color materials. One solution to the problem is to install *voltage regulators* in the electrical supply to the lamps. Be sure, however, that any such units have the capacity to handle the electrical load placed upon them. In any case, get professional advice before taking action in regard to voltage fluctuation.

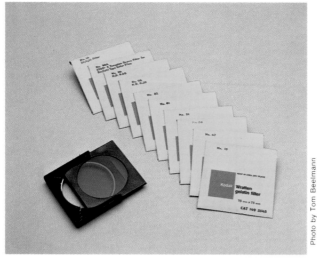

KODAK WRATTEN Gelatin Filters are available in all colors and in many degrees of filtering strength. A KODAK Gelatin Filter Frame Holder and a KODAK Gelatin Filter Frame are shown in the foreground.

Filters

Filters are used extensively in copying and duplicating work to improve the photographic result both in color and in black-and-white. The *action of a filter is to absorb light of certain colors*. For example, a red filter transmits red light and absorbs or stops green and blue light. Any specific filter can be used only with films sensitive to the color of light transmitted by the filter. Generally, closely related hues are permitted to pass through while complementary colors are absorbed or stopped. When this occurs there is a change in both the color and intensity of the light going to expose the film. The proportion of the light absorbed or subtracted depends on the transmission characteristics of the filter, and affects the filter factor.

Filters reduce the light reaching the sensitized material film and therefore an increase in exposure is usually required to compensate either by use of a larger aperture or a slower shutter speed. This change is expressed as a *filter factor*—a number that indicates how many times the exposure without a filter must be multiplied to obtain a satisfactory result with a filter. Filter factors are given on the Color Filter Circle on page 35 for most Kodak panchromatic films, and on the appropriate KODAK Data Sheets for other films.

Filters, whether glass or gelatin (film or cemented), should be kept in dust-free, opaque containers in a cool, dry place. They should always be handled carefully by the edges and be kept free of scratches, dirt or fingerprints, to avoid serious loss in definition. The dyes used in some filters are only moderately stable and should not be exposed to daylight or flourescent light for prolonged periods of time or subjected to extreme temperatures and humidities.

Classes or Types of Filters

There are a considerable number of filter types designed for specific purposes in black-and-white and color copying and duplicating. These are summarized briefly here. More detailed information can be found in these KODAK Publications: E-77, *KODAK Color Films*; KW-13, *Using Filters*; and B-3, *KODAK Filters for Scientific and Technical Uses*.

Contrast Filters: Filters offer one approach to contrast control with black-and-white copying, provided the original is multicolored. The less pure the colors involved the less important is the possible filter effect and the more significant become factors such as film contrast, exposure, paper printing grade and the degree of development. Selection of the most appropriate contrast filter demands considerable judgment and practical tests with several filters and films. Often viewing the original through several likely contrast filters will help, although the eye and film are not exactly alike in their color response. KODAK WRATTEN Gelatin Filters for reproducing common colors as lighter or darker include Nos. 12, 29, 47, 58, 25, 11, 13 and occasionally others.

As a general rule, filters lighten colors (in the final print) that are the same hue or a similar hue to the filter color, and darken colors that are complementary to the filter color. The filter circle on page 35 shows a variety of KODAK WRATTEN Filters, the colors that are lightened and darkened by them, and their filter factors for daylight and tungsten light.

Neutral Density Filters: Generally neutral density filters are used to increase the exposure time and can be used with any black-and-white or color film without materially altering contrast or color balance (in some uses, ND filters may add a slight amount of yellow to the neutrality). Neutral density filters are specified according to the transmission density of each filter. KODAK WRATTEN Neutral Density Filters, No. 96 are manufactured in $1/3 f$-stop increments from a density of .10 to 1.00 and in $1 1/3 f$-stop increments from 1.00 to 4.00. The chart below shows the density of the filter, the percent transmission, and the increase in exposure that results from using each filter.

This old drawing was mounted in an overlay. The exposed area had turned yellowish in color, while the protected area remained white. This copy was made without filtration.

This copy was made with a red filter, KODAK WRATTEN Filter No. 25. The filter has lightened the yellowed area in the copy.

Many reddish colored stains mar this old photograph. This copy was made without a filter on KODAK Technical Pan Film.

This copy, also on KODAK Technical Pan Film, was made through a KODAK WRATTEN Filter No. 25, (red). The filter has lightened the stains considerably, making them easier to retouch.

KODAK WRATTEN Neutral Density Filters

Transmission Density	Percent Transmission	Exposure Change in f-stops
0.10	80%	$1/3$ stop
0.20	63	$2/3$
0.30	50	1
0.40	40	$1 1/3$
0.50	32	$1 2/3$
0.60	25	2
0.70	20	$2 1/3$
0.80	16	$2 2/3$
0.90	13	3
1.00	10	$3 1/3$
2.00	1.0	$4 2/3$
3.00	0.1	6
4.00	0.01	$7 1/3$

Neutral density filters can be used to make an exposure series without changing exposure time or aperture.

They are also commonly used for flashing. If a 1% flash exposure to a white card is desired, a 2.00 KODAK WRATTEN Neutral Density Filter would be put in front of the lens. The flash exposure would be made for the same time and at the same f-number as the main exposure. More information on flashing is provided in the section called "Controlling Contrast of Transparency Films" on page 78.

Conversion Filters: These filters are used to compensate for the color quality of various light sources that are not matched to the color balance of a color film being used. The series 80 WRATTEN Filters are used with the combination of tungsten light and daylight film while the series 85 filters are used with daylight light sources and tungsten film.

Light Balancing Filters: These WRATTEN Filters change the color quality of the illumination to provide a cooler or warmer color rendering. The No. 82 series yields a bluer or cooler result by raising the color temperature; the No. 81 series yields a more yellow or warmer result by lowering the color temperature. These filters provide an adjustment throughout the spectrum so that the energy distribution of the light reaching the film is changed from one color temperature to another.

Factors affecting the color balance of the light source are variable line voltages, the age of lamps, and any color contribution of light diffusers or reflectors used in the system. Any filters recommended for changing the quality of the exposing light should serve as a starting point for a test, prior to actual production work.

Conversion and light balancing filters are preferred to color correction filters to avoid flare increase and possible loss of sharpness. This is because usually no more than two of the former are needed compared to as many as seven color correction filters required to achieve the same degree of color correction. Color correction filters are recommended for correction of fluorescent light sources, however.

Color Printing Filters: These are acetate filters for use in the enlarger between the light source and the transparency or color negative and must not be used in image forming beams of light. They should not be used over a copy camera lens. They are designated, for example, CP20Y, where CP means color printing filter having a density of 0.20 and yellow color. The density applies to the light of the color that the filter is designed to absorb—in this case blue. In other words, the CP20Y filter is a yellow filter, and placed in the light beam reduces the blue light exposure by 0.20 log exposure or acts like a 0.20 neutral density for the blue light exposure.

Color Compensating Filters: These are gelatin filters used in front of the lens. They are available in red, green, blue, cyan, magenta and yellow in a complete range of densities from CC025 to CC50. They are designated in a manner similar to the CP filters. With no more than three of these CC filters it is usually possible to obtain practically any color and density combination needed for color printing or for correcting for fluorescent lights. Up to three CC filters can be used over a camera lens. However, a minimum number of filters should be used. Filters tend to reduce sharpness and increase flare.

With large format cameras, two filters can usually be taped to the rear of the lens and one in front of the lens when three filters are required. This technique is preferred rather than using three filters over the front of the lens. When using filters behind the lens, best focus is achieved by focusing on the ground glass with the filter in place. Do not use rangefinder focusing.

Care must be taken so that filters do not become scratched or dirty. Dirt and scratches cause flare and sharpness loss. When filters become damaged or faded they should be replaced. Gelatin filters should be stored in the dark to minimize fading.

Special quality color compensating filters known as photomechanical (PM) filters are available from graphic arts dealers who handle Kodak products. PM filters are used in mapmaking and other critical photomechanical work where uniform thickness and maximum optical quality are necessary.

This copy was illuminated with tungsten light and copied on KODAK EKTACHROME 64 Film, which is daylight balanced. The lack of balance results in an overall orangey color.

The lights and the film are the same, but a KODAK WRATTEN No. 80A conversion filter has been used to balance the film to the lights.

KODACHROME 40 Film 5070 (Type A) is balanced for photolamps, which have a balance of 3400 K. This copy was made with studio lamps with a 3200 K balance, which has made the copy slightly warm.

The film and lights are the same for this copy, but it was made through a KODAK WRATTEN No. 82A Conversion Filter, which, in the copy, gives a close approximation of the colors in the original print.

Photo by Merye A. Blazer.

Exact color balance is often achieved using color compensating (CC) filters. This copy was illuminated with studio lights (3200 K) and copied on KODAK EKTACHROME 50 Professional Film (Tungsten). This should have given a balanced copy, but the copy is actually slightly more magenta than the original.

Copy by Tom Benson

This copy was made through a 10 green color compensating filter (CC 10G) which has corrected the color balance. The exact original film balance, film aging, the camera lens, the lamp reflectors, the walls in the copy area can all contribute to a lack of exact color balance in copies. Continual monitoring of results is the one way to insure consistent color balance.

Filters in Enlargers

Many color enlargers are equipped with cyan, magenta and yellow dichroic filters. A dichroic filter is made by evaporating multi-layered coatings on a substrate such as glass. They work using the interference principle of light. The advantage of dichroic filters is that they are sharp cutting, so that they are more optically effective than gelatin filters and withstand heat better than gelatin filters, and their use makes the use of filter dials for color control more practical.

Enlarger light sources equipped with such filters can be used as light sources for many color dupli-cating operations. The color of the light source is adjusted using the dichroic filter controls and no other filters are required.

Another type of enlarger light source uses three light sources, one red, one green and one blue. The light is mixed to create white light. The balance of the white light is adjusted by controlling the intensity of each of these lights. This type of enlarger head can also be used as a light source for color duplication. In some automatic printers, balance is achieved by automatic adjustment of the time the filters are inserted into the light beam.

BLACK-AND-WHITE COPYING TECHNIQUES

Copying of photographs to make a high quality copy is often considered a straightforward simple task. In reality there are few jobs in photography that place such high demands on the skill and patience of the photographer. To make good copies from the many different types of originals requires a knowledge of the techniques and materials that yield the best result in a given situation.

As indicated in the glossary, copying refers to the making of a photograph of a reflection-type image. Commonly a photographic negative is made either in black-and-white or color. However, making transparencies of reflection originals is also considered to be copying. Making transparent images of transparent negatives or positive transparencies is considered duplicating, and this subject is covered in the section entitled "Duplicating."

Reflection copy originals include a wide variety of subject matter broadly divided into line originals and continuous-tone originals. They may be either black-and-white or color. They vary in size from very small to very large. Line originals include printed matter, drawings, typewritten originals, handwritten manuscripts, faded manuscripts, documents on yellowed paper (such as old newsprint), halftone originals*, blueprints and colored line originals.

Continuous-tone originals include photographs, crayon and chalk drawings, acrylic, watercolor and oil paintings, and stained prints. Another group of continuous-tone originals include old and/or damaged photographic prints, daguerreotypes, faded prints, ambrotypes, tintypes, and calotypes. There are also some reflection originals that are described as combined line and continuous-tone originals.

Preparation of Originals for Copying

Originals should be handled with the greatest of care and not be subjected to potential damage or loss. They may be historically valuable, irreplaceable or of sentimental value. The best copy negative possible should be made before attempting any pre-copy treatment. Of course, originals in good condition require no preparation. If any pre-treatment is necessary, it is important to get written approval from the owner in case any damage to the original results from the treatment.

---

*While halftone originals are technically line originals (they are made of small areas of black-and-white or colored ink and white) they are usually treated as continuous-tone originals in copying.

Reflections from Buckled or Creased Prints: Originals with a buckled or creased surface are a special problem in copying because they tend to reflect the copying lights in many directions. Ordinary photographic prints that are new or fairly new can be soaked in water and redried between photographic blotters to remove buckles and creases. Do not re-ferrotype a glossy print, because it may stick to the ferrotyping surface and become a total loss. Remember to spot the print if necessary, because the original spotting may have washed off.

If it is not advisable to wet the original completely, creases can often be removed or reduced by dampening the back of the print and then flattening it in a dry mounting press heated to a lower temperature than that used for mounting: approxi-

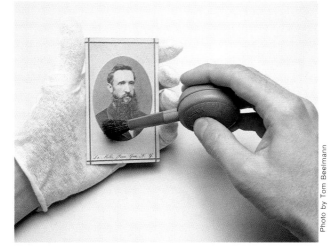

Valuable originals must be handled carefully. Here an antique carte-de-visite is being blown off with an air duster prior to copying.

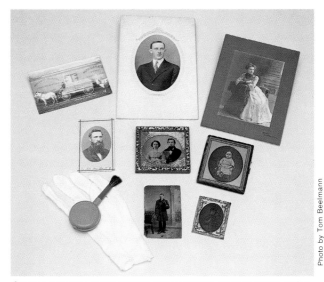

Old photographs may be daguerrotypes, tintypes, albumin prints, ambrotypes, salted paper prints, or old gelatin silver prints made on gas-light paper. All should be handled with great care to avoid damage.

mately 100°F (28°C). The use of polarized light when copying is often helpful in minimizing reflections from buckled prints. Double polarization is often necessary in this instance. (See the section on page 53.)

Cleaning Prints Before Copying: Careful examination of the original under a bright light may reveal surface defects, discoloration, stains, grease spots, dirt, dust, etc. As indicated previously, an examination may indicate the need to clean, restore or retouch the original and permission should be obtained from the owner. In any case the need to make a copy is the first requirement. This point cannot be overemphasized.

Dust and lint can be removed by gently brushing the original with a camel's-hair brush and an air syringe. An artist's kneaded rubber eraser or a gum eraser used lightly will remove dirt and light marks. Erasers or any other abrasive, however, should not be used on an old original or on a valuable photograph. Chemical deposits from the eraser or the abrasion itself may cause harm to the photographic image in time.

Beyond this preliminary examination and cleaning there may be need for some corrective measures such as retouching. Hand work can often be done on the original but **it is generally safer to do the work on the copy negative or a print made from the copy negative. Then make a new copy negative from which the final copy print is made.**

The Copying Procedure

The original to be copied is placed on the copyboard and centered with the optical axis of the copy camera. Lines drawn on the copyboard help to center the original and to align the edges vertically and horizontally when copying on a horizontal copy stand. The edges are aligned with the camera when copying vertically.

The original is held in place with vacuum, magnetic strips, or finger-type spring clamps, or with a plate of glass placed over the original.

Next, the image of the copy must be sized and focused by viewing the image on the viewing screen. Nearly all copying is done with cameras that have a ground glass viewing screen.

When making copies at low magnification (greater than about 1:3 ratio of image size to original size), sizing is done by adjusting the camera to copyboard distance while focusing is done using the camera adjustments. On a small format camera the focusing is done with the helical focusing ring. Focusing on a view camera is done by adjusting the front or rear standard forward or backward.

Sizing and focusing at high magnification (about 1:2 or greater) is performed the opposite way. Sizing is controlled by changing the lens to film distance

and focusing is accomplished by changing the camera to copyboard distance. This adjustment can be made by either moving the camera or the copyboard.

To estimate the lens to film distance for a given magnification use the following formula:

$$\text{Lens-to-Film Distance} = (\text{Magnification} + 1) \times \text{Focal Length}$$

Example: Magnification desired - 1:1 or 1X
Focal length of lens - 6 inches

$$\text{Lens-to-Film Distance} = (1 + 1) \times 6 \text{ inches} = 12 \text{ inches}$$

Magnification is sometimes expressed as the image size divided by the subject size (i.e. 2:1, 3:1, 1:2) and sometimes by the value of the ratio (2:1 = 2X, 3:1 = 3X, 1:2 = 0.5X).

Because it is not always possible to determine the optical center of a lens (principal point), the precise lens to film distance can only be estimated. To check the magnification ratio accurately the image size on the ground glass must be measured and compared to the subject (object) size.

Commonly, the copy photographer must make a negative where the image must measure a certain length (the magnification is not specified). In this case, just measure the image on the ground glass when sizing and focusing.

The next step is to provide even illumination on the copyboard.

Lighting

On page 17 is a section that describes various types of light sources commonly used for copying. In this section we discussed various arrangements of the lights to achieve even illumination, the need for even illumination on the copyboard, and methods of measuring to determine whether the light distribution is uniform.

Lamp Arrangement: Small originals—up to 8 x 10 inches—can be illuminated with two lamps placed about 30 inches from the center of the copyboard and at an angle of about 45 degrees to the lens axis (see illustration). This angle can be varied somewhat if it is necessary to avoid reflections in a cover glass, but it is important that both lamps be at the *same* angle.

Four lamps, one at each corner of the copyboard, provide a better spread of light than the two-lamp setup just described and, at the same time, can be adjusted to give a little extra light intensity at the corners of the board where it is needed to offset the effect of lens falloff.

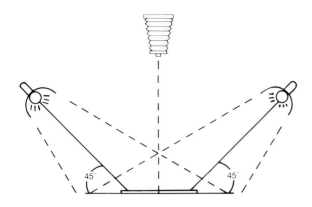

A more even distribution of light across the copyboard may be achieved by aiming the center of the light beam nearer to the edges of the copy area rather than at the center.

Specially designed copy cameras are equipped with lights that illuminate adequately a range of original sizes. However, these lights are adjustable, and the foregoing remarks about copyboard illumination apply equally to the more elaborate equipment.

If the illumination on an original being copied is uneven, both the copy negative and print will show the results of this unevenness. This is true both when making continuous-tone copies and high contrast copies of line originals.

Control of Illumination Evenness: The easiest method to get even copyboard illumination is to measure the intensity of one light (or bank of lights) at a time. The light intensity is then equalized usually by moving the lights closer or farther away from the copyboard at the same angle.

First aim the beam of one light (or bank of lights) at the far side of the copyboard. Then place a KODAK Gray Card on the center of the copyboard and take a light meter reading with a reflected type light meter. The reading can be made directly from the camera if it has a through the lens meter. Turn off the light and repeat the procedure with the other light. Adjust the distance of the lights until each light separately gives the same light meter reading at the center of the copyboard.

The individual light readings can also be measured with an incident light meter that has a hemispherical light diffuser. The light meter is placed in the center of the copyboard parallel to the copyboard for the readings.

The third method is to use an incident meter equipped with a flat diffusing disc. The light meter can measure the individual light intensity by pointing it toward each light. Both lights can be on during the light measurements.

If all the originals to be copied are small, the lamps with either a 2-lamp or 4-lamp setup can be aimed at the center of the copyboard. This will give a high level of illumination and keep the exposures relatively short.

However, when an original is illuminated uniformly over its entire surface, it does not follow that a negative made from it will be uniformly exposed (as discussed on page 16.) This effect is most noticeable with large originals. If a smaller aperture or a lens of longer focal length cannot yield uniform exposure, the alternative is to adjust copyboard illumination by increasing the light intensity at the edges. The amount of this increase can be measured by taking light meter readings in the conventional manner at the copyboard, or by taking light measurements at the focal plane. A light meter for measuring light at the focal plane of large format cameras is illustrated below. This type of meter consists of a light-sensitive cell mounted in clear plastic and connected to an exposure calculator dial. The meter can also be used to calculate exposure by measuring copyboard illumination with the gray

Photo by Tom Beelmann

A special probe is made to be attached to a handheld exposure meter so that illumination at the ground glass of view cameras can be measured.

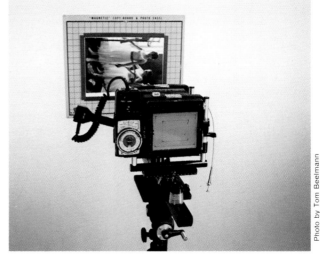

Photo by Tom Beelmann

With ground-glass metering, the evenness of the lighting across the focal plane can be measured. By adjusting the lights on the copyboard, the light as imaged by the lens can be made even. The ground-glass meter can also be used to measure the image of a gray card, or of highlights or shadows as an aid to getting correct exposure.

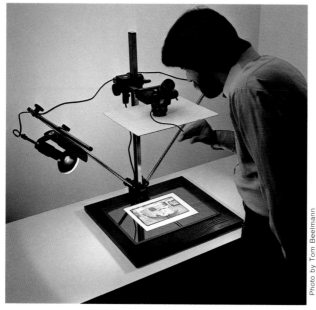

When copying vertically, a piece of clean glass can be used to hold the copy flat. A camera reflection shield, black on the lower side, can be used to avoid a reflection of the camera in the glass. Using polarizing filters is also useful.

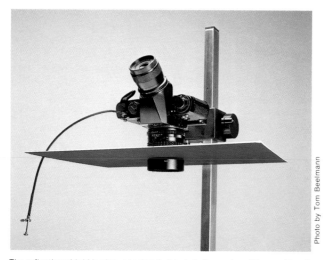

The reflection shield is shown in detail. A hole in the center of the card is cut to just fit the camera lens. Black photographic masking tape can be used to attach the card to the lens, if necessary.

side of the KODAK Gray Card placed on the copyboard. Be sure to stop the lens down to the working aperture before taking measurements. When the most even illumination has been found, mark or record the position of the lights so that the conditions can be repeated when necessary. Because the optical image in the camera is measured, *no change in exposure for magnification should be made* when calculating exposure.

Slight fall off in illumination at the focal plane is not usually serious in copying continuous-tone originals. In fact, the effect is often compensated by a similar effect in the optical system of an enlarger. However, when high contrast film is being used to copy line originals, the effect of differences in light intensity is increased by the short exposure latitude of the film. In this situation, illumination should be adjusted to give the best possible evenness across the focal plane.

Control of Light Around the Copy Setup: Good control of the illumination on and around the copyboard is necessary for consistent high-quality copies. Avoid copying near a window or a white wall. Both may cause a reflection in the surface of the original being copied that would show up in the copy print. Also, both might shine into the camera lens, raising the flare level. It is also a good idea to turn off the room lights, or at least to shield the copy area from them, for the same reasons.

Copying an Original Under Glass: When glass is used to hold an original flat, care must be taken to prevent unwanted reflections from the glass. The most common source of reflections is the camera or tripod. Sometimes these reflections go unnoticed when shooting but appear in the negative or transparency. The reflections may not be noticed because when focusing at a wide aperture they are out of focus. When the exposure is made at a much smaller aperture they are brought into focus much to the photographer's dismay.

To prevent the glass reflection problem a black piece of cardboard with a hole cut out in the middle is placed over the lens. The cardboard should be big enough to cover all reflective parts of the camera. In a vertical copying situation the cardboard can be held on with a lens shade. When a large piece of glass is used with a large copy, reflections can be caused by the tripod. A skirt made from a black focusing cloth will eliminate these reflections.

Dust is another problem encountered when using glass to hold down an original. The sheet of glass provides an extra two surfaces which can attract dust. For these reasons, it is best to avoid using glass if possible.

Flare: Flare is non-image forming light that exposes film. It is caused by reflection of light from lens surfaces, the interior edges of lens mounts, diaphragm blades, and the interiors of cameras. Bright areas near the copy area, such as a white copyboard, windows, and room lights are likely to raise the flare level.

Flare light lowers the contrast of the optical image because light from the brighter portions of the subject (copy original and copyboard) is spread over the entire image, and adds more exposure (as a percentage of the total) to the darker sections of the image. It also tends to reduce the apparent sharpness of the recorded detail.

In copying, it is important to minimize flare. The first step is to have a clean, coated lens on the copy

This tintype was photographed with a white background, and no effort was made to control flare. The shadow tones have been lightened and the contrast reduced by the flare.

Here a dark backing was used, and a lens hood placed on the copy lens to control flare. The shadow tones are darkened slightly, and the contrast increased.

camera. The second step is to ensure that the camera interior is as matte-black as possible. Even a layer of dust on the bottom of a bellows can raise the level of the flare light. The third step is to surround the copy with matte-black material or the copyboard should be painted with a black-matte paint. The fourth-step is to keep any direct light from the copy lights from falling on the camera lens. A lens hood or shade should always be on the lens, and the lights should be baffled so that no light falls on the front of the camera.

Reflector floodlights are most likely to cause flare difficulties. Placing them in metal reflectors is one way of keeping direct light from shining on the camera lens. If this is impractical, matte-black painted metal shields can be made and mounted on the light brackets in such a way as to shield the lens from direct light.

Film Choice

At this point the copy photographer faces one of the most important decisions affecting the quality and nature of the copy: film choice. Choosing the best film for a copy can make the difference between a passable copy and an excellent copy.

Format: The most basic consideration in film choice is format. Format choice is limited by the type of camera equipment available to the copy photographer. A small-format camera can be used in many copying situations with excellent results. There are many advantages, however, in choosing a large (sheet film) format for black-and-white copying.

The larger negative size offers the possibility of making larger prints. Reproduction quality is increased because of the larger negative. Specialized copy films can be used that have a characteristic curve shape most suitable for good tone reproduction in copying. The widest assortment of films used for copying is available in the sheet film formats. Also, larger negatives can be retouched more readily. The table on page 30 lists some of the Kodak black-and-white films useful in copying for each format.

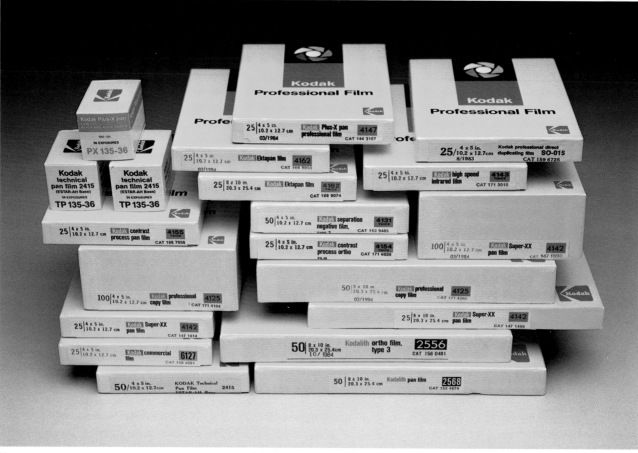

Kodak manufacturers many types of film in a variety of formats that are used for copying.

35 mm—KODAK PLUS-X Pan Film 5062
  KODAK Technical Pan Film 2415 (ESTAR-AH Base)

120/220—KODAK PLUS-X Pan Professional Film
  KODAK VERICHROME Pan Film
  KODAK Technical Pan Film

Long Rolls—KODAK Ortho Copy Film 5125
  KODAK PLUS-X Pan Professional Film 2147
    (ESTAR Base)
  KODALITH Ortho Film 6556, Type 3

Sheet Films-
  KODAK Professional Copy Film 4125
  KODAK Contrast Process Pan Film 4155
  KODAK Contrast Process Ortho Film 4154
  KODAK Technical Pan Film 2415
  KODALITH Ortho 2556, Type 3
  KODALITH Pan Film 2568 (ESTAR Base)
  KODAK Commercial Film 4127, (ESTAR Thick Base)
  KODAK SUPER-XX Pan Film 4142 (ESTAR Thick Base)
  KODAK PLUS-X Pan Professional Film 4147
    (ESTAR Thick Base)
  KODAK Separation Negative Film 4131, Type 1
  KODAK EKTAPAN Film 4162, (ESTAR Thick Base)

Although the choice of films in the 35 mm format is limited, KODAK Technical Pan Film 2415 has proven to be an extremely versatile copy film that can be used in place of several other films. With the appropriate developer it can be used to produce a range of contrasts, from moderate contrast to very high contrast. It also has extremely fine grain allowing enlargements of great magnification. KODAK PLUS-X Pan Film (5062), which is a general purpose film, can also be used for making black-and-white continuous-tone copy negatives. KODAK PANATOMIC-X film gives poorer highlight tone rendition than the above two films.

The 35 mm format is frequently used for copying because of the large variety of equipment available. Many 35 mm cameras can be fitted with close-up equipment and other accessories that make copying quick and convenient.

The 120/220 format has some of the advantages of the 35 mm format but offers an improvement in final print quality resulting from the larger negative size. Negative retouching may also be possible with the larger negative size. Single-lens reflex cameras which are available in this format are convenient to use for copying.

Long rolls (70 mm, 40 mm, & 35 mm) are used primarily for high volume copying, utilizing specialized cameras with bulk film backs. The film, which comes in various lengths from 25 to 400 feet, is processed in an automatic film processor, or cut into lengths and processed in spiral reel tanks.

The copy photographer who has more than one camera available can choose format based upon the end use of the negative. The smaller formats can be used for small to medium enlargements and record keeping. The large sheet film formats can be used for maximum quality copies and large blow-ups.

Image Color: The second most important consideration in film choice is the original to be copied. The image color and contrast of the original determine the type of film to be used. An original that has colors other than black-and-white is normally copied on panchromatic film. Originals that fall into this category are color photographs, tinted black-and-white photographs, stained photographs, brown-toned black-and-white photographs, oil paintings, watercolors, or any other subject with colors. A film with panchromatic sensitivity reproduces in black-and-white a reasonable visual approximation of the brightness of the original color tones. The approximation is improved by the use of a No. 8 (yellow) filter in daylight, or a No. 11 (yellow-green) filter in tungsten light. Most general purpose films are panchromatic and have the term "pan" somewhere in the name. Examples are KODAK PLUS-X Pan Film, KODAK VERICHROME Pan Film, KODAK EKTAPAN Film, and KODAK Technical Pan Film.

A film with panchromatic sensitivity also makes it possible to use filtering techniques to minimize stains and increase contrast. See the section "Special Techniques" on page 49. Filtering techniques may be useful when copying many old faded and stained photographs.

Black-and-white originals can be copied without requiring panchromatic sensitivity. Several special purpose films with orthochromatic or blue sensitivity can be used for these originals. KODAK Professional Copy Film 4125 (available in sheets) or KODAK Ortho Copy Film 5125 (available in 70 mm long rolls) are excellent choices for reproducing black-and-white continuous tone photographs.

We indicated earlier that these two films make possible the best quality copies because of special characteristic curve shapes that give improved highlight tone separation. However, the emulsion (which is similar for both films) is available in only two formats, sheet film and 70 mm unperforated long rolls. For other formats, other films must be used. These special copy films have an orthochromatic emulsion, which makes it impossible to use certain filters, especially red.

Contrast: The contrast of the original is also an important consideration in choosing a film. For a copy photograph to have about the same contrast as a continuous-tone original, a moderate contrast film should be used. Extremely high contrast originals, such as pen-and-ink drawings should be copied on extremely high contrast films such as KODAK Technical Pan Film developed in KODAK Developer D-19, or on a KODALITH Film developed in a KODALITH Developer. When the original contrast is low and should be increased (a faded or yellowed photograph) use a moderately high contrast film such as Technical Pan Film developed in KODAK HC-110 Developer Dilution B, or KODAK Contrast Process Ortho or Pan Film developed in KODAK Developers D-19 or D-11. The Summary of Films, Developers and Filters for Black-and-White Copying table on page DS2 summarizes the film-developer recommendations for different originals. Halftone reproductions in books or magazines should be treated as continuous-tone originals for a pleasing photographic reproduction. (Permission should be obtained before copying from such publications.)

Retouching Surface: An additional consideration is important when choosing a film for copying portraits. Some films have a better retouching surface than others. This characteristic is called "tooth." When a copy negative is going to be retouched a film with good "tooth" should be selected. The negative also must be large enough for a retoucher to work on. This usually requires a sheet film 4 x 5 or larger. Kodak sheet films with good "tooth" are:

Professional Copy Film (Emulsion side)
PLUS-X Pan Professional Film (Both sides)
EKTAPAN Film (Both sides)
SUPER-XX Pan Film (Both sides)

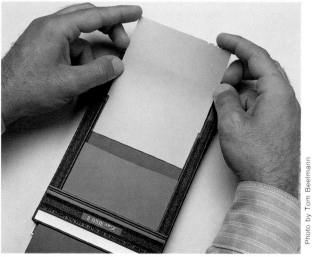

Sheet films are generally loaded into sheet film holders for use in view cameras.

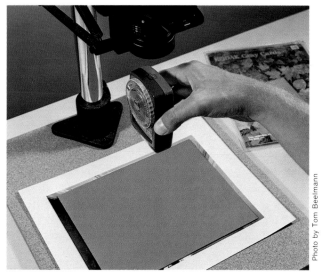

A KODAK Gray Card (Publication No. R-27) is placed on the copyboard and measured with a reflection-type exposure meter to calculate the basic copy exposure. Almost always the basic exposure must be adjusted for magnification.

An incident light meter is often used to measure the incident light as an aid in calculating copy exposures. Note the hemisphere light diffuser.

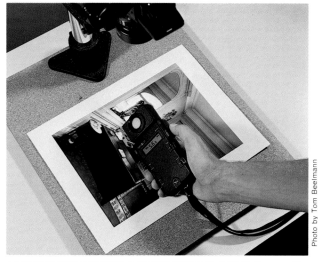

An incident light meter with a flat-disk diffuser is used to compare the intensity of two copy lights.

Exposure

In copying, as with other kinds of photography, correct exposure is a major factor in obtaining high quality results. In a copy setup, a basic exposure can be established that helps determine all subsequent exposures (if lighting and processing conditions remain the same). Once the basic exposure is established for a setup, any changes in exposure resulting from changes in magnification, the use of filters, the type of film, or shutter speed can be based on the basic exposure and a new exposure quickly calculated using the basic exposure as the starting point.

Methods of Determining Exposure:

There are two ways to determine the basic exposure: a) by using an exposure meter and b) running a series of test exposures. In either case a good copy negative should be made from an average original and printed on a normal grade of paper using the printing equipment (enlarger) to be used for all subsequent copy negatives. This verifies the accuracy of the basic exposure so that all subsequent exposures can be determined from it. For processing details see the section *Processing Black-and-White Copy Negatives*.

Using an Exposure Meter to Determine Basic Exposure: As discussed earlier there are two types of exposure meters: incident and reflected-light. An incident meter uses a hemispherical plastic light collector over the meter cell to measure the light falling on the subject (in this case, the copyboard). The meter would be placed on the copyboard with the rounded light collector facing the camera lens to take a reading.

A reflected-light meter measures the light reflected from the subject. In a copying setup a reflected-light meter is most often used with a KODAK Gray Card. A KODAK Gray Card (KODAK Publication No. R-27) is placed on the copy stand and the light reflected from its surface is measured with the meter.

Both meters, used as described, measure the light level and give similar readings. The light reading as indicated on the meter may be in terms such as footcandles, or in an arbitrary number that represents a given light value. The exposure is calculated for this light reading by using the dial calculator on the meter. The dial is set for the film speed and then the reading value. Setting the calculator for these two values provides a series of equivalent exposures in terms of *f*-numbers and shutter speeds. You pick the best *f*-number/shutter-speed combination out of the series for your conditions. Usually in copying, moderate *f*-numbers and moderately long exposure times are selected. Most lenses perform best

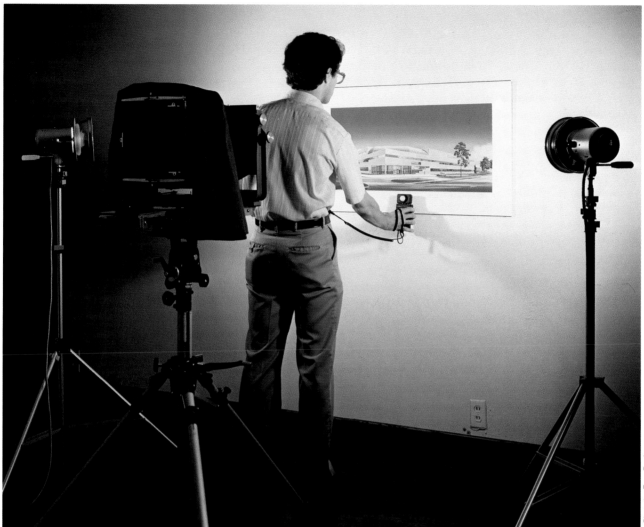

Lighting evenness from top to bottom and from left to right is especially critical with large originals such as this architectural rendering.

at an aperture two or three stops down from the widest aperture. (One stop down may be best with process lenses).

Some newer exposure meters incorporate an electronic calculator instead of the dial calculator. With this type of meter you set the meter for the film speed, choose the shutter speed desired, and take the light reading. The meter then reads out the *f*-stop required.

When a camera that has a through-the-lens meter is used, a KODAK Gray Card is placed on the copyboard as it would be for a hand held reflected-type meter. The reading is taken directly from the card. If the original is large and the KODAK Gray Card occupies a small portion of the frame the camera should be moved in close to the card to take the reading so that the card fills the frame. Do not change the focus when taking the reading or an inaccurate reading may be obtained due to an increase in lens to film distance (this is discussed later in more detail). Use of a spot meter makes it easier to measure the gray card from a distance.

A good method to use when copying printed text material is to measure a white card and to give 5X the exposure indicated by the card, or an increase of $2\frac{1}{3}$ stops. If the printed material is measured, measurements vary as the amount or blackness of the text varies, while the exposure required remains constant. The white card method compensates for this. If the background paper is colored or darker than the white card used for measuring, a slight increase in exposure is necessary.

When electronic flash is used as a light source a flashmeter can be used to determine exposure. Flashmeters are used in a manner similar to that used with conventional light meters except that the only camera adjustment indicated is the *f*-stop.

Once you have measured the light with a light meter and have an *f*-stop/shutter speed combination, you have determined the basic exposure. This basic exposure is modified by making adjustments for magnification, filter factors, and reciprocity law failure before a negative can be exposed.

Determining Basic Exposure with Tests: To determine a basic exposure without a light meter, run a series of tests with the film or films to be used. Use the table below to estimate a starting exposure time. Don't forget to include in your exposure calculations a factor for magnification (bellows extension) if necessary.

From the test series, choose a negative that makes a good reproduction of the original on a normal grade of photographic paper. Record the exposure time, the position of the lights, the lens aperture, the film speed, and the magnification for future reference.

Magnification: The most significant exposure compensation in copying occurs when the lens-to-film distance (often referred to as bellows extension or lens extension) becomes greater than the focal length of the lens. Lens-to-film distance increases rapidly as the reproduction size approaches 100 percent. In this situation, the copy negative image is the same size as the original, the lens-to-film distance is twice the focal length of the lens, and the exposure increase is four times that required with the lens focused at infinity. This is because the lens is twice as far away from the film as it is at infinity focus, and the effective f-numbers are twice the marked values. For example, $f/8$ becomes $f/16$ at 1:1 magnification, requiring 4X the exposure time.

When a hand-held meter is used to calculate the exposure, or when a standard exposure has been found by running tests, an exposure factor for lens extension must be considered to achieve proper exposure when a bellows camera is being used.

However, when the close-focusing is achieved by using a close-up lens in front of the camera lens, no additional exposure is required. When a camera that has through-the-lens metering is used, no additional exposure is required for magnification when the exposure is determined by the camera meter.

The simplest way to find the exposure factor is by the magnification method. Magnification is the ratio of the image size divided by the subject size. A common method of finding magnification is to use a 1-inch subject (such as that provided in the margin) placed on the copyboard. The focusing screen (ground glass) image of the copy is first sized and focused. The 1-inch target is placed on the copyboard. The size of the ground glass image of this target is measured. The magnification is found by dividing the image size by the object size. In this case, the image size is divided by 1, so the image size itself is the magnification.

The exposure factor is found mathematically using the equation.

$$\text{Exposure Factor} = (\text{Magnification} + 1)^2$$

You can find the exposure factors for the common copying range of magnifications using the graph on the next page. The horizontal scale is calibrated both in magnification values and image size values when a 1-inch target is used. There is also a dial in KODAK Publication No. R-28, *KODAK Professional Photoguide*, that helps find exposure factors.

Another method commonly used with bellows type cameras to find the exposure factor is to measure the lens to film distance and use the formula below. F is the focal length of the lens and B is the lens-to-film distance (bellows).

$$\frac{(\text{Lens-to-Film Distance})^2}{(\text{Focal Length})^2} = \frac{B^2}{F^2} = \text{Exposure Factor}$$

The lens-to-film distance should be measured from the approximate center of the lens to the ground glass. For example, when an 8-inch lens (210 mm) is used with a 4x5 camera to copy a print, a 12-inch bellows distance results. To figure out the additional exposure time necessary the preceding formula is used.

$$\frac{(12)^2}{(8)^2} = \text{Exposure Factor} \quad \frac{144}{64} = 2.25$$

If the calculated exposure is 1 second the corrected exposure time would be $2\frac{1}{4}$ seconds. If the film being used has a reciprocity correction necessary at $2\frac{1}{4}$ seconds, this should be considered (discussed in a later section).

Starting Point Exposures for Test Negatives

Individual Lamp Wattage*	400	320	250	200	Film Speeds 125	100	80	50	32	25	12	8
1000 W	f/64	f/56	f/50	f/45	f/35	f/32	f/29	f/22	f/18	f/16	f/11	f/9
500 W	f/45	f/40	f/35	f/32	f/24.5	f/22	f/20	f/16	f/12.5	f/11	f/8	f/6.8
250 W	f/32	f/28	f/24.5	f/22	f/17.5	f/16	f/15	f/11	f/9	f/8	f/5.6	f/4.5

*The chart is based upon the use of two lights, three feet from the copyboard, at an angle of 45° and a shutter speed of ½ sec.

1 INCH

MAGNIFICATION EXPOSURE ADJUSTMENT CHART

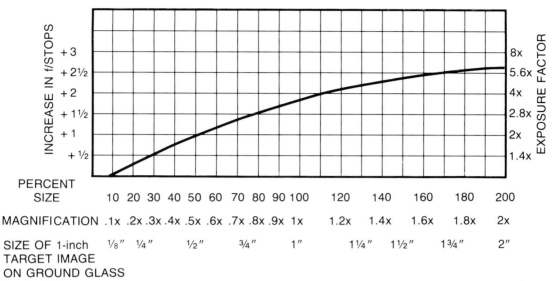

PERCENT SIZE	10	20	30	40	50	60	70	80	90	100	120	140	160	180	200
MAGNIFICATION	.1x	.2x	.3x	.4x	.5x	.6x	.7x	.8x	.9x	1x	1.2x	1.4x	1.6x	1.8x	2x
SIZE OF 1-inch TARGET IMAGE ON GROUND GLASS	⅛″	¼″		½″		¾″				1″	1¼″	1½″	1¾″		2″

This graph can be used to adjust indicated exposures as found by metering or a test for changes in magnification. Adjustment for reciprocity may be needed in addition when long exposure times are required.

Filter Factors: Filters are frequently used in black-and-white copying to help eliminate stains in the copy or to increase contrast. Using a filter also requires increasing the exposure. The filter circle below shows the filter factors required for various colored KODAK WRATTEN Filters when used with normal KODAK Panchromatic Films such as KODAK PLUS-X Pan Film, KODAK EKTAPAN Film 4162 (ESTAR Thick Base), and KODAK SUPER-XX Pan Film 4142

(ESTAR Thick Base). The uses of these films are discussed elsewhere. Some filter factors for other Kodak black-and-white films are given in the KODAK Data Sheets.

The correct exposure time without a filter is multipied by the filter factor to find the exposure time with the filter. For example, if the exposure time

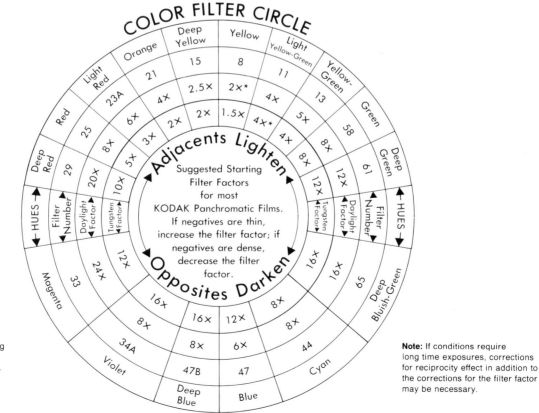

*For a gray-tone rendering of colors approximating their visual brightnesses.

Note: If conditions require long time exposures, corrections for reciprocity effect in addition to the corrections for the filter factor may be necessary.

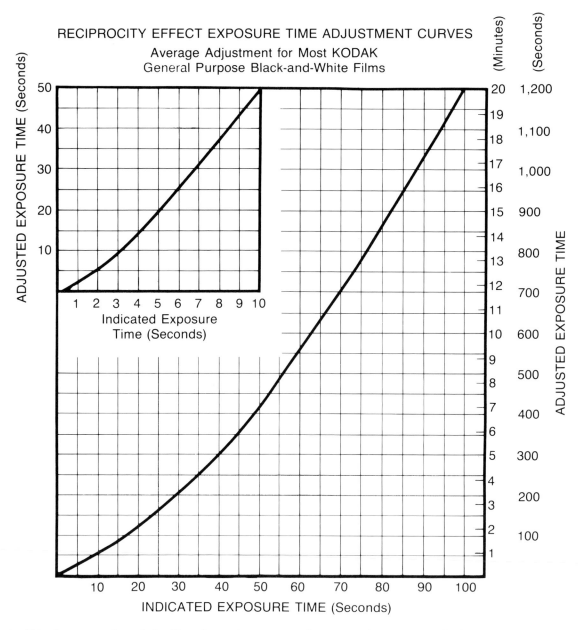

RECIPROCITY EFFECT EXPOSURE TIME ADJUSTMENT CURVES
Average Adjustment for Most KODAK
General Purpose Black-and-White Films

without a filter is 1 second, and the filter factor is 8X, the exposure time with the filter is 8 seconds. As with lens extension exposure factors, an additional correction may be required due to the reciprocity characteristics of film.

Reciprocity Law: The reciprocity law failure effect, sometimes incorrectly called "reciprocity," is frequently encountered in copying. The law of reciprocity is the principle that allows a photographer to choose among many different f-stop and shutter speed combinations at one light level and get essentially the same exposure at all combinations. For example, when taking pictures outdoors with a fast film, an exposure of $f/16$ at 1/250 second might be indicated by your light meter. An equivalent exposure would be obtained using $f/11$ at 1/500 second or $f/22$ at 1/125 second. The reciprocity law is stated as Exposure = Illuminance x Time.

The reciprocity law applies to most films **except for extremely short and extremely long exposure**

times. During extremely long or short exposure times the equation E = IT can become invalid and reciprocity law "failure" occurs. This means that two equivalent f-stop/shutter speed combinations will not produce equal results. Usually, an increase in exposure and less development is required for long exposure times. All films do not respond exactly the same.

Because bellows factors, filter factors, slow film speeds, and relatively small apertures are used in copying, long exposure times are frequently required. Exposures longer than one second usually require a reciprocity-law failure adjustment with most films. Adjustment means an increase in exposure, either by lengthening the exposure time or opening up the diaphragm. The graph shows the reciprocity-law failure exposure time adjustments for many Kodak black-and-white films. Reciprocity curves for other films can be found in the KODAK Data Sheets.

Exposing KODAK Professional Copy Film, 4125

With ordinary black-and-white films, the contrast of negatives is controlled by development. However, with KODAK Professional Copy Film 4125, contrast in the copy negative is controlled by both development and exposure.

Development controls the contrast of the midtone and darktone (shadow) regions of the negative, (and to a slight extent, the highlight region) while exposure primarily controls the contrast of the light-tone region and the density range of the negative.

To determine the correct developing time for your conditions, a test can be performed to find the best exposure-development combination. Using a tray process and KODAK HC-110 Developer (Dil E), the development time range is from 3 to 5 minutes. To find which of these times gives the midtone and darktone (shadow) contrast suitable for your equipment, run a test of five negatives developed at 3, 3½, 4, 4½ and 5 minutes. If you are using a large tank, the times would be 4, 4½, 5, 5½ and 6 minutes. Expose the test negative to an original that has a contrast range that is typical of the type of originals to be copied. It is helpful if the original has a few large representative light, medium and dark tones. Print the negatives using your enlarger and paper that you plan to use, and select the negative that gives the midtone and darktone contrast you prefer.

Repeat the test, but vary the exposure and keep the development constant. Varying the exposure changes the ratio of tones recorded on the two portions of the characteristic curve. Negatives with less exposure will have more of the midtones recorded with normal contrast and fewer of the light tones and highlights recorded with increased contrast. Negatives with more exposure will have more of the midtones recorded with higher contrast. Make prints, and select the print which appears to have the best overall tonal quality. This determines the basic exposure to use. Using a KODAK Gray Card and an exposure meter, calculate backwards to get an exposure index that gives this type of copy negative.

For example, if the meter measurement of the card gives a value of 8, set the meter calculator at this value. Your exposure was 2 seconds at $f/16$. Adjust the calculator as you would set film speed until the exposure of 2 seconds at $f/16$ shows on the dial. By making several adjustments, you find the exposure index is 12. Use this value for future tests.

If a photograph to be copied has turned an even brownish tone, it helps to copy it through a blue filter, such as a KODAK WRATTEN Filter No. 47 or No. 47B. Although there are no recommended filter factors for this film, a factor of about 10X (3¼ stops) for

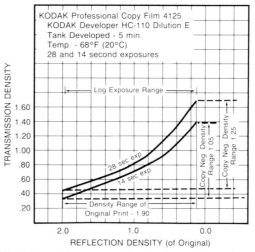

This graph shows how copy-negative density range is adjusted by changing the copy exposure when using KODAK Professional Copy Film. The curves are specific examples of 14 second and 28 second exposure times. Lighting and f-number are constant.

the No. 47 filter and 20X (4¼ stops) for the 47B with tungsten light should be a good starting point. With lights that have a daylight balance, a factor of about 6X (2½ stops) for the 47 and 12X (3½ stops) for the 47B should be close.

Once a basic exposure is found that produces good tone reproduction when the copy negative is printed on a normal-grade paper, the same exposure can be given when copying nearly all continuous tone originals. Adjustments are made, of course, for changes in magnification.

By giving the same exposure, the highlight tones are consistently placed in the upsweep part of the curve, while the midtones and dark tones are recorded on the lower, straight-line portion of the curve.

When using KODAK Professional Copy Film 4125, it is important to place the white tones on the same place on the characteristic curve of the copy film. For negatives to be printed on diffusion enlargers, a copy negative should have a maximum density (image of the whites) of about 1.20, which gives a copy negative density range of about 0.95 when a full scale print (reflection density range of about 1.65) is being copied.

When short-scale prints are being copied, there are two approaches. If the short-scale print (low reflection-density range) is short-scale because the subject was low in contrast, give the same exposure that you would to a full-scale print. The copy print will then come close to having the same tonal range of the original.

However, if the short-scale print is low in contrast as a result of fading, you want the copy print to have normal contrast. If the print looks like the low-contrast print illustrated on page 60, increase the exposure on professional copy film to increase the D-max and the copy negative density range to improve the contrast in the copy print. ½- to 1-stop increase in exposure should give the desired results.

These two illustrations are intended to show the difference between continuous tone and a halftone image; actually the reproduction above is a very fine-screen halftone—a continuous tone image cannot be printed by offset lithography.

Photo by Jean L. Wiley

This halftone has a screen coarse enough to be readily seen. The black dots in light tones are small. Dark tones are small white dots in an all-black surround. The halftone dot size is controlled by the original print tones when the halftone is made.

Photo by Jean L. Wiley

Be sure to adjust the exposure for magnification and reciprocity changes, if necessary.

You may want to try both methods to see which method meets your particular needs.

KODAK Professional Copy Film 4125, is an orthochromatic film, and cannot be used with orange or red filters. Further, this film is not generally recommended for copying colored originals. Reds will copy much darker than they appear. KODAK EKTAPAN Film 4162 in sheets, KODAK Technical Pan Film 2415, KODAK PLUS-X Pan and PLUS-X Pan Professional Films in rolls are recommended for red filter copying and copying colored originals in black-and-white.

KODAK Commercial Film 4127 is a blue-sensitive film. Without a filter it responds as if a blue filter were being used, so that it is a good film to use to copy overall brownish or yellowish faded prints. It also responds well to increasing developing times to increase contrast.

Exposing Line Negatives: An original that consists of tones that are only pure black and pure white is a line original. A line original must be exposed on high contrast film and processed in a high-contrast developer if a reproduction that looks like the original is desired.

When many line negatives are to be made it is a good idea to establish a basic exposure as was done with continuous-tone copies. There are some aspects about line copying that are different from continuous-tone copying.

When choosing an original to establish the basic exposure select an original that has good, rich blacks and clean, bright whites. A piece of type printed on smooth shiny paper is best. Be sure the type has clean sharp edges.

Your exposure can be determined with a light meter or by trial and error tests. To find a starting point for tests consult the chart on page 34 and select an exposure based on the film speed of the high-contrast film being used and the wattage of the light sources.

When a light meter is used to determine exposure, the readings can be made with a gray card and reflected-light meter, or with an incident meter and the indicated exposure is given. If a white card (instead of a gray card) is used with a reflected-light meter, give 5X the indicated exposure (an increase of $2\frac{1}{3}$ stops) as a starting exposure. This is to place the white in the highlight region of the film. The same exposure corrections for magnification, filter factors, and reciprocity failure apply to line and continuous tone copying. Do not forget to include these factors when making your first test.

Illustration Idea

With a little study and practice, the technical end of making photographs becomes natural and even easy. It is solving problems and translating ideas into successful photographs that makes photo illustrations a challenging, enjoyable, and lucrative way of making a living.

The photographs presented here are examples of ideas brought to successful conclusions through

This series of three illustrations is intended to show the effect of exposure on a line copy image. The illustration above received a correct exposure.

Illustration Idea

With a little study and practice, the technical end of making photographs becomes natural and even easy. It is solving problems and translating ideas into successful photographs that makes photo illustrations a challenging, enjoyable, and lucrative way of making a living.

The photographs presented here are examples of ideas brought to successful conclusions through

This copy print was made from an overexposed line negative. Notice how the lines have thinned, and how the letters in the text have become weak.

Illustration Idea

With a little study and practice, the technical end of making photographs becomes natural and even easy. It is solving problems and translating ideas into successful photographs that makes photo illustrations a challenging, enjoyable, and lucrative way of making a living.

The photographs presented here are examples of ideas brought to successful conclusions through

From an underexposed line negative. The lines have broadened, and in some cases, have run together. In the lower portion, the background density in the negative is too light so that some tone shows in the print.

A good line negative will have clear shadow areas (black on the original) and opaque highlights (white on the original) with few pinholes. (Pinholes are tiny clear areas in the dense portion of the negative. Some almost always occur on high-contrast films). It will maintain the same edge sharpness as the original and the same line thickness relationships. In other words, type won't have fuzzy edges, and the characters will be the same thickness in proportion to the original.

In the illustrations on page 39, prints were made from an underexposed line negative, a good negative, and an overexposed negative. The underexposed line negative has an excessive amount of pinholes, and does not have a high enough density in the highlight area. The normal negative makes a print with sharp black lines on a clean white background. The overexposed negative makes a print that loses sharpness and detail. The overexposure caused thin lines to fill in completely on the negative and sharp thick lines to become fuzzy. This is because overexposure causes areas to gain density that should have remained clear.

When a basic exposure has been established that produces a good line negative, this exposure can be used to calculate exposures for most other line negatives. The factors for magnification changes, filters, and reciprocity must be included in the calculations and the lighting and processing conditions should remain constant.

Some variations in negative quality can occur from negative to negative if the whiteness of the original paper stock is not consistent. To compensate for the differences in the whiteness of originals a reflected-light meter can be used to read the exposure from the original. The reading must be taken from a portion of the original that has no type on it. A blank piece of paper of the same type as the original, or the back of the original can also be used. A spot meter may be helpful in this situation. An exposure 5 times the calculated exposure is used as a starting exposure. For example, if the exposure is calculated to be 1 second at $f/16$ (based on the reading of a white portion of the original) the actual exposure would be about 5 seconds at $f/16$. As mentioned earlier, the indicated exposure is multiplied by 5 to find the correct exposure. A check should be made to see whether a correction should be made for reciprocity law failure.

Processing Black-and-White Copy Negatives

The procedures of processing rolls and sheets of copy negatives are just the same as those for processing regular negatives. These procedures are discussed in detail in KODAK Publication No. F-5, *KODAK Professional Black-and-White Films* and are not repeated here. However, some aspects of processing that pertain especially to copy negatives are important to review.

Choosing the Developer

The KODAK Data Sheets in this publication list suitable film developers for each film that can be used for copying. Usually a choice of several developers with recommended developing times are given.

When developing in a tank, it is appropriate to choose one of the recommended developers and dilutions that gives a developing time of five minutes or longer to aid in achieving uniformity of development.

When developing sheet films in a tray, on the other hand, choosing a developer and dilution that gives a moderately short developing time can speed up the process with less likelihood of poor development uniformity.

Uniformity of Development: If an exposure of an evenly lit gray card is made and the film is processed, you would expect to get an even density across the negative. However, especially with copy films, you may find that the density varies across the negative, usually due to agitation effects during development. This shows up more on copy negatives because they are usually developed to a higher contrast than normal negatives. There are two types of nonuniformity encountered.

Random Mottle: If there is a random variation in density that gives a mottled appearance, the negative has usually received inadequate agitation. Increasing the degree, duration or frequency of the agitation will usually correct this type of uneven density, except with very dilute developers.

High Edge Density: When two opposite edges of the negative have higher density than the center of the negative, the negative has received too much agitation.

While this effect usually results from agitation that is too vigorous, it can also occur from agitation that is too frequent or too long.

Developing Procedures

Some workers have found that developing sheet films with hangers in a small tank (one that just fits the hangers) leads to uneven development. Switching from a 4x5-inch tank to an 8x10-inch tank for

Equipment commonly used for small-batch film processing. The processing trays at upper left are used for sheet-film processing, as is the tank and sheet-film hangers at upper right. In the front area are reels and tanks used for roll-film processing.

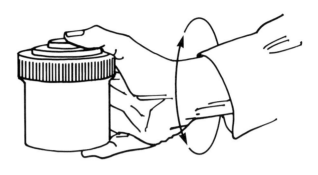

Agitation Method for an Inversion Tank

This type of agitation is called axial inversion because the tank is rotated 180° about an imaginary axis through the center of the tank. Although this method was developed specifically for developing KODAK Technical Pan Film, it is now believed that it gives more even results with all roll films.

4x5-inch films, for example, has been found to make the development more uniform. This is because the larger developer surface area gives less swirl to the developer as the films are agitated.

The recommended procedure for roll films on spiral reels in small tanks is to agitate for 5 seconds every 30 seconds. To aid uniformity the developer is put in the tank first, and in the dark, the loaded reel is lowered into the developer. The tank lid is put on the tank, and the tank is tapped several times on a firm surface to loosen air bells. Agitate for up to 4 cycles using the method appropriate for your tank. Do not agitate for the rest of the first 30 seconds. At the 30-second point, do a 5-second agitation cycle. From here on, at 30-second intervals, repeat 5-second agitation cycles for ththe duration of development. A special procedure is recommended for developing KODAK Technical Pan Film rolls. See page 60.

Several reels of roll film can be developed at a time in a deep tank normally used for sheet films. The reels are strung on a hanger rod and lowered into the developer. Agitation is accomplished by raising and rotating the rod. It is not necessary to lift the reels out of the developer. Agitate for 5 seconds at 1 minute intervals. After agitation, lower the reels slowly to the bottom of the tank.

Agitation Method for a Noninversion Tank

If the roll-film tank cannot be inverted without losing the solution, a horizontal agitation method can be used. The tank is moved back and forth as shown on a flat surface such as a sink bottom with enough force to cause the solution to move back and forth in the tank. Four back and forth movements make one cycle. Cycles are repeated at 30 second intervals. The tank is rotated 90° between each cycle so that the direction of the solution movement is changed.

Insertion Methods For Tray Developing Sheet Films

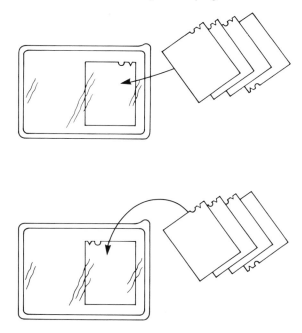

When using interleafing continuous agitation in the tray development of sheet films it is important to go through the stack completely. The first film in the developer is rotated 180° from the rest of the stack so that the notches are at the opposite end. This identifies it as the first film in so that it becomes the first film out, insuring an equal time of development for each film.

Agitation Technique for Sheet-Film Hangers in a Large Tank

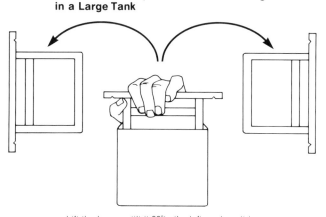

Lift the hanger, tilt it 90° to the left, replace it in tank. Lift it again, tilt it 90° to right, and replace it in tank. Repeat once each minute.

The agitation movements of sheet film hangers in tank development. One cycle is described. In large tank development, the agitation cycle is repeated at 1-minute intervals. Both hands may be used to hold the hangers.

When tray developing sheet films in quantity, the interleaving procedure is recommended. A water bath is prepared at the same temperature as the developer. The films are placed in the water, one at a time, emulsion side down. The stack is turned over so that emulsions are falling upward then the films are interleaved by placing the bottom film on the top of the stack. When the stack is back to its original order, the films are placed in the developer one at a time by the interleaving procedure—that is, the bottom film is removed and placed in the developer emulsion side up. Each successive bottom film is placed on top of the stack. When all are in the developer, the interleaving continues, bottom to top, for the duration of the developing time. They are then interleaved into the stop bath in the same order, bottom-to-top.

Another method is to place the films in the developer, emulsion side up. Each film is placed under the previous ones. When the stack of films is complete, start leafing by taking the bottom film out and placing it on top of the stack. This is repeated continuously for the development period.

Some workers keep counting the films so that each film receives the same number of leafings, and the "first-in, first-out procedure can be used. Others snip off a corner of the first film so that it can be detected in the dark by feel. A third method is to reverse the first film so that the notches are in the opposite corner than the others (see illustration).

When developing a single sheet, agitation is accomplished by a rocking motion of the tray. Each rock is at 90° to the next to provide a random motion to the waves of developer that provide the agitation.

Other Processing Patterns

When films are processed in a vertical position and given inadequate agitation, a condition called "bromide drag" sometimes occurs. If a dense area is above a low density area, bromide released by development of the dense area drops down over the less dense area, inhibiting development. This shows as less dense "streaks" in the lower area. The prevention is proper agitation.

Another directional effect sometimes occurs from physical variations in the film or in film hangers. If perforated film is overagitated, density patterns in negative areas near the perforations can occur, when sheet film being processed in hangers is agitated too vigorously, developer streaming through holes in the hanger can cause "streaks" of increased density. Again, the prevention is proper agitation.

While development uniformity is desirable with all films, KODAK Technical Pan Film is more sensitive to developing nonuniformity, so special care must be taken. See page 60. When the sheet form of

KODAK Technical Pan Film is being used for continuous-tone work, tray development is more likely to produce uniform density than tank development.

Machine Processing

Roller transport processors such as the KODAK VERSAMAT Processors (various models) generally provide very even development across the surfaces of both roll and sheet films. For those who have many films to process, they provide a fine way to process copy films. The amount of development for each type of film is adjusted by varying the speed of the processor film transport. Processing speeds for many Kodak films are available for KODAK VERSAMAT Processors in a *Machine Processing Data Release* which may be obtained from a Kodak Technical Sales Representative or by writing the Eastman Kodak Company, Consumer/Professional & Finishing Markets Publications Department, 343 State Street, Rochester, NY 14650.

For machine processing of high contrast copy negatives KODALITH MPII Ortho Film 2577 and KODALITH MPII Pan Film 2554 are available. They can be processed in the KODALITH Processor, Model 324 using KODALITH MPII Developer and KODALITH MPII Developer Replenisher. KODALITH MPII Films are designed for machine processing but can be processed conventionally also.

Densitometry for Copy Control

As with regular photography, much copying can be done with empirical controls and satisfactory results can be obtained. Judging negative densities and contrast by eye can be a reasonably accurate way to control copy negative quality.

However, when large numbers of copies are being made, or when the utmost copy quality is desired, a measurement control system can be of value. The measuring device used for this purpose is a densitometer.

Density: Density is a measure of the blackness, or light absorbing characteristic of an area in a photograph. Transmission density is a measure of the light absorbing characteristic of an area in a negative or a transparency. Reflection density is a measure of the light absorbing characteristic of an area in a print.

When used to control the copying (or duplicating) process, transmission density (usually just called density) is used.

Technically, density is the logarithm to the base 10 of the opacity, which is the reciprocal of the transmittance.

$$D = \log_{10} 0 = \log_{10} \frac{1}{T}$$

If an area in a negative transmits half the light, it has a transmittance of $\frac{1}{2}$, or 0.50. Thus:

$$\text{Transmittance} = \frac{\text{Transmitted Light}}{\text{Incident Light}}$$

where incident light is the light that falls on the film, and transmitted light is the light that passes through the film.

The percent transmission is 100 times the transmittance. If only half the light is transmitted, there is a transmittance of 0.50, or a 50 percent transmission.

Opacity is the reciprocal of the transmittance.

$$\text{Opacity} = \frac{1}{\text{Transmittance}} \quad \text{or} \quad \frac{\text{Incident Light}}{\text{Transmitted Light}}$$

A film area that has a transmittance of 0.50 has an opacity of $1/0.50 = 2.00$.

Density is the logarithm of the opacity; an area of film that has an opacity of 2.00 has a density of 0.301.

$$\log_{10} \frac{1}{0.50} = \log_{10} 2.00 = 0.301$$

The following table shows transmittance, opacity and density values of a few useful negative or transparency values.

Transmittance	Opacity	Density
1.000	1.000	0.000
.977	1.023	0.010
.891	1.122	0.050
.794	1.259	0.100
.500	2.000	0.301
.316	3.162	.500
.100	10.	1.000
.010	100.	2.000
.001	1,000.	3.000

The incident light generally used in densitometry is diffuse light, so technically in the following discussion densities are diffuse transmission densities.

Fortunately, densitometers are calibrated directly in density units so that it is not necessary to calculate densities from transmittances. These relationships are given to show that densities are valuable in determining how much light goes through a negative area with a measurable density value. It is the varying amounts of light going through the negative areas that expose the photographic paper to make the copy print.

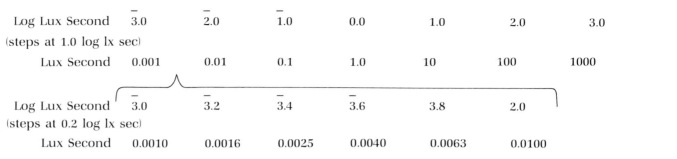

Log Lux Second (steps at 1.0 log lx sec)	$\overline{3.0}$	$\overline{2.0}$	$\overline{1.0}$	0.0	1.0	2.0	3.0
Lux Second	0.001	0.01	0.1	1.0	10	100	1000
Log Lux Second (steps at 0.2 log lx sec)	$\overline{3.0}$	$\overline{3.2}$	$\overline{3.4}$	$\overline{3.6}$	3.8	2.0	
Lux Second	0.0010	0.0016	0.0025	0.0040	0.0063	0.0100	

Characteristic Curves (H&D Curves, or D-Log E Curves): When a film is exposed to varying amounts of light and is developed, various densities result. If known exposures are given, and the resultant densities plotted against the exposures, a characteristic curve results.

Exposure values are given in lux seconds. A lux is a meter candle—that is the illuminance falling on a surface that is 1 meter from a standard candle. Exposure is illuminance X time (E = IT), and since time is calibrated in seconds, exposure values are lux seconds. Because density values are logarithmic, log lux-second values are used as the base units.

When a film is developed, the various amounts of densities have resulted from various amounts of exposure. If each density is plotted on graph paper directly above the log exposure value that produced it, a series of points results. When these points are connected with a smooth curved line, the characteristic curve of that particular film developed in a particular way is produced.

Three characteristic curves are shown on this page. The first is of a typical black-and-white camera film. Notice that the log exposure units on the scale are both in whole numbers and in bar values. Bar logs are minus logs, and represent decimal parts of 1 lux second exposure. The characteristics only are minus, the mantissas remain positive. The table on the top of the page shows the relationship between the log exposure values and the exposure values.

In the first curve illustrated, the toe section and the straight line portion of the curve are shown. In the toe section, the dark tones are recorded. Dark tones are compressed—that is, the separation between the tones is less than it is on the straight line. For copying purposes, it is wise to copy so that the darkest tone is reproduced just above the toe so that all tones are reproduced on the straight line. To accomplish this, a negative must be overexposed moderately. In this case, the tone compressions are only those caused by the paper curve shape.

The second curve shows the characteristics of KODAK Professional Copy Film. The use of this film was discussed earlier in the section "Tone Reproduction in Copying." The upsweep in the curve

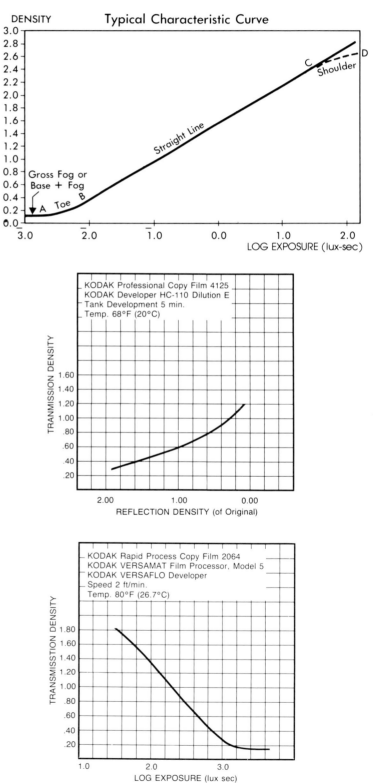

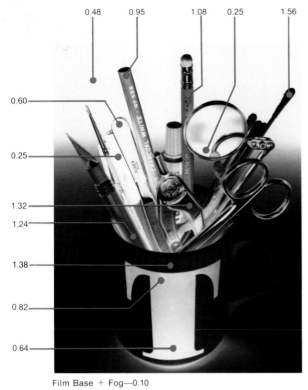

0.48 0.95 1.08 0.25 1.56

0.60

0.25

1.32
1.24

1.38

0.82

0.64

Film Base + Fog—0.10

The resultant negative densities are controlled by the subject illumination and reflectance, the camera exposure, the film, and the development. These factors are controlled by the photographer to obtain negatives with densities that will produce prints with good quality.

1.66 0.87 0.67 1.97 0.09

1.34

1.92

0.36

0.43

0.28

1.02

1.33

Paper Base—0.07

The print reflection densities are controlled by the negative densities, the type of enlarger, the paper, the print exposure and the print development.

where the original highlights are reproduced gives increased separation to the original light tones in the copy negative. This tends to compensate for the highlight compression of tones caused by the printing paper on which the copy negtive will be printed.

The third characteristic curve is of 35 mm direct duplicating film, KODAK Rapid Processing Copy Film 2064. The dark tones are produced by the least exposure, while the light tones are the result of more exposure. The curve slopes in the opposite direction from that of negative films. While designed as a duplicating film, this film can be used to copy prints, thus making blue-based slides in one step. Processing recommendations are given in the Data Sheet. Since this film is blue-sensitive, it is generally suitable for copying black-and-white originals only. As indicated by the curve position on the log exposure scale, this is a very slow film.

Density Range: The density range of a copy negative is the difference between the density of the original white paper highlights which are darkest in the negative, and the density of the deepest original black, which is the lightest area of the negative. Since most copy negatives are moderately overexposed to get the dark tones up off the toe of the characteristic curve, the lightest area in the image of the negative usually has a greater density than the film base.

Density range is useful in determining the printing characteristics of negatives.

Black-and-white negatives with a density range of about 1.05 usually print well on normal grade papers with diffusion enlargers. For condenser enlargers, a lower density range, usually about 0.85, is required. However, with KODAK Technical Pan Film, the 1.05 value works well with both types of enlargers. The grain is so fine that there is little Callier effect, i.e., increase in contrast when enlarging due to light scattering.

When black-and-white KODAK films such as PLUS-X Pan, Commercial, EKTAPAN, SUPER-XX, and Technical Pan, are used for copying, the main control of density range is by the amount of development, or the developer type. Usually the developing time is increased over the standard recommendations given on the instruction sheets packaged with the films because typical real life subjects have greater luminance ranges than the original photographs or artwork normally copied.

As previously mentioned, with KODAK Professional Copy Film, the density range is controlled primarily by exposure. Increasing the exposure places more of the picture tones on the upsweep part of the characteristic curve where the highlight densities increase more rapidly than the shadow densities—giving a greater density range.

When an original print has high quality, and a proper exposure is given on a special copy film, a high-quality copy negative results.

This series of three illustrations illustrates the difference in contrast between different prints. This is a high contrast print with a density range of 1.60.

This is a normal contrast print. The text gives two methods of exposing copy negatives of prints with different contrasts. The density range of the original print is 1.31.

The print from which this illustration was made is a copy print of the print above. The copy negative was made on KODAK Professional Copy Film exposed to give added contrast in the highlights. It is difficult to distinguish the original print from the copy print.

This is a low contrast print. When using KODAK Professional Copy Film, the recommended method is to expose all copy negatives to obtain a constant highlight density. The use of different grades of photographic paper gives the copy print contrast desired. The density range of this print is 1.13.

Reflection Densities: Originals that are copied are not all alike in their luminance ranges. This is caused by variations in their reflection densities. Reflection density is similar to transmission density except that the basic value is *reflectance* instead of transmittance. *Absorptance* is the reciprocal of the reflectance. Reflection density is the logarithm to the base 10 of the *absorptance*.

$$\text{Absorptance} = \frac{1}{\text{Reflectance}} \text{ or } \frac{\text{Incident Light}}{\text{Reflected light}}$$

$$\text{Reflection density} = \text{Log}_{10} \text{absorptance}$$

Reflection density is measured with reflection densitometers. These are calibrated to read reflection densities directly. Color densitometers have a setting with which black-and-white reflection densities can be measured.

If the color settings are marked red, green and blue, the black-and-white setting is likely to be marked amber. If the color settings are marked cyan, magenta and yellow, the black-and-white setting is likely to be marked black. The use of this setting will give the appropriate black-and-white density measurements.

However, if the original print being copied is faded to a yellowish color and is being copied with a blue filter, or with a blue sensitive film, it is better to measure the reflection density range with the blue filter in position in the densitometer. This position may be labeled blue or yellow, depending on the particular densitometer.

When high-quality copying is being done using regular films and the copy negatives are being individually processed, the reflection density range of the originals can be used to determine the developing time to obtain consistent negative density ranges. For example, if a print has a reflection density range of 2.0, and a developing time is found that gives a negative density range of 1.05, prints with less reflection density range should receive a longer developing time to achieve the same negative density range of 1.05. A series of experiments with your own equipment and materials will indicate how much change in developing time is needed for a given change in reflection density range.

However, when using KODAK Professional Copy Film, it is important to place the light to white tones on the same place on the characteristic curve shape of the copy film (and to maintain the same development). Each copy negative is given the same exposure, adjusting only for lens extension and darker than normal "whites" in the original. Negative density range will vary, and adjustment for negative density range is made in the choice of paper contrast when printing.

Densitometers

Both transmission and reflection densities are measured with instruments called densitometers.

Optical densitometers use a visual comparison method to measure density. Electronic densitometers use some type of light-sensitive device (cells, diodes) to measure densities, and range in price from several hundred dollars to thousands. The more costly ones are likely to have a higher degree of these attributes: repeatability, spectral integrity, linear response, dynamic range and low noise-to-signal ratio. Constant calibration and frequent maintenance are required for consistent, accurate measurements.

Densitometers that measure just black-and-white densities are less costly, but color densitometers are more versatile. If the possibility exists that color copying or duplicating may be done, it is probably a good investment to start right out with a color densitometer.

As explained in the text, densitometry can be of aid in achieving high-quality results in copying and in duplicating, in both black-and-white and color. The densitometer shown above measures both transmission and reflection densities.

Another type of densitometer is shown with a reflection density probe.

Both transmission and reflection densities can be measured on this densitometer. The large illuminator surface helps in locating the exact area to be measured.

Following is a partial list of densitometer manufacturers offered as a help in finding the kinds of densitometer useful in copying and duplicating. Eastman Kodak Company does not endorse or recommend specific equipment manufactured by other companies, or otherwise assume responsibility for such equipment.

Berkey Technical Co.
25-15 50th Street
Woodside, NY 11377

Brumac Industries, Inc.
P.O. Box 1786
Huntington Beach, CA 92647

Chesley F. Carlson Co.
2230 Edgewood Avenue
Minneapolis, MN 55426

Cosar Corporation
3121 Benton Street
Garland, TX 75042

ESECO-Speedmaster
East Airport Road
Cushing, OK 74023

Exposure Systems Corporation
265 Asylum Street
Bridgeport, CT 06610

Graphic Arts Manufacturing Company
2518 South Boulevard
Houston, TX 77006

MacBeth Corporation
P.O. Box 950
Little Britain Road
Newburgh, NY 12550

Photographic Sciences, Inc.
770 Basket Road
Webster, NY 14580

Sargent-Welch Scientific Company
7300 North Linder Avenue
Skokie, IL 60077

Tobias Associates, Inc.
50 Industrial Drive
Ivyland, PA 18974

The X-Rite Company
4101 Roger Chaffee Drive SE
Grand Rapids, MI 49508

Special Techniques

Using Filters

Filters are used in a number of ways in black-and-white copying. Contrast filters, polarizing filters and one type of specialized filter (diffusion) are used in this type of work. Only occasionally are conversion, light-balancing and color-compensating filters used except for color copying and duplicating.

Contrast Filters

The color filter circle on page 35 shows the various KODAK WRATTEN Filter numbers of the filters usually considered to be contrast filters.

Contrast filters are strongly colored filters used to change the tonal rendition of colors when photographed in black-and-white. As the color filter circle shows, colors that are similar to the filter being used are made lighter in the final print, while complementary colors, that is, those that are opposite on the circle, are darkened. When a red filter is used, reds, magentas, and yellows are lightened while blue-greens (cyans), blues, and greens are darkened. Filters alter the balance of the wavelengths of light entering the camera. A red filter such as the KODAK WRATTEN Filter No. 25 absorbs most of the blue and green light and transmits much of the red light. The film is only exposed to the red light.

In order to expose the film properly, the exposure (shutter speed and/or aperture) must be increased. How much it is increased is determined by the filter factor. The filter factor for the No. 25 filter is 8X with daylight balanced light and 5X with tungsten balanced light with most panchromatic films.

The Color Filter Circle shows the filter factors for a variety of filters. One way to increase the exposure is to multiply the exposure time (shutter speed) by the filter factor. If the exposure time without a filter is $1/4$ second, and the filter factor is 5X, the time (at the same f-number) is $5 \times 1/4 = 5/4 = 1 1/4 = 1.25$ seconds (for most applications, 1 second would be close enough).

Another way to increase the exposure is to open up the lens, that is, to change the f-number to a lower number. The following table gives the exposure change in stops for a variety of filter factors.

Filter Factor	+Stops	Filter Factor	+Stops	Filter Factors	+Stops
1.25X	+ $1/3$	4X	+2	12X	+ $3^2/3$
1.5X	+ $2/3$	5X	+ $2^1/3$	40X	+ $5^1/3$
2X	+1	6X	+ $2^2/3$	100X	+ $6^2/3$
2.5X	+ $1^1/3$	8X	+3	1000X	+10
3X	+ $1^2/3$	10X	+ $3^1/3$		

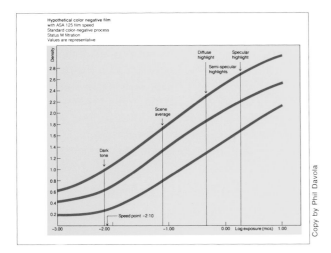

This colored graph serves as an example for the use of contrast filters.

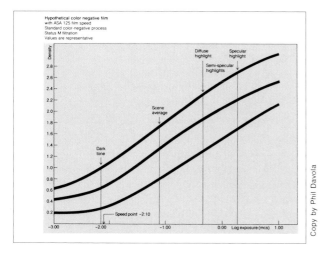

This copy photograph was made on KODAK Contrast Process Pan Film without a filter. Note how the yellow background shows a light tint.

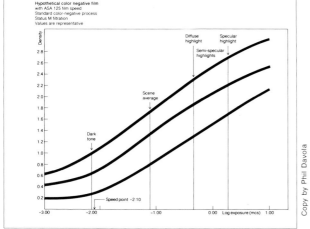

KODALITH Pan Film with a KODAK WRATTEN Filter No. 8 (green) lightens the yellow and darkens the red. This then becomes a clean black-and-white line rendition of the colored graph.

For example, if the filter factor is 5X, the increase in stops is $2^1/_3$. If the original aperture is $f/16$, the aperture corrected for the filter factor would be about $f/7$, or $^1/_3$ stop larger than $f/8$.

Uses of Contrast Filters: The important use of contrast filters is to eliminate or reduce the effects of a colored stain on the original. If an original black-and-white photograph has a red stain on it, and if it is copied through a red (No. 25 or 29) filter, onto a panchromatic film, the copy negative will show a decided lightening of the stain effect. The copy print may even show no evidence of the stain.

The most common stain color is brown. The red filters mentioned above (Nos. 25 and 29) are the best to use to minimize brown stains. If the print is overall brown, a blue filter is used to enhance contrast.

Another use of contrast filters is to provide contrast between colors in an original when making black-and-white copies with panchromatic films. Two areas in the original may be separated well by color, but may photograph as the same tone. By choosing a filter that lightens one color and darkens the other, the same areas will be separated by tone in the copy.

A third use of filters is to enhance the contrast in old, faded, brown-imaged prints. A deep blue filter (No. 47, 47B) increases the image contrast. This use is shown in the series illustrating the use of KODAK Technical Pan Film for copying on page 57. (For local brown stains, a red filter is used.)

Neutral Density, Conversion, Light-Balancing and Color-Compensating Filters: These filters are primarily used in color copying and duplicating, and are rarely used in black-and-white copying.

However, the use of a light-colored filter may be desirable, especially when copying colored originals on black-and-white film.

If two colored areas do not separate in tone when copying without a filter, and separate too much with the strongly colored contrast filters, the lighter colored filters, such as CC (color compensating) filters are useful. If, for example, the No. 25 red filter gives too much tone separation, a CC50R filter may provide the desired moderate tone separation.

The bluish 80 series and orangish 85 series of conversion filters can be used in a like manner.

In rare instances, neutral density filters are used to provide longer copy exposure times with black-and-white (as well as color) copying. Longer exposure times may be needed if color film is balanced for long exposure times. In any copying, it is difficult to give exact exposure times of $1^1/_2$ seconds, for example. A 0.3 neutral density filter reduces the light reaching the film by a factor of 2. If you want to give the $1^1/_2$ second exposure without changing the f-number, place a 0.3 neutral density filter over the lens and expose for 3 seconds. The time error will be reduced. If the film requires it, an additional amount of time may be needed to correct for reciprocity law failure.

Copy by Tom Benson

The illustration above is made from a copy print of a daguerreotype. Daguerreotypes are shiny metallic silver images and require a special arrangement to copy.

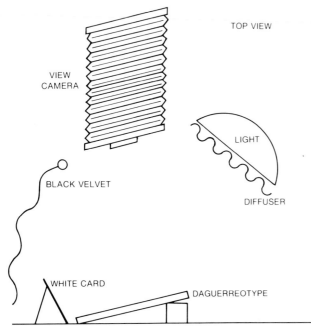

Photographing a Daguerreotype with a View Camera

A diffuse light is placed to illuminate the daguerreotype, which is placed at an angle to the camera axis. A black velvet cloth is placed so that its black image reflects to the camera. A small white reflector is placed to reflect light across the daguerreotype. The camera front and back are tilted at the same angle as the daguerreotype to keep the image rectilinear.

Copying Daguerreotypes

A daguerreotype is a photographic image on a silver-coated copper plate, resulting in a mirror-like surface. To obtain a positive image, the daguerreotype must be reflecting a black surface to the camera. The diagram shows an arrangement that will reflect black to the lens while the diffuse light tones are illuminated. The camera tilts correct for the distortion resulting from the angle of the daguerreotype.

Copying with IR and UV Radiation

Infrared Copying: Infrared radiation is similar to light but occurs at slightly longer wavelengths. KODAK High Speed Infrared Film 4143 (ESTAR Thick Base) in sheets, and its 35 mm equivalent KODAK High Speed Infrared Film 2481 has an infrared sensitivity to wavelengths from about 700 to 900 nanometres. (The eye is sensitive from about 400 to about 700 nanometres). The film is also sensitive to blue light, so it is usually exposed through a red filter such as KODAK WRATTEN Filters No. 87, 25, 29 or 70, or in extreme cases, an infrared filter, No. 87C if a record is required in the infrared region only.

As a result of its unusual sensitivity, infrared film "sees" differently than the eye, and can be used to detect some things that cannot be seen.

One use is to copy paintings where there is a suspicion that there is a painting under that which can be seen. The film may be able to see through the upper painting and show the underpainting—or at least show that there is an underpainting. This method does not work in all cases, but it is one of the methods to try if alterations in a painting are suspected.

Another important use of IR sensitive film is to copy charred or burnt documents where the original writing is invisible. The original writing may be made visible in the infrared copy. Writing made illegible by age, accumulation of dirt, by a stamp applied by a censor, by chemical bleaching, or by mechanical erasure may also be made visible in an infrared copy.

Some inks fluoresce in the infrared region when stimulated with ultraviolet radiation. An infrared copy can make this fluorescence visible.

Filters and Light Sources for Infrared Copying: As indicated above, the No. 87 filter is commonly used for infrared copying. Incandescent bulbs are a good source of infrared radiation for copying. As indicated on The Data Sheet on page DS-11, the exposure index when exposing with the No. 87 Filter in incandescent light is 64; with the No. 87C Filter it is 25. Other filters and indexes are given on the Data Sheet.

Sunlight contains infrared radiation and can be used as a light source for infrared copying. Electronic flash units also emit infrared radiation—low voltage models emit a higher percentage of IR than do high-voltage models.

Focusing for Infrared Copying: Most lenses used for copying are corrected for chromatic aberration with visible light. With infrared radiation, the focal length is longer. Hence, a visual focus will not give a precise infrared focus.

Some lenses have a red mark on the focusing scale for infrared focus. When using an IR filter, the focusing scale is set at the red dot instead of the usual arrows. When using red filters that transmit light as well as IR, set the focusing scale partway between the red dot and the arrow. With lenses not marked, as with view camera lenses, the procedure is to focus visually and then increase the lens to film distance by 0.25 percent.

If the lens to film distance is 10 inches, for example, the increase required would be:

$$0.0025 \times 10 \text{ inches} = 0.025 \text{ inch}$$

.025 inches is slightly less than $\frac{1}{32}$ inch. In most cases, stopping the lens down as is generally done when copying should provide enough depth of field to accommodate the difference in focal length between light and infrared radiation.

Infrared copy negatives may not be as sharp as their visual counterparts because the aberrations of the lens have been corrected for light and not infrared radiation. Stopping the lens down to moderately small apertures will minimize the effects of some of the aberrations and provide improved sharpness.

Infrared luminescence is generally caused by illuminating an object with blue-green light. Certain materials will then emit infrared radiation. While photographing IR luminescence is generally used in scientific photography of biological specimens and minerals, it is sometimes used in law-enforcement photography. Filters or screens made of 9780 Corning Glass color filter, C.S. No. 4-76, molded, 8 mm (blue-green) are generally recommended, but a KODAK WRATTEN Filter No. 44 combined with a KODAK Infrared Cutoff Filter No. 301A can also be used. The 301A filter is placed nearest the light. An infrared filter such as the KODAK WRATTAN Filter No. 87 is placed over the camera lens. Exposure is based on experience gained by running an exposure series.

Copying by Ultraviolet Radiation

While infrared radiation has wavelengths longer than those of light, ultraviolet radiation has wave-

This check was copied on regular film with normal illumination. It looks perfectly normal.

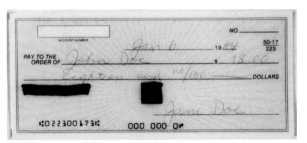

Copied with infrared radiation, it can easily be seen that the value of the check has been raised with a different ink than was originally used. Some trial and error with filters may be necessary. This copy was made on KODAK High Speed Infrared Film using KODAK WRATTEN Filter, No. 89B.

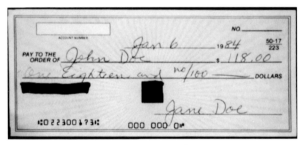

Copied with short wave ultraviolet radiation. The difference between the two inks in the copy is considerably less than with infrared. With other inks, UV copies might show up the difference better than IR copies. This copy was made on KODAK Technical Pan Film developed in KODAK D-19 Developer.

lengths shorter than those of light.

Ultraviolet copy photography has some of the same uses as infrared copying. It is often used to detect faded or vanished writing, chemical erasures and is used in the study of paintings. It is particularly useful in law enforcement photography to detect forgeries.

The wavelengths of the ultraviolet band of radiation extends from about 10 nanometres to 400 nanometres, where light starts. However, the glass in photographic lenses transmits beginning only from about 350 nm to 400 nm, so that this is the region commonly used in UV photography. All normal black-and-white films are sensitive through the entire UV band, so that no special films are required. As with infrared copying, one method is required for copying ultraviolet reflection, while the other is used for ultraviolet fluorescence.

51

Copying Infrared Reflectance

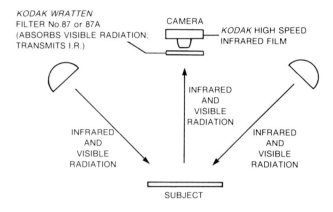

The basic setup for reflectance infrared copying. Tungsten lamps are a good source of IR radiation.

Copying Infrared Luminescence

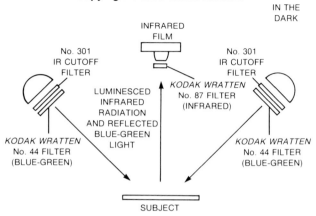

When copying luminescence caused by IR radiation, the subject is illuminated with blue-green light by using a No. 44 filter over each light. The camera lens is filtered with a No. 87 filter so only infrared radiation is transmitted to the lens. The copying is done in the dark.

Copying Ultraviolet Reflectance

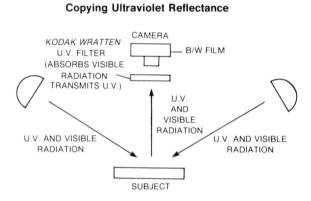

Lights rich in UV radiation, such as arc lights, fluorescent lights, or pulsed xenon lights are used for UV copying. The UV filter over the lens allows only UV to record on the film.

Copying Ultraviolet Fluorescence

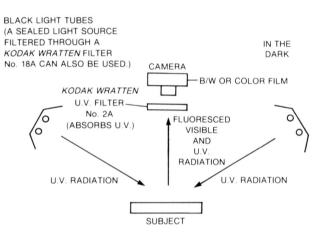

When copying luminescence caused by ultraviolet radiation, the subject is illuminated by ultraviolet radiation and no light. A filter that absorbs UV is placed over the lens. The fluorescence is in wavelengths of light, and is photographed with a regular black-and-white or color film.

Ultraviolet Reflection Copying: This is the primary method used in copying to detect forgeries. In this method, the copy is illuminated with any light source that contains ultraviolet radiation, and a filter is placed over the lens that transmits only ultraviolet radiation. An alternative method is to illuminate the copy with a source that emits only ultraviolet radiation, and to copy with no filter over the lens. This must be done in total darkness.

The black lights sold for special visual effects with fluorescent posters can be used for casual UV copying, but may not be suitable for critical use. A General Electric UVIARC or other UV source can be fitted into a lighttight box equipped with a suitable UV filter to emit ultraviolet radiation only. The KODAK WRATTEN Ultraviolet Filter No. 18A (Glass) is available on special order. The CORNING Glass Filter No. 5860 (Violet Ultra 10 mm thick) is another.

The KODAK WRATTEN Ultraviolet Filter No. 18A (Glass) is also available in 50 mm (2-inch) and 75 mm (3-inch) squares to be used over the camera lens.

Ultraviolet Fluorescence Copying: Certain materials absorb ultraviolet radiation and emit light—they fluoresce. For copying this fluorescence, the copy must be illuminated by ultraviolet radiation only, and the copying must be done in the dark. Such UV sources are described above.

A filter that absorbs ultraviolet radiation is used over the camera lens so that only the fluoresced light is copied. Such filters are the KODAK WRATTEN Filters No. 2A, 2B and 2E.

Some inks tend to fluoresce under UV stimulation. This method should be tried when the writing on a document has faded badly. It may fluoresce, giving a better copy image of the writing. A high-contrast film such as KODAK Contrast Process Ortho Film 4154 (ESTAR Thick Base) or KODAK Technical Pan film, 2415 are recommended for this type of photography.

Color film can be used to copy the fluorescence of posters printed with fluorescent printing inks, as well as the fluorescence of certain minerals.

No focusing correction is usually required for ultraviolet copying, but small apertures are recommended for minimizing aberrations and providing enough depth-of-field to compensate for a slight focus shift between visible and UV focus. Fairly long exposure times on the order of 1 minute at $f/16$ are required.

More information on the specialized techniques of Infrared and Ultraviolet photography can be found in KODAK Publication M-28, *Applied Infrared Photography* and M-27, *Ultraviolet and Fluorescence Photography*.

Using Polarizing Filters

The use of polarizing filters* is a valuable technique in copying. The main purpose for polarizing filters is to control reflections. Polarization also increases color saturation in color copying, and often increases contrast.

Polarizing filters work by taking advantage of the wave nature of light. Unpolarized light vibrates in all directions, with the direction of the wave vibration being perpendicular to the direction of the path of light in all planes. Polarized light vibrates in only one direction. It occurs when light is reflected at an oblique angle off polished, non-metallic surfaces such as those of glass, water, glossy photographs or shiny painted surfaces.

Polarization also occurs when light passes through a polarizing filter. Because the light reflecting from a shiny surface at oblique angles vibrates in one direction, a polarizing filter can block that light by only allowing light to pass that vibrates in a different direction. The first two illustrations show how unpolarized light is polarized by a shiny surface and by a polarizing filter. The third drawing illustrates how a polarizing filter eliminates a reflection.

Originals that are not shiny surfaced will not fully polarize the light as it is reflected. With such originals it is helpful to have polarizing screens over the light sources. Maximum polarization, however, is obtained by using polarizing screens over the lights and a polarizing filter over the camera lens. This technique is called double or crossed polarization. A schematic of this technique is illustrated on page 54.

*We have used the convention that *polarizing filters* are used over the camera lens, and *polarizing screens* are used over the lights although the polarizing material is the same.

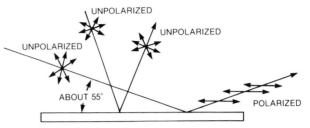

Polarized and Unpolarized Light

The diagram shows the angle of maximum polarization from a plate-glass surface. The angle with a water surface is about 47°.

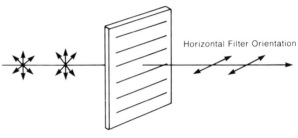

Polarizing Filter

The light beam coming in from the left is unpolarized light and the light waves vibrate in all directions at 90° to the beam path. After going through the polarizer, the light waves vibrate in only one direction, in the drawing, horizontally.

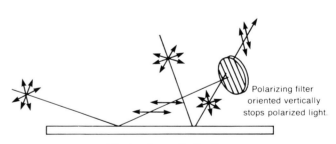

Eliminating a Reflection

A horizontal sheet of glass polarizes the light horizontally. If a polarizing filter is placed over the lens with its polarization vertical, the reflected polarized light is absorbed, effectively eliminating the reflection.

Adjusting polarizers is relatively simple. When a polarizing filter is used over the lens only, the filter is rotated until the image on the camera ground glass or viewfinder in a single-lens reflex camera shows the least amount of reflection. Cameras with beam-splitter mirrors are not suitable for use with polarizers. For cameras that do not have through-the-lens viewing systems the adjustment can be made by viewing the copy from the camera's vantage point and rotating the filter in front of the eye until the reflections are minimized. The position of the filter is noted, and it is then placed on the camera lens with the same orientation.

In a vertical copy setup when polarizing screens are used over the lights *only*, the maximum effect is gained by orienting the polarizing screens so that they polarize horizontally. In a horizontal copy set-up the maximum effect would be gained by orienting the screens to polarize vertically. The orientation of the screen refers to the direction in which light must vibrate in order to be able to pass through the screen. To determine the vertical orientation of a screen, look at a reflection from a horizontal surface through the screen. Rotate the polarizing screen until the reflection is eliminated. This is the vertical orientation of the screen. Rotate the screen ninety degrees to put the screen in horizontal orientation. Label the screen at the top for its polarization direction for future reference. The screens should be placed in the proper orientation in front of the lights before shooting.

When double polarization is used for maximum reflection control, the polarizing screens on the light sources should be oriented first (one at a time), then the polarizing filter on the lens can be rotated until the reflection is minimized. A shiny-surfaced sphere placed on the copyboard helps to detect the effects of the polarizers. The procedure can be reversed, adjusting the polarizing filter on the lens first.

When artwork that has cels or transparent overlays is copied with polarizing filters, stress patterns from the overlay material may appear in the copy. To avoid this effect, acetate cels should be used for the artwork or polarizers should not be used.

Polarization is often essential for the highest quality copy work. There are many situations in which polarizing provides the difference between an unacceptable copy and a copy of high quality. Polarization is helpful for eliminating "silvering" when copying old photographic prints. It helps eliminate or minimize the texture of rough-surfaced prints. When transparent or translucent tape has been used on the surface of a print to repair a tear (a destructive practice) polarization can make the tape almost invisible in the copy. Polarization is also extremely helpful when copying paintings. Illustra-

Lights with polarizing screens are used when double or crossed polarization is needed to eliminate specular reflections. These are KODAK Pola-Lights, Model 2 equipped with KODAK POLA-SCREENS for KODAK Pola-Lights.

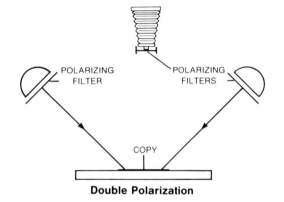

Double Polarization

Copying lights are often at angles to the copy surface other than the angle of maximum polarization. Putting polarizing screens over the lights and a polarizing filter over the lens can eliminate reflections. The text explains how to orient the polarizers.

tions showing applications of polarization are on page 55.

Whenever polarizing filters are used an exposure compensation must be made (unless a through-the-lens meter is used). Most polarizing filters have a filter factor of 2.5X to 3.0X and require an exposure increase of about one and one half f-stops. When polarizing screens are used over the lights an additional increase in exposure is necessary. This increase can be measured by taking a light meter reading with the screens over the lights and comparing it to a reading without the screens over the lights*. The difference in measured exposure should be added to the tested basic exposure in use. The exposure required with crossed polarization may be 20 times the exposure without the polarizers. It may also be necessary to include an increase for the reciprocity characteristics of the film when exposure times get long.

An increase in color saturation may also be noticed as a result of polarization. This is because the polarization filter removes specular reflections from the image which would otherwise dilute the colors.

*This does not work with cameras that have beam splitters in the optical path.

Some old photographs "silver-out," that is, they develop a mirror-like silver surface in certain high density areas. Note the loss of blacks, especially in the lower part of the picture in this copy photograph made with unpolarized light.

If copied with double polarization, the effects of the silvering-out are minimized in the copy.

Another use of polarizers is to minimize texture in copying prints made on a textured paper. This print was copied without polarizers.

The same print was copied using double polarization. The texture on the original print has been reduced in the copy.

Copy by Tom Benson

Copy by Tom Benson

At the same time, the contrast of the copy image is increased because the specular reflection would othewise lower the contrast. This increased image contrast helps increase shadow tone separation in the copy. With single-lens-reflex cameras that have beam-splitting mirrors, these effects may not occur, or may occur but with incorrect exposure. Circular polarizers are available for such cameras.

Polarizing filters that are used in front of camera lenses are easily obtained in camera stores or from other photographic suppliers. Polarizing filters (screens) that are used in front of lights must be large enough to span the width of the front of the light. For this, large sheets of polarizing filter material are necessary and are sometimes difficult to get. At least two companies sell large sheets of polarizing material: Edmund Scientific Company, Barrington, NJ and Spiratone, Inc., New York City. KODAK Pola-Lights are lights that are made specifically for photographing with polarized light. These may be ordered from a Professional Stockhouse Dealer who handles Kodak products. The catalog number of the KODAK Pola-Light, Model 2 is 147 5797.

A Method of Copying Yellowed and Faded Originals with KODAK Technical Pan Film 2415

Possibly one of the most perplexing problems in copying yellowed and faded photographs, especially for the inexperienced, is the choice of film, filter, and developer. Usually a considerable amount of time, in trial and error experimentation, is required.

A very versatile film, KODAK Technical Pan Film 2415, makes this an easier and more pleasant task. The film has extremely fine grain, extremely high resolution, and uncommon flexibility in processing. The fine grain characteristic of this film makes it ideal for copying medium to low contrast originals with 35 mm and 4 x 5 inch format cameras. Developed in KODAK Developer D-19 or KODAK DEKTOL Developer, it can be used to copy high-contrast originals like pen and ink drawings. With a concentrated developer such as KODAK HC-110 Developer, it is possible to use a range of developer dilutions to accommodate originals with varying density ranges.

In the illustrations on the following pages, originals were selected that had various density ranges. They represent photographs in progressive degrees of fading, from prints that are almost normal to severely faded and yellowed specimens. A negative was made from each of the originals that had good printing characteristics. Each of the reproductions made from the negatives showed an improvement in tone rendition over the original.

The chart below shows how the different originals were handled with two developer dilutions using KODAK HC-110 Developer. KODAK POLYCONTRAST Rapid II RC Paper with KODAK POLYCONTRAST Filters was used to make the prints. The originals that were extremely yellowed required the use of a KODAK WRATTEN Filter No. 47B (blue) over the camera lens. The developing time was 8 minutes for all the films in both of the dilutions. This developing time is a starting point and should be used as a guide only.

Original	Filter	Developer Dilution	KODAK POLYCONTRAST Printing Filter	Density Range of Original
#1	—	HC-110F	1	1.12
#2	—	HC-110F	2	1.05
#3	47B	HC-110B	2½	.99
#4	47B	HC-110B	3	.94
#5	47B	HC-110B	3½	.61
#6	47B	HC-110B	3½	.50

All negatives developed in a large tank for 8 minutes at 68°F (20°C).

KODAK Technical Pan Film 2415 also has extended red sensitivity. Technical Pan Film without the use of any filters, will record the reddish areas so that they are slightly lighter than normal in the print. If it is not desirable to lighten the reddish areas, a KODAK WRATTEN Filter No. 38 or a KODAK Color Compensating Filter, CC40C may be used to neutralize the extended red sensitivity of the film. A filter factor of 1.5X can be used for the CC40C filter while a filter factor of 2X in tungsten and 4X in daylight must be used for the No. 38 filter. It may be helpful to do this when copying color prints, hand colored photographs or warm toned prints.

Some old deteriorated photographs may have reddish patches or spots. Commonly, when reddish patches or spots occur they are stains. It is usually desirable to eliminate or minimize the tone of the stain. The extended red sensitivity of Technical Pan Film is an advantage in this case. Used in conjunction with a red filter, such as a KODAK WRATTEN Filter No. 25, it is a very effective tool for minimizing reddish stains. However, if a red or reddish brown spot occurs in a dense area, it may be due to oxidation and should not be lightened by the use of a red filter. Copy with no filter or with a CC40C filter.

Filter factors for these filters and others are given on the next page. These filter factors only apply to KODAK Technical Pan Film because of its extended red sensitivity.

Set 1. In this series, KODAK Technical Pan Film developed in KODAK HC-110 Developer is used to compensate for variations in original print contrast. This print is only slightly faded, and is copied in a manner similar to copying regular prints.

The copy print has close to the same tonal characteristics as the original print. See the table opposite for filter and developing data.

Set 2. This print has slightly less contrast than the first original. Exposure and processing were the same, however, and the contrast gain was achieved in printing.

The copy print has been brought back to a normal contrast. If a brown color is desirable, the copy prints can be toned.

| KODAK WRATTEN Filter | Filter Factors | |
	Tungsten	Daylight
No. 8	1.2X	1.5X
No. 25	2 X	3 X
No. 38	2 X	3 X
No. 47	25 X	12 X

Because of the extremely fine grain and high resolving power of this film it is a valuable film for copying with small format cameras. When copying with roll film, group originals together according to contrast so that low contrast originals are shot on one roll of film, normal contrast originals on anoth-er, etc. Then the roll that contains the low contrast originals can be developed longer (or in a stronger developer dilution), the roll that contains normal originals can be developed for the normal time, etc. Using the example provided above, it is possible to group the originals into two categories for copying so that only two rolls of film would be necessary: the extremely low contrast originals requiring a strong developer (i.e. less dilute), and originals that are near normal in contrast requiring a more dilute developer. Contrast refinements can be made for negatives within these groups during printing by using appropriate paper grades or KODAK POLYCONTRAST Filters (with KODAK POLYFIBER Paper).

Set 3. The contrast of this print has been reduced considerably by the effects of time and fumes in the air. Perhaps it was not washed adequately when it was made.

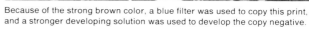

Because of the strong brown color, a blue filter was used to copy this print, and a stronger developing solution was used to develop the copy negative.

Set 4. The contrast of this print is lower yet, probably due to the effects of time and fumes. In this print, the highlights have stained, lowering the reflection density range.

This print was copied the same as set 3, but printed with more contrast. Because the highlights have been raised in tone, and the dark tones deepened, a normal tonal range has been restored.

Set 5. The same things have happened to this original as happened to the set 4 original, only more so. While the image is discernible, the print has a very low contrast.

The copy print has brought back the contrast, but the shadow detail has been nearly lost. (It may not have been in the print originally.)

Set 6. This print has browned and faded so badly that the image is very difficult to make out. However, the flexibility of this method of copying is useful, even with this type of original.

By using the blue filter, a full development, and by printing with a high contrast POLYCONTRAST filter, the image in the copy print has been made quite visible.

Photographer unknown

Copy by Kodak Research Laboratories

An alternative to using KODAK Technical Pan Film when copying low contrast originals is to use KODAK Process Pan or KODAK Process Ortho Film. This faded print was copied on KODAK Process Pan Film.

This copy print was made with normal contrast paper (a PC2 filter on KODAK POLYCONTRAST Rapid II RC Paper F-Surface).

Developing KODAK Technical Pan Film: Small and medium format Technical Pan Film can be developed in a tank on spiral metal or plastic reels. As illustrated, KODAK TECHNIDOL Liquid Developer and KODAK TECHNIDOL LC Developer (powder) require different agitation techniques.

1. Before loading the film on the reels, fill the developing tank with the amount of developer needed to fill the tank. Leave enough space at the top to allow for later insertion of the loaded reel without overflowing.

2. After the reels are loaded, place the loaded reels smoothly and quickly into the tank filled as above with developer.

3. Replace the top on the developer tank. Tap the tank once or twice on a hard surface to dislodge air bells from the surface of the film.

4. *For TECHNIDOL Liquid Developer*: Agitate for 2 seconds with "paint-can" shake described in illustration.

   For TECHNIDOL LC Developer (powder): Agitate up to 4 inversions of tank using axial inversion as described in illustration.

5. Let the tank sit for the remainder of the first thirty seconds.

6. At intervals of 30 seconds for the rest of the development, agitate for:
   a. 2 seconds using "paint-can" shake if using TECHNIDOL Liquid Developer.
   b. 5 seconds using axial inversion if using TECHNIDOL LC Developer (powder).

Agitation Technique for TECHNIDOL Liquid Developer

Rapidly shake tank up and down over a distance of a few inches as if you were shaking a paint can. Do not rotate the tank.

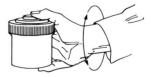

Agitation Technique for TECHNIDOL LC Developer (powder)

Extend your arm. Turn the tank upside down by rotating your arm (with no lateral arm movement) and then return the tank to an upright position. During a 5-second agitation cycle, you should invert the tank 2 to 5 times depending upon contrast desired and individual technique.

Agitation may vary from individual to individual depending upon that person's technique and depending upon the amount of contrast desired. More agitation will produce more contrast; less agitation will produce less contrast.

Overagitation, particularly during the first minute of development, can cause uneven development. Often, the uneven development is characterized by areas of extra density near the sprocket holes of the film. Insufficient agitation during the first minute of development will cause uneven development or mottle over the entire surface of the film.

Large format Technical Pan Film should be processed in a tray for best results. Development of Technical Pan Film in sheet film hangers tends to produce unacceptable unevenness of development. Developing times shorter than five minutes should be avoided for both rolls and sheets of KODAK Technical Pan Film. It is difficult to develop sheets of Technical Pan Film to a contrast-index of 0.56 or lower without getting uneven densities.

Improving Highlight Tone Rendition

As discussed earlier, one of the frequent tone-rendition occurrences in copying is the compression of highlight tones so that they look muddy, making the copy print lose sparkle. KODAK Professional Copy Film usually improves highlight tone rendition, but for several reasons there are instances where this cannot be used. It may not be available in a size to fit the copy camera, the originals may be in color so that a panchromatic film is needed, or only occasional copies are made and Professional Copy Film is not available at the time.

Highlight rendition by conventional black-and-white films can be improved in several ways.

Chemical Method: The copy negative can be locally intensified in the highlight areas (densest areas in the negative). A single solution intensifier is applied locally to the negative in the highlight areas, increasing the density and contrast in these areas. A cotton swab or spotting brush can be used to apply the intensifier. The gain in density can be controlled by placing the negative over an illuminator during the intensification. KODAK Intensifier IN-6 is a satisfactory intensifier for this procedure. The formula and instructions for use of this intensifier can be found in KODAK Publication No. J-1, *Processing Chemicals and Formulas*. KODAK Selenium Toner can also be used as a local intensifier for this purpose. The density-contrast increase with a particular toning is shown in the graph.

Dye Methods: The highlight areas of the copy negative can be increased in density by applying dyes such as KODAK Crocein Scarlet or neutral spotting dyes. The dye is applied locally using a cotton swab and spotting brushes. While increasing the effective negative density of the highlights, this method does not increase their contrast, as does the intensifier method.

Photographic Masking: The density and contrast of the copy negative highlight regions can be enhanced by use of a highlight mask.

A single step masking procedure consists of contact printing the negative onto a black-and-white direct duplicating film. KODAK Professional B/W Duplicating Film (ESTAR Thick Base) can be used. A relatively long exposure and long developing time is used to provide densities only in the highlight regions, and to provide adequate contrast to the mask. When processed, the highlight mask is registered with the copy negative, and taped into place.

Another suitable film for single-step masking is KODALITH Duplicating Film 2574 (ESTAR Base) which can be obtained from a dealer handling Kodak graphics arts materials. Development in KODAK Developer D-11 or KODAK DEKTOL Developer is satisfactory. Exposure and development should be such as to provide moderately low densities in the highlight areas only. This is accomplished by overexposure because this is a direct positive film. The finished mask is registered and taped to the copy negative for printing.

The two-step method of making a highlight mask consists of making a contact positive transparency image first, and then using this transparency to make a negative highlight mask.

The positive can be made on such films as KODAK Commercial Film or SUPER-XX Pan Film by the same

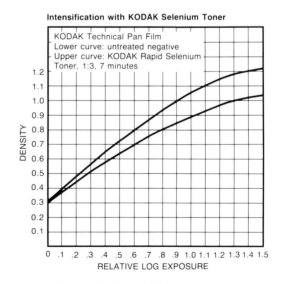

Intensification with KODAK Selenium Toner

KODAK Technical Pan Film
Lower curve: untreated negative
Upper curve: KODAK Rapid Selenium Toner, 1:3, 7 minutes

DENSITY / RELATIVE LOG EXPOSURE

This graph illustrates the increase in density and contrast achieved by treating negatives with KODAK Rapid Selenium Toner. If the negative highlights in a copy negative are locally intensified by toning, the tonal separation lost in copying can be restored.

procedures described in the section on making duplicate black-and-white negatives by the two-step process on page 123.

The highlight mask is made by contact printing the positive on a high contrast film such as KODALITH Ortho Film, Type 3. Development can be in KODAK Developer D-11 (see Data Sheet DS12). Exposure should be just enough that only the highlights show in the mask, and the maximum density is about 0.25 to 0.50. When the highlight mask is registered and taped to the original negative, the highlight densities will appear enhanced.

If the highlights appear washed out in the copy print, the highlight mask densities are too great. If they still appear muddy, the highlight mask densities are not great enough.

A third technique is the in-camera method. The regular copy negative is exposed. Then a sheet of KODALITH Film is exposed lightly to record just the highlight areas. This in-camera mask is developed as above in KODAK Developer D-11. After both negatives are dry, they are registered. Obviously this requires a view camera on a rock-steady support.

Photo by Bob Clemens.
Copy by Dennis Thompson

Another method of restoring highlight contrast to copies, is to use a highlight mask. This is a print from the original negative without masking.

Mask by Dennis Thompson

A highlight mask has densities only in the highlight areas. See the text for details on making these masks.

The mask is registered with the original negative, giving added density and contrast to the highlight areas. A print made from the masked negative shows the improvement in highlight tonal separation.

Using Diffusion Techniques

In most copying, every effort is made to retain the sharpness of the original in the copy print. However, there are situations where a slight degree of diffusion in the copy image becomes desirable.

When the final print is a copy restoration, there is often hand work on the intermediate print, or on the copy negative. If the copy print is enlarged, a slight degree of diffusion minimizes the chances of the hand work showing.

Copying may be used to transform a snapshot of a person into a portrait-type photograph. Diffusion can change the image characteristics in such a way as to enhance the facial portrayal.

If the original is on a textured paper, and the usual methods of reducing the reproduction of the texture are only partially successful, diffusion of the copy image can reduce the visibility of the texture in the copy print.

These methods can be used successfully to diffuse the images:

1. Use of a soft-focus portrait lens for copying.

2. Use of commercially available diffusion filters or fog filters.

3. Use of homemade diffusion filters.
   Following are some pointers about diffusing.

- Soft-focus portrait lenses usually provide variable amounts of diffusion, depending on the aperture used. Stopped down, such lenses usually provide sharper images; wide open, they provide a maximum amount of diffusion; at intermediate apertures, various intermediate degrees of diffusion are provided.

- The copy negative is made in the usual way, using the portrait lens as the copy lens. Initially several copy negatives can be made at different apertures to find the degree of diffusion that works best. With experience, the proper aperture can be selected directly.

- Commercially made diffusion filters (or discs) are available from a number of sources. They are made in different degrees of diffusion. Changing the aperture provides an additional control on the degree of diffusion.

- With normal diffusion filters, a soft image is superimposed over a sharp image. With the stronger diffusion filters, the soft image is emphasized over the sharp image.

- With fog filters, the entire image is softened. The filter is like a fine-ground glass—with a stronger fog filter, the grinding is coarser.

- A number of homemade devices can be used to soften, or diffuse, the image. Thin transparent sheeting, like the outer wrapping on a pack of cigarettes, can be crumpled lightly and straightened out. When used in front of the normal copy lens, the crumple lines provide the image diffusion. The straightened out material can be stretched on a filter ring and trimmed, making a semipermanent diffusion filter.

- Black tulle is an open hexagonal weave material used for veils. Bridal veils are often white tulle. This can be dyed black, or blackened with a felt-tip marking pen. Two layers stretched over a filter frame or embroidery hoop can make a semi-permanent diffusion filter. Nylon hosiery material used in the same way gives a greater degree of diffusion.

- Diffusion can be thought of as spreading light areas of the image over the dark areas. The effect is different when starting with a positive image than with a negative image. Generally the effect is most pleasing when making the original copy negative. Diffusion can be done when enlarging the copy negative by holding the diffusing filter just under the enlarging lens during the print exposure. However, since the shadows are light in the negative, this results in spreading the shadows over the highlights, often causing a dull looking print.

- Because image light is spread by diffusion, the contrast of the image is usually lowered. The contrast can be adjusted in the usual ways, by increasing the negative developing time, by increasing the exposure on KODAK Professional Copy Film, or simply by printing on a higher-contrast grade paper.

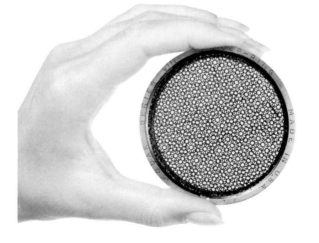

This diffuser is made with two layers of black tulle. It can be used over the camera lens while copying, or over the enlarger lens when making the copy print. It should be kept moving during the exposure.

Printing Black-and-White Copy Negatives

The same principles and techniques that apply to printing camera original negatives are used to print copy negatives. KODAK Publication G-1, *Quality Enlarging with KODAK B/W Papers* explains in detail the technique of black-and-white printing and offers many tips for improving print quality.

There are some aspects worth mentioning here that make printing a copy negative different from printing an original negative. The first aspect is that only in certain situations will a copy print be better in quality than the original. An improvement in quality is possible most often with poor originals where the use of a special technique eliminates a gross defect. For example a stained print will show a dramatic improvement when filtering is used to eliminate the stain. A torn print will look dramatically better if the tear can be cropped in copying or if it is retouched in a restoration technique. A low contrast original will show a great improvement if the contrast is increased in copying. With a high quality original, under ideal conditions, the best that a copy photographer can aim for is a black-and-white print that nearly equals the original in quality. When printing a copy negative the result is somewhat limited by the quality of the original. The importance of careful technique in copying cannot be overemphasized.

A second aspect in printing copy negatives is the importance of printing highlights to the proper density. With a poor quality copy negative workers often make the mistake of printing the highlights darker than normal, in order to increase highlight tonal separation. The resultant print often looks muddy with little improvement in highlight detail. It is easily identified as a copy. With this type of copy negative it usually improves the overall appearance of the print if the highlights are printed quite light in tone and the loss in highlight detail is accepted. A good copy negative with increased highlight contrast can be printed with normal highlight density and retain much of the detail that was in the original. (As previously mentioned KODAK Professional Copy Film 4125 and KODAK Ortho Copy Film 5125 are designed to minimize the problem of muddy or low contrast highlights by utilizing a

The main sections in the publication *Quality Enlarging with KODAK B/W Papers* are:

Sensitized Paper, the Basic Material
Darkrooms and Enlarging Equipment
Printmaking Procedures
Finishing and Mounting
Print Quality

characteristic curve shape that increases the contrast of highlight tones.) In either case good judgement is necessary when determining highlight density because highlights are often the most important tones in determining good print quality.

A third aspect is the contrast of the copy print. If the original is a high quality original, it is desirable to match the contrast of the copy print to the original. Some burning in or dodging may be necessary to match the density of the shadows and highlights to the original print or other local areas.

A final point is that most black-and-white papers increase slightly in density when they dry. This slight increase in density should be anticipated when judging wet prints for overall print quality. A copy print that matches the original when wet may appear too dark when it dries. This dry-down effect is generally most noticeable in the highlights.

COLOR COPYING TECHNIQUES

The procedures for copying with color films are similar to those of copying with black-and-white films. Of course, processing is different. Another difference is that, in color copying, contrast cannot be controlled by adjusting developing times.

The major difference, however, in color copying is the necessity to maintain color balance throughout the copying procedure.

It is necessary to match the color balance of the lights and film when copying in color either by the choice of lights and film or by the use of filters.

Color Balance, Films and Lights

When tungsten bulbs are used as the light source, it is best to use tungsten balanced films. For occasional copying, a conversion filter can be used to balance tungsten lights to daylight film. The following KODAK WRATTEN Gelatin Filters can be used to balance lights of various color temperatures for use with daylight balanced films.

    3000 K (Enlarger bulbs) 80A + 82A
    3200 K (Studio lamps) 80A
    3400 K (Photolamps) 80B

An exact balance is desirable when copying on color transparency and slide films. Color negative camera films can be exposed with the wrong lamps and correction made when making prints. However, this makes color printing more difficult and can lower the color print quality as the result of different exposure levels in the three color emulsion layers of the film which gives different density ranges in the different layers. KODAK VERICOLOR Internegative Films must be exposed to the correct balance illumination.

Although KODAK VERICOLOR II Professional Film 4108, Type L and the several KODAK VERICOLOR Internegative Films are basically tungsten-balanced, they usually require exact balancing with CC filters. The other KODAK VERICOLOR Films designed for camera use and the KODACOLOR Films are daylight-balanced. KODAK EKTAFLEX Materials and KODAK EKTACHROME Papers used for direct-print copying are also tungsten balanced, but also usually require fine tuning with filters.

When color copies are being made for halftone reproduction, transparency films are usually chosen. Slide films are normally used for copies being made for projection. The Kodak films for tungsten use are EKTACHROME Professional 6118 (Tungsten), EKTACHROME 50 Professional Film (Tungsten), EKTACHROME 160 Professional Film (Tungsten), EKTACHROME 160 (Tungsten) and KODACHROME 40 Film 5070 (Type A).

Electronic flash is the daylight balanced source commonly used.* Pulsed xenon is not recommeded for use with color films. All of the daylight balance films, both negative and transparency, can be used with electronic flash with minimal color balance filtration. Some arc lamps are suitable for color copying with daylight films. They provide high levels of illumination, but require special installation and considerable filtration, which varies with the type of arc.

When an overall balance is achieved by proper choice of lamps and film, minor variations in balance are not generally required for color negative camera films. However, with transparency and slide films and with KODAK VERICOLOR Internegative Films, it is usually necessary to control color reproduction to a fairly close balance using light balancing filters and/or color-compensating filters.

Handling the Original

Color prints, printed illustrations, artwork, and fabrics are all commonly copied in color. Originals that are unmounted or large present the most difficult handling problems.

Color prints can be damaged very easily, particularly if they are unmounted. Unmounted prints are susceptible to crimp marks and bends from handling. Once a crimp or a bend has been made in a color print it cannot be removed, and it will almost certainly show up in the copy. Fingerprints are also a hazard. Color prints can be marred by fingerprints very easily. Because of this, it is a prudent measure to wear white cotton gloves when handling color prints. Color prints can be dusted clean with a camel's hair brush or a soft cloth.

Unmounted printed originals are also susceptible to crimps and bends, particularly large sheets of thin, coated paper. Unmounted originals can be positioned for shooting in a vertical copy setup by simply laying the original flat on the copyboard. If the original has a tendency to curl, low profile weights or tacks can be used to hold it flat. Vacuum easels or copyboards are useful for holding thin originals flat.

A clean sheet of glass can also be used to hold an unmounted original flat.

In a horizontal copy setup unmounted originals must be pinned or tacked. A magnetic copyboard may also be used.

---

*Blue flashbulbs are also daylight balanced, but are rarely used for copying because of cost.

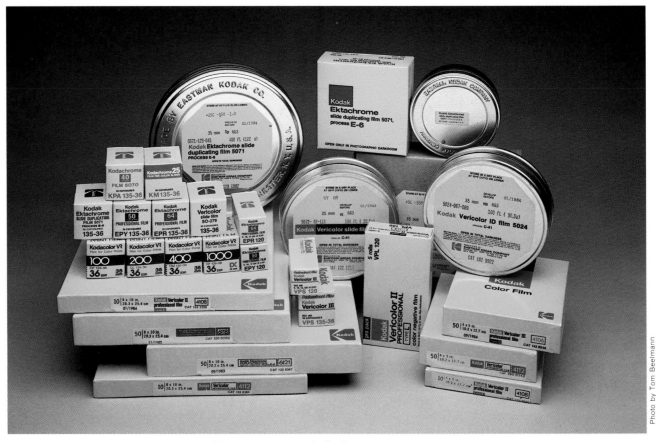

Kodak makes all these films and more that are useful in color copying and duplicating.

Artwork such as paintings, drawings, or advertising comprehensives deserve special care. The value of such an original makes careful handling important. Do not attempt to clean or erase a mark on artwork.

Tapestries or textiles usually must be stretched taut before they can be photographed. In most instances, glass cannot be used to hold fabrics flat if the fabric has much texture. The glass tends to crush or flatten the fibers that impart the three dimensional quality to the fabric.

A good way to mount a fabric for copying is to pin it in several places so that it does not show evidence of stretching.

Large unmounted color originals can be handled in the same way that a blueprint or a map would be handled. The original can be pinned or tacked to a large board when copying horizontally, or laid flat for vertical copying.

Choosing a KODAK Color Film for Copying

As indicated earlier in connection with black-and-white copying, the first criteria of a film is that it fit the camera. Not all color films are available in all formats.

Camera Formats and KODAK Color Films: Most custom color copying is done with view cameras that use sheet films. The 4 x 5-inch size is the most commonly used. When process cameras are used, 8 x 10-inch and larger film sizes may be used (11 x 14-inch, 30 x 40 cm). Nearly all the color films that are used for copying are available in sheet film formats.

Sheet-film cameras are the only ones suitable for direct copying on reversal color papers such as KODAK EKTAFLEX PCT Reversal Film, and KODAK EKTACHROME Papers.

Most copying films are also available in the long roll format used in high production copy cameras. The 35 mm, 46 mm and 70 mm widths, both perforated and unperforated, are made in many color emulsions. Larger width rolls are also available.

VERICOLOR and KODACOLOR Negative Color Films are available in 35 mm magazines. The VERICOLOR Internegative Films are available in 35 mm perforated long-rolls. All the color slide films in both EKTACHROME and KODACHROME emulsions are available in 135 size magazines.

Not many color copy films are available for cameras that use 120 or 220 size film. One VERICOLOR Film is available in 220, three in the 120 size. Two KODACOLOR Films are available in 120 size. (See Data Sheets).

Two KODAK EKTACHROME Films are available in 220, while four are available in 120. (See Data Sheets).

Choosing Films for Color Prints

Color negative films are recommended if the end product is a color print. The tone reproduction is more accurate than copying on a color transparency film and printing on a color reversal paper. However, copying on KODAK EKTAFLEX PCT Reversal Film can give quite good results.

KODAK VERICOLOR Internegative Films are designed specifically to copy transparencies or color prints. As with black-and-white KODAK Professional Copy Film discussed earlier, these films are designed to give added contrast in the highlights to compensate for the compression of highlight tones that occurs when the negative is printed.

For this reason, more accurate copy tone reproduction can be achieved with VERICOLOR Internegative Films when they are properly used. KODAK VERICOLOR Internegative Film 4112 (ESTAR Thick Base) in sheets, and KODAK VERICOLOR Internegative Film 6011 in rolls are the films recommended for copying prints (and transparencies). KODAK VERICOLOR Internegative Film 4114, Type 2 (ESTAR Thick Base), is recommended for copying transparencies only. These films are the only color films made by Kodak for the specific purpose of color copying, and, in general, are the best films available for this purpose.

The successful use of KODAK VERICOLOR Internegative Films requires critical exposure balance control achieved primarily through the use of color densitometry. Without this type of control, mismatched contrast in the three dye layers is highly probable, resulting in negatives that are impossible to print without tinted highlights or shadows. If no such control is available, it is more practical to aim for the next best quality level by the use of a KODACOLOR or VERICOLOR Films for cameras.

The following listings give the Kodak color films generally used for copying, with some information about the particular copying uses and characteristics. Further information will be found in the Summary of Films for Color Copying, and the Data Sheets.

Color Negative Films

- KODAK VERICOLOR Internegative Film 4112 (ESTAR Thick Base), Sheets
- KODAK VERICOLOR Internegative Film 6011, Rolls

These films give fine tone reproduction in copies of prints, other full-tone reflection copy, and transparencies. They are used where the final result is to be a copy print. Their use will provide the best reproduction of highlights and pastel colors from full-tone originals. All the color internegative films are balanced to be used with tungsten (3200 K) lamps. Some color compensating filter balancing is usually required.

VERICOLOR Internegative Film is capable of producing the best color copy negatives, but its use requires great care. The exposure must be precise to maintain the proper tone reproduction, and the color balance must be precise to keep the same contrast in the three dye images. This means that more measurement and testing needs to be done to obtain consistent working conditions for optimum results. Use of exposure meters for determining exposure and a color densitometer to control the negative density ranges in each dye layer are almost mandatory. Details of these controls are given starting on page 70.

- KODAK VERICOLOR Internegative Film 4114, Type 2 is a relatively new film that is recommended for best results when copying KODACHROME and EKTACHROME Film color transparencies. The density-difference method of exposure balancing control is suggested. Details of this method are given in a later section.

This internegative film has the same basic curve shape as the other internegative films. It has an upsweep in the curve to give expanded highlight-region tone reproduction to correct for the tone compression in the papers on which prints are made.

When this film is balanced, exposed and processed accurately it produces very high-quality results.

KODAK Camera Color Negative Films: As with black-and-white copying, color negative camera films intended for photographic use outside the laboratory can also be used for color copying. In general, these camera films have straight line characteristic curves and tend to give compressed shadow and highlight tones, and expanded middle tones in the copy prints. This gives good color reproduction in the middle tones, but tends to wash out the light tones and block-up the dark tones. If a color densitometer is not available to control the use of the VERICOLOR Internegative Films, it may be better to use a camera color film even though the potential tone-reproduction quality may not be as high. Details are given on page 76. The advantages offered by the use of the KODAK VERICOLOR Internegative Films are highly dependent on correct usage with densitometric control. Used without this control, results are very likely to be poorer than if a KODAK VERICOLOR camera Film were used.

KODAK Transparency and Slide Films

As mentioned earlier, copy transparencies are useful when the copy is to be used to make halftone reproductions or when the transparencies (slides) are to be projected. When transparencies are used to make reflection copy prints, quality losses occur that are greater than those that occur when color negative films are used. Copy slides are generally made when the copies are to be used for projection. A flashing technique can be used to lower the contrast, if necessary. See page 79.

KODAK EKTACHROME Duplicating Film 6121 (Process E-6) and KODAK EKTACHROME Slide Duplicating Film 5071 are the laboratory films of choice for making transparency duplicates. Their use is discussed later in detail. Some camera films are occasionally used to "copy" transparencies.

KODAK EKTACHROME Films are available in many formats: sheets, rolls, long rolls, and 35 mm magazines. KODACHROME Films are only available in 35 mm magazines.

Tungsten Films: KODAK EKTACHROME Professional Film 6118 (Tungsten) in sheets is designed to be used with exposure times near 5 seconds although it can be used over a range of $^1/_{10}$ second to 100 seconds, and, of course, with tungsten illumination (3200 K). The effective speed of this film changes with the exposure time, and specific speeds are given on the instruction sheet packaged with the film for exposure times of $^1/_2$, 5, 30, and 100 seconds. The speeds given include the exposure increase required by the CC filter(s) recommended to compensate for reciprocity effects.

KODAK EKTACHROME 50 Professional Film (Tungsten) in rolls is a similar film, but is color balanced for an exposure time of $^1/_{10}$ second. Its recommended range of exposure times is from $^1/_{100}$ sec to 1 second. The effective speed of each roll is printed on the instruction sheet.

KODACHROME 40 Film 5070 (Type A) is balanced for photolamps (3400 K). It is designed for exposure times for $^1/_{10,000}$ second to 10 seconds. Exposure times longer than $^1/_{10}$ second require a correction for reciprocity. KODACHROME Films are especially recommended when long term dark storage stability is desired, although current EKTACHROME Films also have excellent dark storage stability.

Daylight Films: KODAK EKTACHROME 64 Professional Film 6117 (Daylight) in sheets is a good choice when the copy transparencies are to be used for halftone reproduction and when electronic flash is the illumination. It is useable for exposure times from $^1/_{10,000}$ second to 10 seconds. Reciprocity exposure time correction and CC filter correction is necessary at the shortest time, and for times 1 second and longer. KODAK EKTACHROME 64 Professional Film 5017 (Daylight) is available in 120- and 220-size rolls, long rolls (6017)and 35 mm magazines (5017). EKTACHROME 64 Film (Daylight) is available in 35 mm magazines.

KODACHROME 25 Film (Daylight) and KODACHROME 64 Film (Daylight) are available only in 35 mm magazines. KODACHROME 25 is usable for exposure times of from $^1/_{10,000}$ second to 100 seconds, while KODACHROME 64 Film is usable for exposure times from $^1/_{10,000}$ second to 1 second. Corrections for reciprocity are required with the longer exposure times. The contrast of copies made on KODACHROME Films is high, and is generally reduced by flashing. See page 79.

Using Faster Color Films for Copying: As indicated earlier, it is usually an advantage to use the slower speed films for copying because finer grain and increased sharpness are usually achieved.

However, there are times when a faster film offers considerable advantage with either color negative or transparency film. One situation is where lighting levels are such that extremely long exposure times are necessary such as in dimly-lit museums where the use of a tripod and/or auxiliary lights is forbidden. Another is when correction or polarizing filters are used that reduce the effective film speed considerably. This is especially true when polarizing screens are placed over the lights and a polarizing filter is placed over the camera lens. Under these circumstances, the finer grain and increased sharpness of the slower film can be exchanged for a faster film speed. The following films can be used in these circumstances, but the user must be willing to accept the attendant lowering of quality.

Faster KODAK Color Negative Films

VERICOLOR III Professional Film, Type S	ISO 160 Daylight
KODACOLOR VR 1000	ISO 1000 Daylight
KODACOLOR VR 400	ISO 400 Daylight
KODACOLOR VR 200	ISO 200 Daylight

Faster KODAK Color Transparency Films

EKTACHROME 200
Professional Film 6176   ISO 200 Daylight
EKTACHROME 200
Professional Film   ISO 200 Daylight
EKTACHROME 400
Film   ISO 400 Daylight
EKTACHROME 160
Professional Film   ISO 160 Tungsten

The films mentioned in this section are Kodak color films suitable for copying that are available as this book is written. Eastman Kodak Company reserves the right to change and improve products at any time. It is therefore likely that some of the films mentioned above may have been replaced by the time you read this. The replacement films may work for copying and duplicating purposes just as well as the current films. It is wise to make a choice of films based on the principles presented in this book, and to run tests to see that the new choice produces satisfactory results. Be sure to match the balance of the lights to the balance to the film, to base the exposure on the listed film speed, to choose properly between fast films and slow film, and between color negative films and transparency films.

Lighting and Exposure

The basic concepts of lighting and exposure are the same as in black-and-white copying. The biggest difference when copying in color is that the spectral sensitivity of the film (color balance) should be selected to match the color temperature of the light source.

Kodak color films are usually balanced for exposure to 5500 K light sources or 3200 K light sources. Film balanced for exposure to 5500 K illumination is referred to as daylight balanced film. Film balanced for 3200 K illumination is referred to as tungsten-balanced film. One film that does not fall into these two categories is KODACHROME 40 Film 5070 (Type A). This film is color-balanced for 3400 K illumination. KODAK VERICOLOR Internegative Films are balanced for 3200 K illumination but nearly always require the use of CC filters to balance the dye layer contrast.

Color balancing filters can be used to match unlike films and light sources. A list on page 18 shows what filters are necessary with several film and light source combinations.

Some light sources that work well with black-and-white materials are unsuitable for critical color photography. Fluorescent light sources and pulsed-xenon sources, for example, should be avoided because of the difficulty in obtaining good color balance.

In general, color negative camera films with straight line characteristic curves have much more latitude with film/light-source color match than VERICOLOR Internegative Films. The latter, however, give improved highlight tone reproduction. A great deal of color control can be exercised in the printing step. Color transparency films require much closer attention to color balance.

When color transparency films are used in copying it is a very good idea to expose and process a test transparency first before shooting many originals. Even when the light source and the film type have been matched as recommended, critical color balance usually requires that color correction filters be used. Color balance corrections can be determined with the KODAK *Color Print Viewing Filter Kit*, KODAK Publication No. R-25. This is a kit containing magenta, red, yellow, green, cyan, and blue filters. The correct color balance of a transparency or print can be determined by viewing it through the filter that neutralizes the color cast.

Several light source variables can affect the color balance of the reproduction. The age of the light bulbs (especially tungsten light sources other than quartz iodide or tungsten halogen) can have an effect on the color balance. The color balance of the lights may shift through the life of the bulbs. Electronic flash units emit varying amounts of ultraviolet radiation which may photograph bluish on color film. Diffusers and reflectors can also impart a color cast to a copy. The flash from automatic units can also change color balance when taking extreme close-ups because the flash duration is shortened considerably.

Minor speed corrections for KODAK EKTACHROME Professional Films are printed on the instruction sheets packaged with the film. This is information about the particular emulsion and is based on manufacturing tests.

KODAK Color Control Patches and a KODAK Gray Scale are helpful guides to the reproduction of a color original. Both are available in a kit as KODAK Publication Q-13 ($7^7/_8$ inches or 20 cm long) or Q-14 (14 inches or 35.6 cm long). These guides, along with a KODAK Gray Card, can be placed next to the original to monitor color reproduction and tone reproduction. The MACBETH Color Checker Chart is also a useful monitoring tool. (See the illustration on page 79). The reproduction of these guides can be compared to the original to observe color balance, color saturation, and tonal compression. The guides are especially useful when comparing films or when trying special techniques such as flashing. The guides are also helpful when the copy is to be reproduced photomechanically. The printer can use the color control patches as a guide for color reproduction.

Reflections and Color Contamination

For color copying, control over copyboard illumination is even more critical than with black-and-white copying. Room lights should be turned off even if they are dim. Room lights are seldom the correct color temperature and can cause a color cast or reflections in the copy either by direct illumination or by illuminating a wall that may reflect the wrong color light on the original. This color cast is called color contamination, because it is caused by a source of illumination other than the copy lights.

Other sources of color contamination are windows (daylight), colored walls, colored ceilings, and colored furniture. These objects should not be located next to a copy set up.

Ideally, a color copying room should have black walls and a black ceiling with no windows. If a window is located near a copy set up, opaque black shades can be used to minimize the daylight illumination.

Processing Color Films

KODACOLOR Films and KODAK VERICOLOR Films (including the internegative films) are processed in the C-41 Process with KODAK FLEXICOLOR Chemicals. KODAK EKTACHROME Films are processed in the Process E-6 process using KODAK EKTACHROME Chemicals, Process E-6. It is not practical for most users to process KODACHROME Films because of the complicated process. Kodak and some other large processing laboratories are set up to process KODACHROME Films.

The Processes C-41 and E-6 are of such a nature that they can, with care, be performed by any fairly proficient person. Many photofinishing and commercial laboratories provide processing services for those who do not wish to process their own films.

Processing instructions for using the Processes C-41 and E-6 are given in several KODAK Publications:

> *Identifying E-6 Processing Errors*, E-65
> KODAK *Color Films*, E-77
> KODAK *Color Darkroom* DATAGUIDE, R-19
> *Introduction to Color Photographic*
>   *Processing*, J-3

In addition, concise instructions are packaged with E-6 and C-41 chemical kits, and with the developers in the larger sizes of chemicals and with the HOBBY-PAC™ Color Slide Kit.

For large volume processing with replenishment, control strip quality control procedures are required. The following manuals give instructions for these procedures:

> *Introduction to Color Process*
>   *Monitoring*   Z-99
> *Using Process E-6*   Z-119
> *Using Process C-41*   Z-121

For those already processing color films, there are no basic differences between processing copy negatives and regular camera negatives.

Special Techniques

Copying Reflection Copy with KODAK VERICOLOR Internegative Film 6011 (Rolls) and 4112 (ESTAR Thick Base), Sheets

KODAK VERICOLOR Internegative Films have the highest potential for producing quality copy negatives from which color copy prints are made, but the characteristics that give it this potential make it somewhat difficult to use. However, with adequate time spent learning the procedures for controlling exposure and color balance, any careful worker should be able to make high quality copy negatives with one of these films.

In order to build in the desired characteristics, six emulsion layers, plus nine separation, protective and filter layers are required, making them the most complex color films manufactured by Eastman Kodak Company. See illustration on page 111.

Because of the unique curve shapes, each layer must receive just the correct exposure by the user, both to put the exposure at the right place for the inflection point in the film curve shape to provide the best tone reproduction, and to balance all dye layers so that they print correctly.

Use of these films for optimum results for copying both reflection originals and transparencies requires precise exposure and light balancing, and constant monitoring of results, and a level of technical competence to measure and control the results.

Tungsten illumination (3200 K studio lamps) is recommended for copying reflection flat-art originals on either of these VERICOLOR Internegative Films. Also recommended is the use of a KODAK WRATTEN Filter No. 2B over the camera lens to absorb the ultraviolet radiation.

It is important that the three basic layers receive the same relative exposures. To do this, KODAK Color Compensating Filters must usually be used over the camera lens. The correction varies with different emulsion numbers of internegative film, a starting pack is recommended for each package on the instruction sheet. If this is not available, use a starting pack of 30M + 30Y. This applies to all the VERICOLOR Internegative Films.

For the sheet film, the lights should be placed so that the copyboard receives about 100 footcandles of illumination. If a 18% KODAK Gray Card is placed on the copyboard and the lights adjusted until a reflected-light meter reading based on a film speed of ISO 125 indicates an exposure of $1/8$ second at $f/8$, the 100-footcandle aim is achieved. This setting

This reproduction was made directly from a color print made on KODAK EKTACOLOR 74 Paper from an original color negative. This subject was chosen because of the variety of colors to show how well color prints of all colors can be copied.

This reproduction was made from a copy color print. The print above was copied on KODAK VERICOLOR Internegative Film 4112 (ESTAR Thick Base) and the copy print on EKTACOLOR 74 Paper. Control of the internegative was provided by the curve plotting method. The color match between the copy print and the original is generally good, but some colors do not match exactly.

is used only to get the light level correct, and is not an exposure reading. An exposure time of 10 seconds is nominal for this film.

For the roll film, the copyboard should receive 500 footcandles, a gray card reading with an exposure meter should indicate an exposure of $^1/_8$ second at $f/16-f/22$ based on a film speed of ISO 125. An exposure of 1 second at $f/5.6$ is nominal for this film when the copy receives 500 footcandles of illumination.

The starting exposure on the VERICOLOR Internegative 4112 Sheet Film emulsion should be about 10 seconds at $f/5.6$. The optimum range of exposure times is 7 seconds to 15 seconds. The optimum time range for the roll film 6011 emulsion is from $^1/_2$ to 2 seconds with a nominal time of 1 second.

A KODAK Gray Scale, such as that supplied in the KODAK Color Separation Guide and Gray Scale (KODAK Publication No. Q-13 or Q-14), should be included with the copy. The image on the film should be large enough so that the images of the gray-scale steps can be measured with a densitometer.

With roll film, close-ups of the steps may be required. Three frames can be exposed to make the step image large enough, exposing just part of the gray scale on each frame. Exposure compensation for the close-up condition must be carefully included in these exposures.

The following basic exposure series should be made:

At $f/8$ 4112 sheet film:
5, 7, 10, 14 and 20 seconds.
(100 fc illum)

At $f/5.6$ 6011 roll film:
$^1/_4$, $^1/_2$, 1, 2, and 4 seconds.
(500 fc illum)

The test films are processed normally in Process C-41 using KODAK FLEXICOLOR Chemicals. The negatives are then checked to see that the cyan, magenta, and yellow dye images are very closely the same in contrast.

Kodak suggests two methods of checking copy color negatives made from reflection copy with KODAK VERICOLOR Internegative Films. The first is a visual method, the second is a measurement—plotting method called the reference curve method.

Visual Check of Color Internegatives

The visual check method must be used if you do not have a color densitometer. It may take many trials to achieve a balanced negative using this method alone. The other use of the visual check method is to verify the results of the other two methods.

This method requires making test color prints. The first test is made on KODAK EKTACOLOR Paper and is balanced for the middle gray tones on the reproduction of the gray scale. It may take several filter adjustments and trial prints to achieve the balanced neutrals.

If the highlight and shadow tones are neutral when the midtones are neutral, the negative has satisfactory color balance, that is, the three dye images have the same contrast and the curves are said to be parallel and not crossed.

If, however, the highlights have a cast of one color while the shadows have a cast of the complementary color, the negative is out of balance and is said to have crossed curves. The strength of the color cast gives a clue to how far it is out of balance.

The filter pack on the copy camera is changed to correct the balance. The correction is made by subtracting filtration of the color cast in the highlights. If the highlights are yellowish, for example, yellow filtration is subtracted from the pack. If there is no yellow in the pack, filtration of the complementary color is added to the packs. In our example, blue filtration is added.

The table on page 73 summarizes this procedure, gives guidance on how great a filter change to make, and indicates how to change the camera exposure in order to compensate for the change in filtration.

A new internegative is then made. Another test print is made, again balanced for the middle gray tones on the gray scale. This new print is evaluated.

If the print highlights have the same color as the first print, but less of it, the filter change was in the right direction, but was not great enough. In our example, more yellow should be subtracted from the packs. If the highlights are now blue, too much yellow was subtracted, and some yellow filtration is added back in the camera pack. Of course, when the highlights and shadows are neutral, the correction was just right.

This procedure is repeated until an acceptably neutral gray scale is achieved.

When a balance is obtained for a given emulsion of the film, many copies can be made as long as all the factors stay the same—emulsion number, lights, camera filter pack, process, etc. When one of the factors changes, a new test may be required to find the proper balance for the changed conditions.

Curve Plotting Method of Balancing

To balance internegative film by plotting curves, a series of copy negatives of the KODAK Gray Scale (Publication No. Q-13 or Q-14) is made on KODAK VERICOLOR Internegative Film as described earlier.

After processing, the A steps on the gray scale of the negatives are measured with the red filter (status M) on the densitometer. The negative is chosen that has a density value in this step of between 1.30 to 1.50, preferably about 1.40.

Guide for Adjusting Filter Pack When Making Internegatives

If Highlights in Print Are	If Shadows in Print Are	Either		Or	
		Subtract These Filters from Pack	And Multiply Exposure by	Add These Filters to Pack	And Multiply Exposure by
Cyan	Red	20C	0.91	20R	1.5
Magenta	Green	20M	0.91	20G	1.3
Yellow	Blue	20Y	0.91	20B	1.6
Red	Cyan	20R	0.67	20C	1.1
Green	Magenta	20G	0.77	20M	1.1
Blue	Yellow	20B	0.59	20Y	1.1
Cyan	Red	10C	0.91	10R	1.3
Magenta	Green	10M	0.91	10G	1.2
Yellow	Blue	10Y	0.91	10B	1.3
Red	Cyan	10R	0.77	10C	1.1
Green	Magenta	10G	0.83	10M	1.1
Blue	Yellow	10B	0.77	10Y	1.1

Note: It is generally more desirable to modify a filter pack by subtracting filters rather than by adding them.

The red, green and blue densities of each of the steps in this negative are measured on a color densitometer with status M filters. Each density is plotted on KODAK Curve-Plotting Graph Paper, KODAK Publication No. E-64.

Row C on the curve plotting paper lists the steps of the Q-13 or Q-14 gray scale.

A smooth curve is then drawn through a line of best fit for the plotted points creating characteristic curves of the cyan, magenta and yellow layers. The curve for the cyan dye layer is usually called the red curve, because it is measured with the red filter on the densitometer and is a record of the red content of the original. Likewise the magenta dye-layer curve is called the green curve, and the yellow dye-layer curve is called the blue curve.

The plotted curves represent the inherent characteristics of the particular emulsion combined with the modifying effects of the photographic system including camera flare, film process, etc. In an earlier section on copy camera setup, attention was called to the various factors that reduce the flare level. These are especially important in copying on VERICOLOR Internegative Film.

• Clean camera lens

• Clean and relatively scratch-free filters.

• Black copyboard surround for the original copy material.

• Effective lens hood.

• Clean and matte-black camera interior.

• Matte black walls, ceiling, floor, window shades, etc. in the copy area.

When the three curves are plotted on the KODAK Curve Plotting Graph Paper, the paper is placed over the KODAK Internegative Film (Reflection) reference curves shown in the illustration on page 74. The reference lines of the graph are aligned over the reference lines in the illustration on the next page. Where the *upper part of* test curves fall in relation to the reference curves indicates how well the test negative has been balanced and exposed.

If all three test curves are higher than the reference curves, the negative is overexposed. A new test negative is made with less exposure. If all three test curves are lower than the reference curves, the negative is underexposed and a new test negative is made with more exposure. The red curve is the key to the basic exposure. If the red curve is too high, reduce the overall exposure. If the red curve is too low, increase the overall exposure. When the red curve aligns with the reference curves, look at the other two curves for alignment. Misalignment of either curve means that the negative is out of balance. Correcting the balanced is accomplished by using KODAK Color Compensating (CC) Filters over the camera lens.

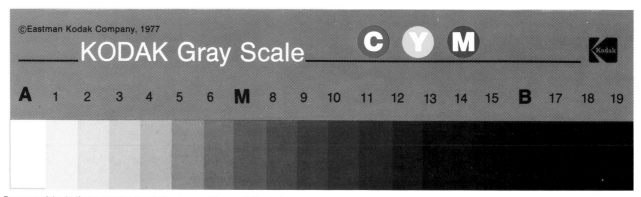

KODAK Gray Scale

C Y M

A 1 2 3 4 5 6 M 8 9 10 11 12 13 14 15 B 17 18 19

Because of the halftone process in printing, some of the gradation between the steps of the KODAK Gray Scale is lost.

The curves change shape as the exposure is changed. In the illustration, note that the overexposed curve has a longer section of upsweep at the high density end. The underexposed curve has a shorter section of upsweep. Balancing the three curves using CC filters makes all three curves have the same amount of upsweep.

If the blue curve is high, that layer received too much exposure. Blue light is absorbed by yellow filters. Therefore, yellow filtration must be added to the pack (or blue filtration subtracted) to move the curve down.

If the blue curve is low, it received too little exposure, and the exposure is increased by removing yellow filtration.

If the green curve is high, add magenta filtration; if the green curve is low, take out magenta filtration.

The filter pack will generally contain yellow and magenta filtration to produce balanced copy negatives, so the changes will almost always be in these two colors. Green and blue are included in the table for the unusual circumstances when these colors are in the pack.

The following table summarizes the changes.

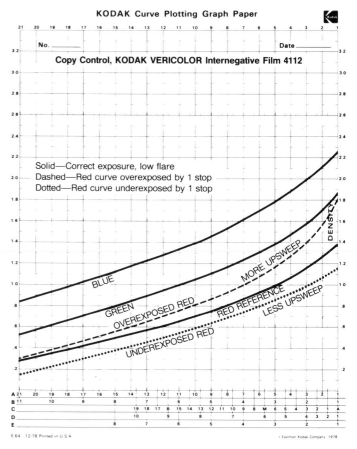

The solid curve lines are the plots of correctly exposed red, green and blue curves. The dashed line represents the plot of an overexposed red curve, while the dotted line represents the plot of an underexposed red curve.

Curve Color	Curve Location	Correction Add Filtration or Subtract Filtration	
Red*	Too High	Cyan	Red
	Too Low	Red	Cyan
Green	Too High	Magenta	Green
	Too Low	Green	Magenta
Blue	Too High	Yellow	Blue
	Too Low	Blue	Yellow

*This correction is rarely used. Changing the camera exposure raises and lowers the red curve.

When the changes needed have been calculated, a new exposure is made incorporating these changes. The densities of the step images are measured and a new set of curves plotted. These curves should fall closer to the reference curves. Additional corrections and yet a third negative may be needed before all these curves come close to the reference curves. KODAK Publication No. E-24S, *Interim Balancing Procedure for KODAK VERICOLOR Internegative Films 4112 (ESTAR Thick Base) and 6011* gives detailed instructions for balancing internegative films by the curve plotting method.

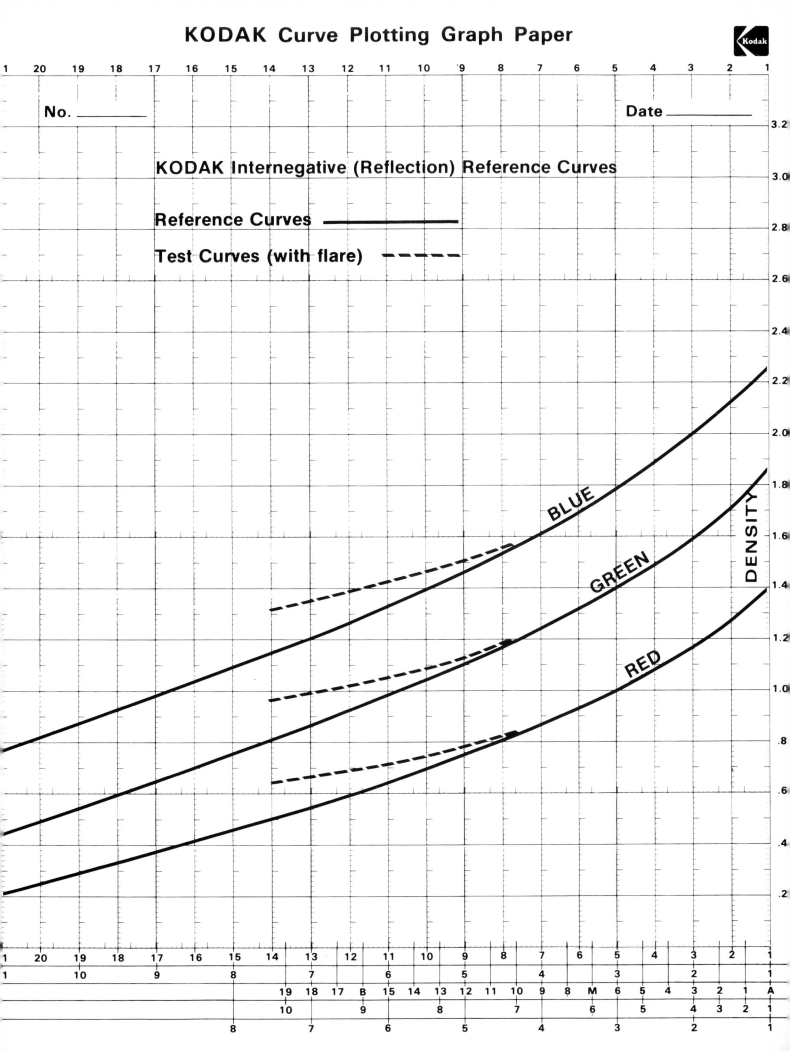

Copying Faded Color Prints

The technique of copying color prints on KODAK VERICOLOR Internegative Films 4112 and 6011 offers a method of restoring faded color prints. Overall exposure increase is used to restore the lowered print contrast caused by the fading.

Usually one of the dye colors fades more than the others, resulting in a print that is no longer in balance. Using color compensating filters, a filter pack adjustment is made to give the most faded color layer additional exposure to raise its contrast (density range) to be equal to the others.

Detailed instructions of this procedure are given in KODAK *Current Information Summary CIS-55*. A copy may be obtained by writing to:

> Dept. 412-L
> Eastman Kodak Company
> 343 State Street
> Rochester, NY l4650

Copying with Other KODAK Color Films

Camera Color Negative Films

The special curve shape of KODAK VERICOLOR Internegative Films offers the possibility of improved tone reproduction in the highlight tones of copy prints made from them. As we have seen, this curve shape requires that the exposure of the three color images be fairly exact and very closely matched or the density differences as finally seen by the print material of the three layers will not match, making it impossible to balance the prints made from them. Thus careful control is required when copying with the internegative films.

Regular camera color negative films do not have this special curve shape because they are designed to photograph original subjects whose tone reproduction has not been distorted by having already

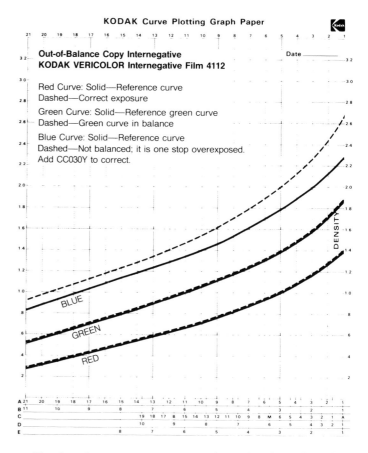

Out-of-Balance Copy Internegative
KODAK VERICOLOR Internegative Film 4112   Date

Red Curve: Solid—Reference curve
Dashed—Correct exposure
Green Curve: Solid—Reference green curve
Dashed—Green curve in balance
Blue Curve: Solid—Reference curve
Dashed—Not balanced; it is one stop overexposed.
Add CC030Y to correct.

When the red curve on your test copy negative overlaps the standard red curve, the basic exposure is correct. In this plot, the green curve also overlaps the standard curve, indicating that the magenta balance is correct. However, the blue curve indicates overexposure of the blue layer, so the yellow balance is off. With the blue curve too high, yellow filtration should be added to the pack to lower the blue curve in the next test.

been through one photographic process. The characteristic curves of camera films have nearly straight-line characteristic curves above the toe level. Therefore, within a limited range, when one imaging layer receives relatively more exposure than another, as when the light and film may be slightly out of balance, the one layer will have more density overall than the other layers, but will have essentially the same density difference. Special filtering will be required in making the print, but the special filtering will produce a print that does not shift appreciably in color from highlight to shadow tones.

Thus, color camera negative films are much easier to use than the internegative films, and do not require the very careful densitometric control described earlier.

In addition to highlight compression, another difficulty with using camera color negative film for copying is that the contrast is too high for most originals. The midtone contrast is increased in the copy print, and the negative density range is too great, leading to burned-out highlights and loss of shadow detail in the print.

This page compares color copies made with KODAK VERICOLOR Internegative Film and a regular camera film, KODAK VERICOLOR II Professional Film 4108, Type L. This illustration was made from the original print.

This illustration was made from a copy print made from a copy negative on KODAK VERICOLOR Internegative Film 4112 (ESTAR Thick Base).

Using a camera color negative film as a copy film increases the contrast considerably. This illustration was made from a copy print from a copy negative on KODAK VERICOLOR II Professional Film 4108, Type L without flashing.

Giving a flash exposure to the regular color negative camera film reduces the contrast of the copy print. This illustration was made from a copy print on KODAK VERICOLOR II Film 4108, Tungsten, with a flash exposure of a white paper with 1.2 neutral density filtration. See text for details.

The answer to this problem is to give a flash exposure or fogging exposure to the film at the time the copy exposure is given. The following procedure seems to work satisfactorily with most KODAK camera color negative films.

1. Give normal copy exposure.

2. Place white paper on the copy board. Fixed-out white photographic black-and-white paper works well.

3. Place 1.2 neutral density filters over the lens.

4. Give the film the same exposure (same exposure time, same f-number) for the flash exposure.

5. Process normally.

KODAK VERICOLOR III Film, Type S has slightly lower contrast than the other Kodak color negative films, so requires less flash exposure. A 1.3 to 1.4 neutral density filtration should work well with this film.

If the negative contrast is too low, *increase* the value of the neutral density filtration, or if the contrast is too high, *decrease* the amount of neutral density filtration.

In summary, the highest quality copies can be made with VERICOLOR Internegative Film, with densitometric control. Quite satisfactory copies can be made with flashed color negative camera films without densitometric control.

The different color negative camera films have different reciprocity characteristics. In general, Type S films are designed for short exposure times while Type L films are designed for longer exposure times. Exposure time adjustment curves are shown in the Data Sheets.

There is usually no need to use high speed color negative films. However, when copying in a museum where no additional lights are allowed the use of KODACOLOR VR 400 or KODACOLOR VR 1000 Films should be considered.

The camera negative color films are processed normally and the negatives are printed normally. There are two KODAK EKTACOLOR Papers, and some degree of contrast control can be achieved by the choice of paper. EKTACOLOR Professional Paper has slightly less contrast than EKTACOLOR PLUS Paper. Printing on EKTACOLOR Professional Paper will therefore produce slightly lower contrast prints.

Copying on Transparency Film

Copying reflection originals using transparency film is different than copying with negative film because there is only one opportunity to make exposure and color correction adjustments. The exposure and color correction must be correct the first time. Unlike color negative films, there is very little overexposure latitude. It is better to underexpose slightly, rather than to overexpose. If the color balance is off slightly, it must be corrected by reshooting or by duplicating. Lighting unevenness cannot be corrected by burning-in or dodging, as it can be during the printing of a color negative.

As mentioned previously, because of the need for precise exposure and color correction it is advisable to make a test before copying many originals. The test will confirm exposure and color balance. Color transparency film requires correct color balance more than most color negative camera films. KODAK Color Compensating Filters, used over the the camera lens, can be used for fine tuning color balance. The KODAK *Color Print Viewing Filter Kit*, KODAK Publication No. R-25, is helpful for determining the exact filtration.

It is also helpful to include KODAK Color Control Patches and a KODAK Gray Scale to monitor the reproduction of colors and tones.

Controlling Contrast of Transparency Films: The contrast of various KODAK EKTACHROME Films can be varied by changing the first development time or temperature (push or pull processing) of the Process E-6. A moderate change in color balance may occur when the process is changed. This can be corrected by the use of color compensating filters. The following table can be used as a starting point for experimentation.

Exposure-Development Changes for Control With Proces E-6

Contrast Change	Exposure Index Change	First Development Time Change	or	Temperature Change
Maximum Increase	+3 stops	+10 minutes		+16 F
Moderate Increase	+2 stops	+ 5 minutes		+12 F
Slight Increase	+1 stop	+ 2 minutes		+ 8 F
Slight Decrease	−1 stop	− 2 minutes		− 6 F
Moderate Decrease	−2 stops	− 3 minutes		−13 F
Considerable Decrease	−3 stops	Not recommended		−16 F
Maximum Decrease	−4 stops	Not recommended		−19 F

A first development adjustment to raise contrast results in lower D-max and warm color balance. Temperature adjustment to lower contrast is preferred to time adjustment because there is less highlight degradation. Compensation to lower contrast results in cold color balance, especially in the highlight region.

Flashing is a method of lowering contrast that can be used with both EKTACHROME and KODACHROME Films*. A brief exposure to a white card is commonly used. A neutral density filter with a density value of from 1.6 to 2.0 is put over the lens, the white card is placed in front of the original copy, and an exposure of the same shutter speed and *f*-number as the main exposure is given. This lowers the D-max and the contrast. Using a 2.0 neutral density filter gives a minimum effect, using a 1.6 density filter lowers the contrast considerably. If the shadows appear "milky" the flash exposure is too great, and is lessened by using a higher value ND filter. When the contrast is changed by flashing, normal processing is used.

Where lower contrast transparencies are desired, KODAK EKTACHROME Duplicating Film or KODAK EKTACHROME Duplicating Slide Film can be used as a copy film. The contrast of these films is lower than camera transparency color films because it is made to duplicate (copy) color transparencies which are generally higher in contrast than original subjects. It is not necessary to flash this film to achieve low contrast results.

Another control that is available to increase contrast moderately is polarizing filters. When polarizing filters are used both over the lens and the lights, as described in the section on "Using Polarizing Filters," contrast increases noticeably. To a lesser extent, contrast also increases when using a polarizing filter over the lens only.

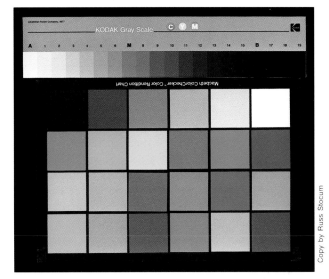

Flashing is useful to lower the copy contrast when copying with transparency films as well as with color negative films. The above illustration was made from a copy transparency on KODAK EKTACHROME Professional Film 6118 (Tungsten) without flashing.

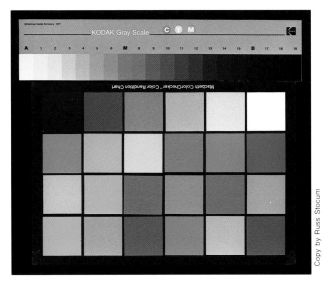

This illustration was made from a copy transparency on the same film but an additional flash exposure of white paper was given using 1.7 neutral density filtration.

---

*This procedure is similar to that used with color negative films. A higher neutral density value is used with transparency films.

Direct Copying with KODAK EKTAFLEX PCT Reversal Film and EKTACHROME 21 Paper

Photographers and art directors are often in a rush to obtain copies of color photographs, artwork, or layouts. Fast turnaround times can be achieved by copying directly onto KODAK EKTAFLEX PCT Reversal Film or KODAK EKTACHROME 21 Paper. Both are available in several sizes. The copy is made by exposing the reversal material in a view or process camera focused on the original.

With EKTACHROME 21 Paper laterally reversed images will occur unless a mirror is used in front of the camera lens to correct the image orientation. This can be accomplished by positioning a front-surface mirror at a 45° angle in front of the lens. With EKTAFLEX PCT Reversal Film, a mirror is not necessary because the image is transferred from the film to paper during processing, producing a correctly oriented image. EKTACHROME 21 Paper can also be used in some copy machines that combine camera and processor into one unit. Available from other manufacturers, these units can be used in normal roomlight.

EKTAFLEX PCT Reversal Film is processed using a KODAK EKTAFLEX Printmaker, Model 8, or the EKTAFLEX PCT Processor, Model 12, or equivalent. It's a one-step process in which the film is bathed in an activating solution and then laminated to a receiving sheet. Several minutes later the sheet is peeled from the film to produce the final print or transparency. No running water or plumbing is required. EKTACHROME 21 Paper can be processed in a drum or a tray with KODAK EKTACHROME R-3000 Chemicals or in a machine processor with EKTACHROME R-3 Chemicals.

Standard copying equipment will fulfill most needs. Tungsten-balanced lights (3200 K) are preferred because these reversal materials are tungsten balanced. Other items that might be used are a tripod, a copyboard, KODAK Color Compensating (CC) Filters and a KODAK Color Print Viewing Filter Kit (KODAK Publication R-25).

The copy set-up can be arranged like any other copy set-up using the view camera. The color copy is secured to the copyboard, and the image is sized and focused on the ground glass. A sheet film holder is loaded with either EKTAFLEX PCT Reversal Film or EKTACHROME 21 Paper and exposed in the camera. A camera equipped with a vacuum film back (such as a large graphic arts copy camera) can hold all sizes of film or paper without a film holder.

Determine exposure with an exposure test. A convenient method of making a test exposure is to

KODAK EKTACHROME 21 Paper works well when copying continuous-tone originals or, as in this example, originals that have both continuous tone and line copy.

use a piece of black copyboard over the copy to step off a series of exposures on one sheet of film. Intervals of five or ten seconds can be used. A starting point for making a test, copying at 1:1, using two 250 W photolamps placed 3 feet from the copyboard (on both sides at 45°), would be 5, 10, 15, and 20 seconds at f/8.

From the processed test sheet, the best exposure can be determined by choosing the time required to produce the most pleasing density (with reversal film or paper, more exposure gives less density).

Color balance can be evaluated by viewing the print with filters from the KODAK Color Print Viewing Kit. The evaluation should be made by viewing the print under the same type of illumination that will be used to display the print. It is usually helpful to compare the color balance of the copy to the original. Select a filter from the kit that makes the midtones of the copy appear close in color to the original. The value of the selected filter is the value of the CC filter required over the camera lens. In general, if the print looks cool, warm-colored filters (magenta, red, or yellow) will correct the color. If the print appears warm, cool-colored filters (green, cyan, or blue) will correct the color.

Once color balance has been established for a given set of circumstances, the color balance for successive copies should be very close. Minor adjustments may be necessary with different packages of film or paper and as the copy lights age.

Original illustration

Photo by John C. Kimkel

Copy made on KODAK EKTAFLEX PCT Reversal Film.

Copy by Tom Benson

Copying Paintings and Other Art Originals

Copying paintings and artwork is one of the most difficult types of copying. Each original must be photographed with the sensitivity and skill that would be required of a portrait or a studio illustration. Each original presents different technical problems that must be overcome.

Art is photographed for many different purposes. The most common purpose is for halftone reproduction. A print or a transparency is much more convenient and useful to give to a printer than the original artwork. Whenever halftone illustrations are required for book illustrations, posters, or catalogs a photographic print or transparency is made first. The color balance of the copy, the contrast, and the lighting are all extremely important.

Another purpose for photographing art is for documentation. Photographs are often needed for insurance records or for inventory files. Several views might be required showing scale, thickness, condition, or significant details. The intent is different than when photographing to make an illustration. Cosmetic appearance is not as important as detail and scale. For this type of photograph a ruler or other object that has size recognition is helpful to include in the frame of the picture to identify the size of the original. Close-up views that help show such features as condition or authenticity may also be helpful.

Also, damage to artwork from an accident or vandalism is often photographed for file and insurance records.

Photographs may be required prior to the restoration of a painting. Cracks, scratches, dents, or other blemishes would be emphasized so that a before and after comparison can be made. The back side of a painting must be photographed when it is to be put on a new stretcher or if it will be relined with new canvas so that any important historical information is recorded.

Artwork must be handled with extreme care. When positioning artwork for copying the method for securing the artwork must not in any way damage the original or interfere with the lighting. Several methods for securing paper artworks are illustrated here. The idea behind each method is to ensure that the securing system does not puncture or create a dent in the surface of the paper but still provides a safe method for holding the original flat. For this reason pins and tacks should never be used directly on a valuable original. Adhesives should not be used for securing art work because certain adhesives may cause permanent damage. Also, it is important that tacks or pins, used as illustrated, are positioned so that they do not cast shadows on the

When many copies of flat art are being copied on a vertical copy stand, two weighted straps can be made as a quick and safe way to hold the art flat. The art must have margins.

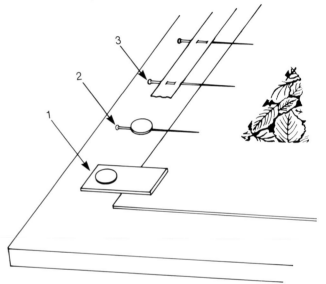

Three methods are shown for holding unmounted art without putting pinholes in it. (1) a tab of stiff cardboard is held with beeswax, (2) a pin is pushed through a small dab of beeswax, and (3) pins are pushed through masking tape which is then stuck to the copy stand.

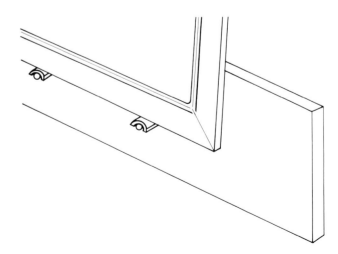

Framed art can be held against a wall for horizontal copying. Small pads placed on the nails protect the frame. These can be made of masking tape rolled into small cylinders with the sticky side inside.

copy. Push pins or other high profile tacks may be unsatisfactory because of the shadows they cast.

A heavy framed painting can be supported on a sturdy easel for photographing or it can be supported on two large nails in a wall. A small piece of padding between the frame and the nails is necessary to prevent damage to the frame.

No attempt should be made to clean a painting or other art original. If the appearance of a painting needs to be improved for reproduction the job should be left to an expert. An inexperienced person cleaning a painting could cause considerable damage that might result in a lawsuit being brought against the photographer.

When storing artwork that is to be photographed keep it away from extremes of heat, humidity, and light. It is a good practice to cover or enclose artwork when it is not being photographed to provide protection from dust and dirt.

Techniques: Once the painting or other type of artwork is mounted securely the next task is to light it. The basic setup is the same as for a routine copy. Two lights on each side of the original at 45 degrees to the copyboard will suffice for many types of flat art. Many of the precautions for avoiding flare and unwanted reflections that would be taken in any good copy setup should also be observed here. Room lights should be made as dim as possible, and the surrounding walls should either be painted a dark neutral color or should be far enough away from the copy so that reflections and color contamination are not a problem. Gobos (a shading device on a goose neck), lens shades, and barn doors (black metal flaps on the front of spotlights to control light spread), are all useful to help control unwanted, stray light.

The format of the copy film is generally determined by the end use of the copy. For high quality color reproductions (posters, book illustrations) a large format film is preferred. A color transparency is usually more acceptable than a print for photomechanical reproduction. 35 mm slides are commonly used for less critical purposes and for audio visual shows.

Oil or acrylic paintings that have a glossy surface must be handled with special care to avoid reflections or color contamination.

The ideal environment for photographing paintings is in a black room with a dark floor. The illustration on page 84 shows how one photographer who specializes in photographing artwork has solved these problems. In his studio portable matte black flats are used to block off stray light to the sides of the painting. They are also used to shade the camera from stray light that may come from the back of

the lights. A flat is a large panel that is self-supporting. It may or may not have wheels.

A black background is provided behind the paintings to reduce flare in the camera. A dark neutral colored cloth is used to cover the floor in front of the painting to avoid a reflection from the floor. In this studio the ceiling is also painted black to prevent reflections. These precautions are not necessary for every painting that is copied, but they are necessary when a large shiny-surfaced painting is to be photographed and in many other instances.

When paintings are copied for reproduction they are most often copied in color. In order to judge the quality of the copy and to monitor the reproduction process, it is helpful to include a gray scale and a color scale. KODAK Publications Q-13 (small), and Q-14 (large) include both of these scales. A gray scale is helpful for judging exposure and contrast. The color scale is useful for determining color balance. The scales can be positioned along the edge of the original, just outside the image area.

A technique that is very helpful in copying paintings is flashing. Flashing is particularly useful for reducing contrast when copying with color reversal films or camera color negative films. For more information on flashing, turn to pages 78 and 79 in the Color Copying section. KODAK EKTACHROME Duplicating Film 6121 or EKTACHROME Slide Duplicating Film 5071 can be used to achieve a nearly 1:1 contrast ratio. These films are relatively slow, however.

Using Polarizers: Polarizers can be very helpful in copying artwork. Both double polarization and single polarization are helpful techniques. These techniques are explained in the previous section Polarizers. Polarizers, however, must be used with discretion. They will eliminate reflections or the sheen that is sometimes important in the artist's conception of the painting. Double polarized light will eliminate the tiny reflections that occur on the texture of the surface of an oil painting. Removing the reflections may not be desirable if the gloss and texture of the paint is important in the appearance of the painting. The use of polarizers usually increases the contrast and color saturation of the copy. If it is important to maintain these attributes close to those of the original, partial polarization or no polarization can be considered.

Generally, older paintings usually require full polarization but discretion must be used when photographing a more recent painting. On older paintings, the surface varnish may have cracked and polarization can minimize reflection from the crazing in the copy. Also, texture as part of the artistic presentation is more common in modern work.

Museographics is a studio that copies art objects. Here proprietor Earl Kage photographs a painting from the Memorial Art Gallery of the University of Rochester using polarizing screens over the lights and a polarizing filter over the camera lens. Note the use of black cloth, drapes, and flats to control reflections.

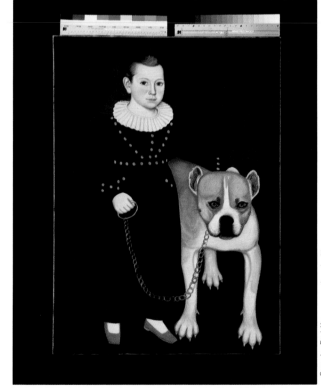

This copy of the American primitive painting *Pierrepont Edward Lacey* by Noah North was made with quartz lights on KODAK EKTACHROME 50 Professional Film 5018 (Tungsten) without polarizers. Note the uneven milkiness of the glaze on the painting surface.

Using double polarization, the surface veiling has been removed, and the contrast has been increased. Flashing could be used to lower the contrast, but Mr. Kage rarely finds it necessary in his work.

One-Light Technique for an Impasto Painting

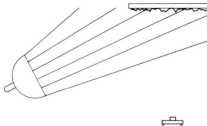

Artists often use the heavy texture of oil paint as part of the artistic experience. Copying the painting with only one light can emphasize the texture. This is called interpretive lighting.

Earl Kage turns a painting on its side and lights from the left, which has become the top of the painting, to show the impasto texture.

When copied with standard two-side lighting, the texture effect of the painting *Plum Island Cottage* by Ward Mann is lost.

More of the effect of a textured painting is retained in the copy when copied with interpretive lighting. KODAK EKTACHROME 50 Professional Film 5018 (Tungsten) was used to make these copies.

Interpretive Lighting: Occasionally the standard copy lighting arrangement does not illustrate a painting as it was intended to appear. This problem can occur when a three dimensional effect is present in the painting. When a painter uses the impasto technqiue for example, the shadows created by the paint are an important element in producing the illusion of depth. The shadows also create dark areas that the painter uses instead of dark paint. The wrong lighting of a painting of this sort would not display the painting as the artist intended it to be displayed.

The illustrations above show an example of how correct lighting can change the appearance of a painting. In this case the photographer observed that the artist would have had a diffuse overhead light as he painted. (The artist works outdoors.) The photographer then attempted to simulate the lighting conditions for the copy. This was accomplished by turning the painting on its side and lighting it with one light from the "sky" side. The light had to be moved a greater distance from the painting than normal to obtain even illumination.

This concept must be considered when photographing art that is not entirely two dimensional. The distinction between the artforms of painting and sculpture has become blurred in recent years making this situation more common. In each situation, the photographer must interpret the way in which to light the artwork with sensitivity and skill.

To show texture, this painting required a grazing light in addition to the regular copy lights. This light is placed at a narrow angle to the surface plane of the painting. It was positioned so that a ridge of paint on the shoulder of the arm picked up a highlight, which adds sparkle to the copy.

When a painting is mounted in a deep frame, it may be nearly impossible to copy it properly. If permission is granted, the painting can be removed from the frame to be copied. Often the museum staff has an expert to perform this task. If the frame is to appear in the final reproduction, it can be photographed separately to the same scale, and the two copies are combined for the final reproduction.

Shooting on Location: Unfortunately artwork cannot always be taken to a studio to be photographed. A museum curator is not likely to let a priceless painting be taken to a photographer's studio regardless of the advantages. Also, when a large number of items are to be photographed it is easier to set up on location and photograph there. This saves the cost and risk of transporting a large number of valuable pieces.

Good planning is essential for any kind of location photography. Copying artwork in a museum or institution is no exception. If possible, a preliminary visit to the location is very helpful. During the visit one should take notice of the existing light (artificial or daylight), the room available, the availability of electrical outlets, and the volume of traffic (human) that the area has. This will help to generate a list of items to bring on location. Such items as extension cords, various focal length lenses, large black flats, and a ladder may be useful.

By checking out the location in advance one can plan to avoid difficult lighting situations. For example, it may be necessary to have a maintenance man turn out the room lights in the area for shooting (but not the electrical outlets). Or it may be necessary to arrange for a piece to be moved if it is located near a window—or other source of lighting.

If access to the museum is available at night, copying paintings at that time offers many advantages. There is no daylight coming through windows to contend with (reflections and mixed sources), light sources that might be troublesome can be turned off, and there may be no traffic of visitors to contend with.

Copying Paintings with Infrared and Ultraviolet Radiation: It is occasionally helpful to photograph with infrared or ultraviolet radiation for an investigation or an analysis of a painting. Infrared photography generally refers to the technique of using film that is sensitized into the infrared region of the electromagnetic spectrum for photographing an object. Infrared photography can be used for detecting overpainting, or forgeries. The principle is that different pigments may not reflect or transmit infrared radiation the same as visible radiation. As a result, two pigments that appear as identical tones to the eye may record as two very different tones on infrared film. In addition, infrared radiation has the ability to pass though some opaque pigments, making it possible to "see through" several layers of paint. Kodak manufactures infrared film in black-and-white and color. KODAK High Speed Infrared Film 2481, a black-and-white film, is available in 35 mm magazines and long rolls. A similar film, KODAK High Speed Infrared Film 4143 is available in 4 x 5 sheets. KODAK EKTACHROME Infrared 2236 Film is a

Above: when paintings must be copied on location because they are too large or too valuable to be moved, the photographer must move his equipment to the painting—in this case to the Memorial Art Gallery of the University of Rochester. Portable lights, polarizing screens, black flats, and a sturdy tripod are required. Here Earl Kage is photographing the painting shown below and on the inside front cover.

color reversal film available in 35 mm magazines. This film is processed with a Process E-4.

Ultraviolet radiation may also be used to photograph a painting for an investigation. The principle of UV reflection photography is similar to the principle for infrared photography. Two materials (or pigments in this case) may reflect (or transmit) different amounts of ultraviolet radiation yet reflect (or transmit) the same amount of visible light. An ultraviolet source of radiation must be used, and a filter must be used over the lens to eliminate all of the visible light. A normal panchromatic or color film can be used, although color film will generally not be needed. The techniques of copying with ultraviolet and infrared radiation are detailed in the section "Copying with IR and UV Radiation" starting on page 50.

Right: The copy on KODAK EKTACHROME 50 Professional Film 5018 (Tungsten) that is being made in the illustration above. The painting is a portrait of the Archbishop of Paris Hyacinth Rigand painted in 1731. The room lights have to be turned off for the exposure, and long extension cords were necessary to get power to the lights. The lights had to be brought fairly close to the camera to avoid a shadow of the frame on the painting. Double polarization was used to eliminate the reflection of the light from the painting surface.

Color Microfiche Copying

Museums, government agencies, industries, and educational institutions often have many large, detailed color originals such as maps, manuscripts, and records that present preservation and storage problems, as well as photocopying problems.

Two methods have been developed for copying such originals using rolls of 105 mm color film at a maximum reduction of 10X (magnification 0.10X) with unusually high image quality. One method uses a standard transparency film, while the other uses a special color-negative film.

The processed rolls can be stored, viewed or printed, and the originals can either be destroyed, reducing the storage area required, or dedicated to long-term, undisturbed storage. See page 130 for a procedure on copying maps and charts.

Printing Color Copy Negatives

Color negatives are exposed onto negative working color print paper and processed to make color prints. Mass produced prints are printed from rolls of negatives on computer controlled printers that expose thousands of prints per hour. The color balance of each negative is measured automatically and filters in the printer are automatically adjusted to control the color balance of the print. The rolls of exposed paper are processed in continuous roll processors and the processed prints are cut automatically. Where color copying is a large volume business, such equipment is practical for making copy prints.

However, most copying is of lesser volume, and the color negatives are generally enlarged and processed individually.

Color enlargers are usually diffusion-type enlargers with built-in cyan, magenta, and yellow dichroic filtration. The density and color balance of color prints can be controlled by on-easel densitometry, or by running tests, evaluating results, and making changes based on the evaluation. This might be called the "trial and error" method. Some laboratories use KODAK Video Color Negative Analyzers that make it fairly easy to find the correct filter packs to get closely balanced prints on the first attempt.

The primary emphasis of this book is on the copying (and duplicating) procedures. Kodak publishes a number of books on the details of color printing; these details will not be repeated here. If further information is needed on color printing, refer to the following publications.

KODAK Publications	Title
No. AE-13	*Basic Developing, Printing, Enlarging in Color*
No. E-66	*Printing Color Negatives*
No. E-172	*Making Color Prints with KODAK EKTAFLEX PCT Film and Paper*
No. E-173	*Color Print Evaluating Guide for KODAK EKTAFLEX PCT Products*
No. KW-16	*Color Printing Techniques*

In another section direct color copying with KODAK EKTAFLEX PCT Reversal Film and Paper is described. KODAK EKTAFLEX PCT Negative Film and Paper are used to make color prints from color negatives. KODAK Publications No. E-172 and E-173 listed above describe the procedures for printing, processing and evaluating color prints made in this manner. While it costs somewhat more to make color prints from copy negatives with EKTAFLEX PCT Negative materials, the processing is considerably simpler than that for processing EKTACOLOR Papers. For those starting out to make color prints, a careful comparison between the two methods should be made.

With either method, many of the same techniques used in black-and-white enlarging can be used such as cropping, dodging, burning in, and diffusion.

DUPLICATING

Introduction to Duplicating

In this book we use the term "duplicating" to mean the reproduction of transparent originals (negatives or transparencies) with photographic materials that yield either film positives or negatives. In the photographic trade, making "dupes" or duplicates usually refers to copying color transparencies with color reversal film. We prefer to use the term duplicating in the broader sense because the techniques and equipment necessary are similar whether negatives, positives, color or black-and-white images are being reproduced. The section "Duplicating" is divided into two parts: One-Step Duplicating (Direct Duplicating on Reversal Films) and Two-Step Duplicating (Negative-Positive process).

In photographic work it is often necessary or convenient to use a duplicate of an original. Duplicates are expendable, originals are usually not expendable. Valuable photographic originals are generally protected and carefully preserved. This applies to both black-and-white and color originals.

There are many reasons why a duplicate negative or transparency may be desirable. For example, by using a duplicate negative to make a large quantity of prints instead of the original negative, the risk of damage to the valuable original is reduced. In this manner, the duplicates serve as working negatives while the original is kept in a safe place. This is a particularly useful procedure for valuable color originals. Long and repeated exposures to intense light sources (as would be encountered in an enlarger or slide projector) can cause fading of the dyes in color negatives and transparencies. By making duplicates, the originals can be kept in cold storage while the more expendable duplicates are used for printing or projection. This procedure is particularly useful for galleries or museums that have large collections of valuable color negatives and transparencies. It is equally useful for the valuable originals of professional and fine-arts photographers.

Duplicates of color transparencies are often needed for slide shows when one slide is to be used several times or when an entire slide show must be shown in several locations at once. It is also useful to duplicate the entire show if it is to be shown repeatedly because fading can occur from repeated projection, and physical damage from repeated handling is also a possiblity. Similarly, duplicate negatives can enable the distribution, storage, and simultaneous use of color negatives in many separate geographical locations.

An enlarged duplicate negative is also helpful in reducing printing time and improving sharpness when a very large mural-sized print is required from a small format negative. It is also useful if the small negative requires retouching.

Museums and other large institutions also find it helpful to have duplicates made of valuable original negatives and transparencies as a precautionary measure in case the original is stolen, accidentally damaged or destroyed. When an original color negative, transparency or print is made on a photographic product that is known to fade, or if it has faded, it is useful to make a duplicate on a newer more stable product to preserve the image or to aid in restoring it.

Making a duplicate is a standard cautionary procedure used by restoration technicians prior to any work on an original. Most restorative techniques involve some degree of risk to the original. A good quality duplicate provides insurance that if the original is damaged or destroyed during restoration at least the duplicate will remain.

Also, some restoration techniques make use of a duplicate for the restoration. For example, a duplicate of a damaged negative can be retouched by an artist. The retouched duplicate can then be used to make a print that will be retouched or airbrushed with dyes.

These examples demonstrate the importance of good quality duplicates in many areas of photography.

Duplicating techniques range from single-step to elaborate and complex duplicating with masks. Most of the equipment types described earlier are employed providing image-size change, cropping potential, and contrast or density adjustment to suit the reproduction system in use. The potential user should become familiar with the various techniques and materials and then select those that best suit his needs and available equipment.

Whether the duplicating is to be done in black-and-white or in color, careful preliminary testing is necessary if predictable results are desired.

The chart on the next page graphically illustrates most of the procedures available for making duplicate negatives and transparencies.

Diagram of Duplicating Procedures

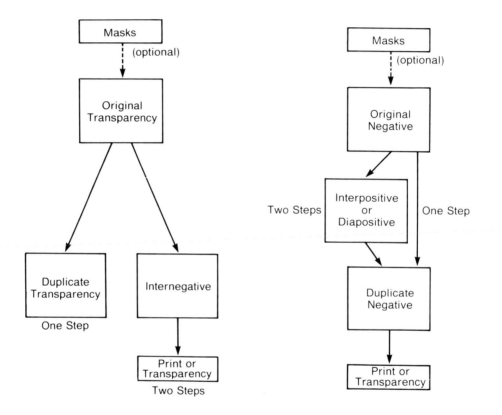

ONE-STEP DUPLICATING

Duplicating Black-and-White Negatives

There are a number of reasons for making duplicates of black-and-white negatives:

- As a restoration of old negatives on which the nitrate base is deteriorating.

- To change negative size—this may be to enlarge small negatives to a larger size so that retouching can be done, or reducing old large-size film or glass-plate negatives to a size that is convenient to store and compatible with available equipment.

- To change the contrast (density range) of a negative. Old wet-plate negatives, for example, can have a density range of well over 2.0. These cannot be printed on any current photographic paper. When a duplicate with a lower density range is made, prints on current papers can be made.

- When thousands of prints are to be made, it is often more efficient to multiple print fewer times than to print more times from a single negative.

- Some laboratories are equipped with automatic contact printers to make large quantities of prints, especially in an 8 x 10-inch size. Negatives of any size can be duplicated by enlarging to make a negative that can be contact printed.

- Master negatives all alike are sometimes needed as setup or standard negatives in many labs located geographically apart. Such negatives can be made by duplicating an original negative.

Kodak manufactures two black-and-white films used to make general-purpose direct duplicates. That is, the original negative is exposed on the direct duplicating film, which is developed to produce a negative image. (This is *not* reversal processing which requires a bleach and a redevelopment.)

KODAK Rapid Process Copy Film (2064) is available in 35 mm size and KODAK Professional B/W Duplicating Film (4168) is available in 4 x 5-inch, 5 x 7-inch and 8 x 10-inch sheets. Their use is quite similar. Both are blue sensitive and can be handled under red, yellow-green or deep amber safelight filters. Both can be exposed in a camera, contact-printed, or exposed in an enlarger. They can be processed in tanks or in roller transport processors such as one of the KODAK VERSAMAT Film Processor or KODAK RP X-OMAT Processors. See the Data Sheets for processing details.

In contact printing, it is essential to have good contact between the original negative and the du-

plicating film to maintain sharpness. Vacuum printing frames are recommended. Spring-back print frames can be used, but care must be taken to insure good contact. When good contact is obtained, the exposure can be made with a diffuse source such as with a contact printer, with an enlarger used as a light source, or with an exposing light on the ceiling over the exposure area.

When contact printing, Newton's rings often form between the glass of the printing frame and the base of the negative. These may then show up on the negative.

If the negative is to be contact printed, the glass in the frame can be replaced with anti-Newton ring glass.* This has a texture that prevents the rings from forming, but leaves a fine pattern on the duplicate negative that can show up on enlargement.

An alternative is the use of a lithographers offset powder, one example of which is Flo-Mix Non-Offset Powder, available at dealers in graphics arts ma-

Lithographer's Offset Powder in Squeeze Bottle

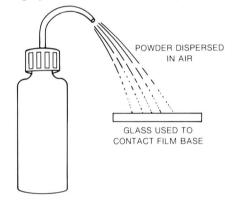

POWDER DISPERSED IN AIR

GLASS USED TO CONTACT FILM BASE

The special powder is puffed into the air and a very light coating is allowed to fall on the clean glass.

Anti-Newton Ring Glass Used in Duplicating

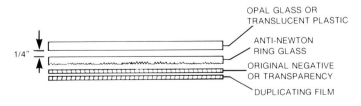

1/4"

OPAL GLASS OR TRANSLUCENT PLASTIC

ANTI-NEWTON RING GLASS

ORIGINAL NEGATIVE OR TRANSPARENCY

DUPLICATING FILM

Use of the spaced diffusing sheet minimizes the texture of the anti-Newton ring glass in the duplicate.

---

*4 x 5-inch sheets are available (larger sizes are special order) from Berkey Marketing, 25-20 Brooklyn-Queens Expressway, Woodside, NY 11377.

terials. The powder is very lightly "puffed" on to the clean glass surface with a squeeze bottle. Puff a little into the air to make a light cloud, and pass the glass through this cloud. This technique will almost always eliminate the Newton's-ring problem.

A third approach is to lightly spray the glass with a dilute solution of gum arabic, using an atomizer. A 14% solution of gum arabic can be purchased at art supply stores or drugstores. Add 1/2 oz of this gum arabic solution to 4 oz of water, stir, and place in the atomizer spray bottle. The glass is then held horizontally and the spray is aimed upward at the glass so that only a very fine spray reaches the glass. When dry, this coated surface is placed against the base side of the negative. The dry surface can be dusted, but if it requires wet cleaning, wash off the gum arabic, dry the glass, and replace the gum arabic spray.

Contrast is controlled by the degree of development. Shorter developing times result in lower contrast, while longer developing times produce more contrast. The recommended times produce an average contrast.

When using a camera to duplicate negatives, the original is placed on an illuminator and 'copied' by the camera. The copying methods of sizing and focusing on the ground glass are used. The same care to reduce flare and reflections from the surface of the negative must be taken.

Exposure is determined by making a series of test exposures. Because these direct duplicating films are quite slow, (an exposure index of about 0.10 for KODAK Rapid Process Copy Film and about 0.25 for Professional B/W Duplicating Film) exposures are relatively long. Exposure meters cannot be used directly for calculating exposures because they do not usually have settings for such low film speeds. However, by running tests, a correlation between exposure meter readings and the proper exposure can be worked out so that differences in exposure required for negatives of varying densities can be predicted. A method of using a factor of 100X the film speed is described on the instruction sheet packaged with the Rapid Process Copy Film.

When making duplicate negatives that will be used for making prints, expose so that the negative minimum density is about 0.30. This practice minimizes the compression of highlight tones by making sure the toe of the original negative falls above the toe of the duplicating film.

When making duplicates with an enlarger, KODAK Professional B/W Duplicating Film is handled in a manner similar to that used to make prints with photographic paper. The original negative is put in the negative carrier and is sized and focused on the easel. Because duplicate negatives must be as sharp

as possible, it is advisable to use a focusing aid such as a micrograin focuser.

After the image is focused and sized, the film is placed on the easel with a piece of black backing paper. The speed of the film used this way is similar to a moderate speed enlarging paper, such as KODAK EKTALURE Paper. A test-strip exposure is given the film. A final exposure is made based on the results of the test strip.

With these two direct positive films, overexposure produces light results while underexposure produces dark results.

Control of Contrast: One of the reasons for making duplicate negatives with KODAK Professional B/W Duplicating Film is to control negative contrast or density range. This can be done along with size change and the making of multiple duplicates.

A negative with a density range of about 1.05 is considered normal for printing with a diffusion enlarger. The following table can be used as a guide for making negatives with this density range with a considerable range of original negatives.

KODAK Professional B/W Duplicating Film (4168)

Suggested Starting Developing Times to Achieve Negatives with a 1.05 Density Range.
Large Tank Development at 68°F (20°C) with Agitation at 1-minute Intervals.

Original Negative Density Range*	Develop to Gamma	DK-50 (in minutes)	DK-50 (1:1) (in minutes)
0.70	1.60	8	12
0.80	1.40	6½	10
0.90	1.20	5½	8½
1.00	1.10	5	7½
1.10†	1.00	4¾	6¾
1.20	0.90	4½	6¼
1.30	0.85	4¼	6
1.40	0.80		5¾
1.50	0.75		5½
1.60	0.70		5¼
1.70	0.65		5
1.80	0.62		4¾††
1.90	0.58		4½††
2.00	0.55		4 ††

Note: Tray developing times are about 25% less.

*When negatives are overall yellow as from a Pyro developer, use the blue filter setting on the densitometer.

†Use these times to duplicate original negative density range.

††May produce uneven densities and low D-max.

When the original negative has a density range greater than 2.00, the two-step duplicating method can be used. See page 123.

As with almost any photographic process, a particular set of conditions can produce different results. It is wise to monitor results and make changes to achieve the exact results desired.

Occasionally, tank agitation effects can result in uneven densities in the negatives, especially with relatively short developing times. If sheet film hangers are used for developing, use an oversize tank to minimize these effects. If they still occur, change to tray development.

If negatives made on KODAK Professional B/W Duplicating Film 4168 are likely to be subjected to abnormally high levels of prolonged illumination, they should be treated to enhance the stability of the silver image.

After fixing and washing the duplicate negatives, they are treated for 3 minutes in the following 1:19 solution of KODAK Rapid Selenium Toner.

Water	950 mL
KODAK Rapid Selenium Toner	50 mL
Solution	1 L

Up to 160 4x5-inch negatives can be treated in a litre of solution. After the treatment, wash the negatives for 30 minutes and dry in the usual manner. Treated duplicate negatives have excellent light and dark keeping characteristics. The use of washing aids such as KODAK Hypo Clearing Agent, either before or after treatment, is **not** recommended. Reduced image stability is very likely to result from the use of washing aids with this film.

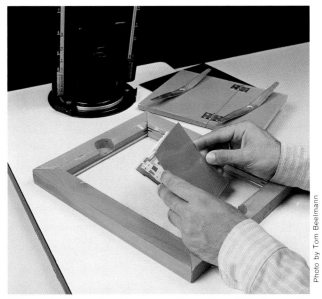

Photo by Tom Beelmann

A black-and-white negative is being placed in a contact-printing frame along with a sheet of KODAK Professional B/W Duplicating Film 4168. The enlarger serves as a light source. Of course, this takes place in the dark or under red safelight conditions.

Duplicating Color Transparencies

Duplicating color transparencies or "duping" is usually accomplished by photographing the original transparency with a color reversal duplicating film. The reproduction is made with one-step duplication.

Specialized equipment is commonly used for duplicating. If the amount of duplicating is small, the equipment need not be very sophisticated to get good results. When 35 mm slides are being duplicated, the basic equipment required, in addition to the camera, is a method of magnifying the image to 1:1 proportions or greater. As illustrated previously in the equipment section, close-up equipment for 35 mm cameras can be purchased in a broad range of sophistication. The cost of this equipment varies proportionally. Expensive equipment is not necessarily a prerequisite for good results. The more expensive equipment is more likely to have features that would increase speed of operation, the versatility, or durability of the equipment, but not necessarily the quality of the duplicate.

The one piece of equipment that is important is the lens. A lens that is designed for picture taking at normal distances will not be extremely sharp when focused at 1:1. For close-up photography a lens designed for close focusing will produce sharper results. More information on close focusing lenses and equipment is provided in the *Equipment* section.

Transparencies can be duplicated in a number of ways. The duplicating film can be exposed by contact, with an enlarger, or in a camera. The method that is chosen depends upon a number of user requirements such as speed, volume, and equipment available.

General Procedures

Contact: The method of duplicating by contact is similar to any other method of contact printing film to film. In the dark, the duplicating film is placed on a sheet of black paper with the emulsion up. The transparency is placed on top with the emulsion down. A piece of glass is used to hold the combination flat during exposure. *Cleanliness is important during this operation or dust spots will appear in the duplicate.* A printing frame can also be used. It is convenient to use an enlarger with a set of color filters as the light source. The color balance can be adjusted by adjusting the enlarger filtration. This method is most often used to duplicate large format transparencies.

Projection: Duplicates can also be exposed with an enlarger by projection. The exposing technique is similar to making prints except a transparency is placed in the negative carrier instead of a negative and duplicating film is placed on the easel instead of photographic paper. The filter pack can be adjusted with dichroic filters if the enlarger is so equipped, or with KODAK Color Printing (CP) Filters in the filter drawer of the enlarger. If filters must be used in front of the lens of the enlarger KODAK Color Compensating (CC) Filters should be used.

Camera: Same size duplicates of small format transparencies are most often exposed in a camera. The equipment available for this task can be very specialized or merely a rudimentary adaption of a simple camera. The basic requirements and procedures remain the same. A device for holding and illuminating the transparency is necessary when making duplicates with a camera. The light source should have some method of diffusing the light before it strikes the transparency. The light source must provide even illumination across the transparency. A place for inserting filters is also necessary.

In all cases, the transparency should be cleaned with compressed ionized air or an anti-static device prior to duplicating. Oil or stubborn dirt can often be removed using KODAK Film Cleaner* and a cotton swab. Fingerprints cannot always be removed by cleaning. Using a diffuse light source will help minimize all of these problems.

When focusing close-up equipment at distances near 1:1 the lens movement changes image size while the movement of the camera body changes the focus. This is the opposite of the procedure used in normal picture taking.

When the slide or transparency is positioned for copying it should be oriented so that the emulsion is facing away from the camera so that the duplicate is not laterally reversed when compared to the original.

For optimum sharpness in duplicating 35 mm slides, the originals can be mounted in glass slide mounts. This will help keep the originals flat. Flatness is important at close focusing distances where depth of field is limited.

A color reversal duplicating film is preferred for copying transparencies instead of a general purpose camera film. A duplicating film produces lower contrast and has a characteristic curve shape that is designed for good tone reproduction when copying transparencies. These films produce better highlight and shadow tone reproduction in duplicates than do camera films. See illustrations on pages 98 and 99.

Kodak makes several color reversal duplicating films. KODAK EKTACHROME Duplicating Film 6121 is a

sheet film intended for use with tungsten light sources. It is available in sizes from 4 x 5-inch (10.1 x 12.7 cm) to 16 x 20-inch (40.6 x 50.8 cm).

KODAK EKTACHROME Slide Duplicating Film 5071 is a roll film that is also balanced for tungsten light sources. It is available in 135 size magazines, 35 mm and 46 mm long rolls. KODAK EKTACHROME SE Duplicating Film SO-366 is also a roll film but is intended for use with short duration illumination. The SE film is tungsten balanced, so it requires considerable filtration for electronic flash (see chart on page 100). It is available in 135 size magazines and 35 mm long rolls. The 36-exposure magazine is CAT No. 159 0223 while the 35 mm 100-foot-long roll is CAT No. 159 0256.

It is essential that the proper light source be used with each film product. The chart on page 96 gives the light sources that are intended for each film product along with starting filter guidelines.

The filtration necessary for each film varies with the type of film that is used as an original. A different filter pack is usually required for duplicating originals on KODACHROME Film than for EKTACHROME Film. The filter pack requirements are also different for older films of the same type (KODACHROME Film Process K-12, EKTACHROME Film Process E-4 etc.)

These differences can be minimized by using a KODAK Infrared Cutoff Filter No. 304 between the light source and the transparency. This filter should be positioned perpendicular to the light source with the coated side facing the bulb. The filter should be in front of any diffusion material, nearest to the light source.

A disadvantage of using this filter is that the intensity of the light is reduced greatly. This might require excessively long exposures in some situations. Another disadvantage is that the color reproduction may not be as good as it would be using a normal filter pack. There can be red contrast difficulties.

Adjusting the Filter Pack: Critical color evaluation of slides should be made with a projector if the slides are to be projected. A standard 5000 K illuminator is also helpful for evaluating color balance, particularly if the transparencies are to be reproduced photomechanically. Fluorescent tubes that have an equivalent color balance of 5000 K can be purchased for light boxes.*

5000 K illumination with a high color rendering index is an industry standard for evaluating color by photographers, printers, and photographic manufacturers.

---

*One manufacturer of such fluorescent tubes is:

Macbeth Color & Photometry
P.O. Box 950
Little Britain Road
Newburgh, New York 12550

---

*Do not use motion picture film cleaners which contain a lubricant.

35-mm duplicates can be simply made with this duplicating equipment. Courtesy Spiratone.

A type of illuminator that is used for vertical duplication. This Testrite Illuminator contains a modeling light for framing and focusing, and an electronic flash for exposure.

A vertical copy stand in use as a duplicator.

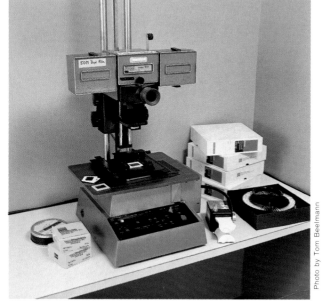

This Forox SD Duplicator is designed for large scale slide duplication. The camera back holds long rolls of duplicating film.

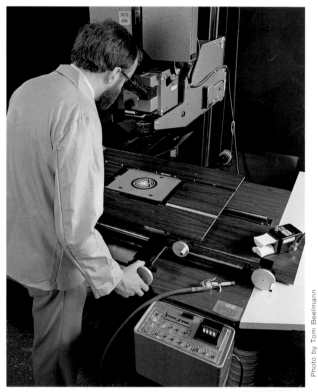

Oxberry professional duplicating equipment is flexible and adaptable. Here a slide duplicate is being made from a large transparency. The camera holds long rolls of duplicating film.

Photo by Tom Beelmann

A filter pack can be adjusted by evaluating a test duplicate. A test duplicate should be made from a slide that has a large neutral midtone area. The test should include several exposures made at different lens apertures at the same exposure time. The color balance of the duplicate can be evaluated by judging the predominant color balance of the neutral midtone areas. To correct a color imbalance a filter that is complementary to the predominant hue must be added. For example, if the neutral areas of the test duplicate appeared magenta, more green filtration or less magenta filtration would be required.

The KODAK *Color Print Viewing Filter Kit*, KODAK Publication R-25, is helpful for determining the exact hue that is present, and the value of the color compensating filter that is required to correct it. It is particularly helpful in determining the unwanted hue when the exact hue that is present is not obvious. For example, if the unwanted hue is either cyan or blue, either a red or a yellow filter respectively from the filter kit will make the off-neutral tone appear neutral.

If the color imbalance is strong, a combination of filters may be necessary for good color rendition. It is best to keep the number of filters to a minimum. If

KODAK Film	Light Source	KODAK WRATTEN Filters	Intended Exposure Time
EKTACHROME Duplicating Film 6121	Tungsten	2B, + CC filters as needed. Starting pack given in instruction sheet with film.	10 sec.
EKTACHROME Duplicating Films 5071, 7071	Tungsten*	2B + CC filters as needed. See Data Sheet DS-40	1 sec.
EKTACHROME SE Duplicating Film SO-366	Electronic Flash	2B + CC110Y + CC15C†	$1/1000$ sec.

* Although KODAK EKTACHROME Duplicating Film 5071 is intended for tungsten illumination at exposures of one second, some workers have had satisfactory results using electronic flash illumination and an 85B filter. Color rendition may not be as accurate as with EKTACHROME SE Duplicating Film SO-366 due to the effects produced by the reciprocity-law failure.

† This will vary with the type of original slide being duplicated, with the color output of the electronic flash and with different batches of film. Tests must be run.

all three subtractive colors are present in a filter pack (cyan, magenta, yellow) the lowest value filter can be removed and the other filters reduced by the same value. If the filter pack consisted of 40C + 40M + 20Y, then 20 points of neutral density could be removed. The filter pack could be reduced to 20C + 20M. Because cyan and magenta make up blue, this filter pack could be represented by only one filter: a 20B. The table below illustrates these relationships.

Filter Changes for Transparency Duplicating

Overall Color Balance	Subtract these Filters*	or Add these Filters*
Yellow	Yellow	Magenta + Cyan (or Blue)
Magenta	Magenta	Yellow + Cyan (or Green)
Cyan	Cyan	Yellow + Magenta (or Red)
Blue	Magenta + Cyan (or Blue)	Yellow
Green	Yellow + Cyan (or Green)	Magenta
Red	Yellow + Magenta (or Red)	Cyan

*It is necessary to make exposure corrections as the filter pack is changed.

The filter pack for one type of duplicating film may vary from emulsion to emulsion. If a large quantity of duplicating is done with one type of film it is advisable to buy a 3- to 6-month supply of one emulsion so that filter pack changes are limited to variations in originals. Kodak color reversal duplicating films should be stored at 55°F (13°C) or lower in the original sealed container until just before use. Allow sufficient warm-up time at room temperature before opening for use to prevent condensation.

Emulsion numbers are printed on the outside box of most duplicating films.

When a new film emulsion is to be used where the filter pack for the previous emulsion has been established, a change in the filtration and exposure index may be necessary. To make these changes easier, crossover data is printed on the outside

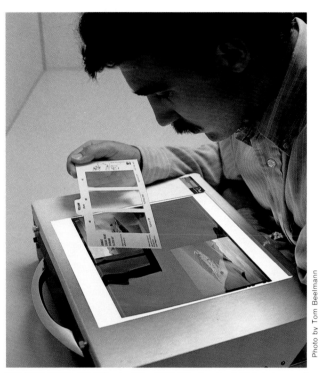

The KODAK Color Print Viewing Filter Kit, Publication No. R-25, is being used to evaluate the color balance of a duplicate transparency.

Photo by Tom Beelmann

package of the film near the emulsion number or on the data sheet. The crossover data consists of three numbers: a cyan value, a yellow value and an exposure factor (in f-stops). All filtration changes are expressed in positive or negative cyan and yellow values.

The filter and exposure adjustments are calculated by subtracting the crossover data from the package of the old film emulsion from the data on the package of the new film emulsion. This may require subtracting a minus value which is the same as adding.

Example:
$$-05C + 10Y + 0.5 \quad \text{New emulsion}$$
$$-(+10C - 05Y - 0.5) \quad \text{Old emulsion}$$
$$-15C + 15Y + 1.0 \quad \text{Change in filtration and exposure}$$

From original transparency.

From duplicate made on regular transparency film. Increased contrast is apparent.

The illustration above was made directly from a duplicate on KODAK EKTACHROME Duplicating Film. When carefully made, duplicate transparencies made on KODAK EKTACHROME Duplicating Film 6121 can closely match the originals. A subject with a long scale was selected for this series of illustrations because this type of subject is most difficult to duplicate satisfactorily.

This change would be added to the present filter pack for the film.

Example:

30C	+	50Y 1 sec. @ f/11	Old filter pack and exposure
−15C	+	15Y + 1.0 stop	Change
15C	+	65Y 1 sec. @ f/8	New filter pack and exposure

If there is not enough cyan or yellow filtration to subtract then add red (for cyan) or blue (for yellow).

Example:		
10C + 50Y	Old filter pack
−15C + 15Y	Change
05R + 65Y	New filter pack

Determining Exposure Index: When a camera is used that has a through-the-lens light meter it is convenient to get a starting exposure by using the camera meter. While there are no official speeds given for this film, the table below gives approximate exposure indexes for the duplicating films that would normally be used with this type of camera.

KODAK Film	Starting Exposure Index
EKTACHROME Slide Duplicating Film 5071 & 7071	6
EKTACHROME SE Duplicating Film SO-366	8

Meter readings can be made from an average slide or a 1.0 KODAK WRATTEN Neutral Density Filter No. 96. (This is similar to using an 18-percent gray card when copying.)

When an exposure adjustment appears with the crossover information, it can be used to adjust the exposure index. If the exposure index is 6 and the exposure adjustment is +1.0 then one f/stop more exposure is necessary. The new exposure index would be 3. If the adjustment was -1.0 the new exposure index would be 12.

For consistent results exposure changes should be made with the lens aperture and the shutter speed should remain constant.

KODAK EKTACHROME Duplicating Films should be processed in Process E-6. The duplicating films are process-compatible with other Process E-6 KODAK EKTACHROME Films.

Improving the Original: As in other forms of copying, it is not always best to duplicate the original exactly. Often improvements can be made. It is possible to improve an off-color original, increase contrast, reduce contrast, crop, or add special effects. Usually, improvements are subject to customer ap-

proval. When duplicating for a client, it is important to determine what changes will be attempted before the work is done. Otherwise the client may be disappointed that his original was not reproduced exactly as it appeared.

An off-color original can be improved by filtering with color filters during the exposure. Filters can be used over the lens (KODAK Color Compensating Filters) or over the light source (KODAK Color Printing Filters). To determine the proper filter, just view the transparency with a filter that is complementary to the color cast. When the transparency looks neutral you have selected the correct filter. The KODAK Color Print Viewing Filter Kit, mentioned previously, is an aid in determining the correct hue and the proper value of the filter. When the proper filter is determined, add it to the standard filter pack for the duplicating film being used.

Some originals may benefit from an increase in contrast. A transparency that is slightly flat will gain contrast and color saturation if duplicated on KODACHROME or KODAK EKTACHROME Films for cameras (instead of duplicating films). The correct filter pack must first be determined for the camera film in the same manner as for a duplicating film. Some photographers copy transparencies several times using KODACHROME Film. Each succeeding copy gains a little in contrast.

Contrast can also be manipulated in the other direction. The primary technique is flashing. Flashing is a technique of reducing contrast by the use of a second, non-image exposure to the film. The easiest way to flash, when making a duplicate, is to make the main exposure in the normal manner first. Remove the slide leaving an even white-light area to photograph. Then put a neutral density filter in front of the lens and expose again. Use the same f-number and exposure time. A KODAK WRATTEN Neutral Density Filter No. 96 with a density of 2.00 is a good filter to start with. A 2.00 neutral density filter will transmit only one percent of the light that falls on it. The amount of neutral density or exposure may have to be adjusted to get the correct amount of flash exposure. If the shadows in the duplicate are light and have a smoky appearance, the flash exposure is too strong. Increase the amount of neutral density filter for the next attempt. If the shadows in the duplicate are black and the contrast is still too high, run another test with less neutral density. With some cameras, it may be necessary to use a film advance override to make the second exposure.

Some slide copying devices have a feature that makes it possible to flash during the main exposure. This can save time in a production situation.

Another simple technique for improving an image that is often overlooked is cropping. Often an

Photo by M. A. Geissinger

The illustration above was made directly from a slide on POLACHROME Film. It was reproduced dark to show its original appearance. Such slides can be reproduced to a normal density even though their densities are considerably higher than that of slides on KODACHROME or EKTACHROME Films.

Duplicate by Dakin Chamberlain

This illustration was made of a duplicate of the slide made on POLACHROME Film. The duplicate was made on KODAK EKTACHROME Slide Duplicating Film. Such duplicate slides can be intermixed with other slides on transparency films for normal projection brightness.

original will contain extraneous elements or extra space that can be cropped out to increase the importance of the subject matter. Many good photographs can be made to have more impact when cropped. Other techniques that may be useful are double exposures, sandwiching slides, adding color with color filters, or using special-effects filters.

Duplicating Slides Made on POLACHROME Film: POLACHROME Film is an additive film rather than subtractive like KODACHROME and EKTACHROME Film. As a result, the slides made on POLACHROME Film are much darker than conventional slides. This makes them unsuitable for regular projection intermixed with regular slides. However, duplicate slides can be made from POLACHROME Film slides that have the same density characteristics as normal slides.

When duplicating on KODAK EKTACHROME Slide Duplicating Film, POLACHROME Film slides require about 3 stops more or 8X the exposure for regular slides. In addition, they require a filtration of about CC25G greater than that used for duplicating EKTACHROME Film slides. Properly balanced and exposed duplicates make quite good slides for projection.

Duplicating Color Negatives

Many reasons for making duplicate negatives are given on page 89. The simplest and most direct way to duplicate a color negative is to print it on a color reversal film. KODAK EKTACHROME Duplicating Film 6121 (sheets) and KODAK EKTACHROME Slide Duplicating Film 5071 (rolls) are excellent films for this purpose.

Duplicating films generally make better duplicates than camera films because their sensitometric characteristics provide better contrast and tone reproduction for this purpose.

The same general procedure that is used for duplicating color transparencies is used for duplicating color negatives with KODAK EKTACHROME Duplicating Films. The original negative is treated as if it were a transparency to be duplicated. The same filtration that is used for making duplicate color transparencies should be used as a starting point in making duplicate color negatives. To determine if the color balance is acceptable a color print must be made. The color balance can also be evaluated on a densitometer or a color analyzer. The duplicate should have similar red, green, and blue density ranges as the original (measured with Status M filtration). Most areas in the duplicate should have densities about 0.10 higher than the original, in order to get the tone reproduction up off the toe of the duplicating film.

An exposure adjustment of one-half to one full stop underexposure is necessary when duplicating color negatives with this method. This puts most of the tones of the reproduction on the relatively straight portion of the characteristic curve of the duplicating film. By placing the reproduction on the straight line portion of the curve the duplicate will reproduce the original almost tone for tone.

Some loss of color saturation can be expected, but as the illustration above shows the loss is minimal. Underexposing as recommended above will help to reduce any loss of color saturation.

When a small-sized duplicate negative is to be used for making enlarged color prints, the duplicate negative should be enlarged to about three times the size of the original negative to maintain about the same visual graininess as in a print from the original.

Although the grain on EKTACHROME Duplicating Film is extremely fine, when duplicate negatives are made the same size there is an enhancement of graininess. But when the duplicate negative is enlarged several times, the enlarged grain of the original negative image becomes large compared to that of the duplicating film and the effect is eliminated.

If the original negative is quite contrasty, a positive contrast-reducing mask can be made to fit in register with the original. The technique for making contrast-reducing masks can be found on page 108.

Duplicate negatives usually require a different printing filtration from the originals. If a negative evaluating equipment such as a KODAK Video Color Negative Analyzer is being used, a new correlation between analyzer results and printing filters is usually required.

Another method of making duplicate color negatives is to neutralize the orange colored minimum density with filtration. Complete neutralizing may require CC90C + CC30M filtration. If this leads to excessively long exposures, as little as CC50C can be used with adequate results. With dichroic filters in an enlarger head, less filtration may be required.

Both methods, duplicating as is and duplicating with neutralizing filtration are being used successfully. If you have any quantity of color negative duplication to do, you might try both methods and compare results. For more information write for CIS-59, *Color Duplicates of KODAK Color Negative Films* to:

> Dept. 412-L
> C/P & FM
> Eastman Kodak Company
> 343 State Street
> Rochester, New York 14650

KODAK Direct Positive Paper

Black-and-white prints can be made directly from color transparencies in one step by printing them on KODAK Direct Positive Paper. This paper has an orthochromatic emulsion so that the gray tone rendering of colors will be distorted. Reds will be darkened and blues lightened.

The transparency is enlarged or contact printed on the paper, and the paper is given a reversal processing, resulting in a direct positive print. The tone-reproduction quality is generally not quite as high as that of prints made from black-and-white internegatives by a two-step process.

Details of the process are given in KODAK Publication No. G-14, *Direct Positive Photography with KODAK Direct Positive Paper*.

This illustration was made from a color print made from the original color negative.

TWO-STEP DUPLICATING

B/W Internegatives from Color Transparencies

Black-and-white prints are often needed from color transparencies for a variety of purposes. For example, a black-and-white print is necessary when a picture is to be photomechanically printed in black-and-white but the original is a color transparency.

In order to make a black-and-white print from a transparency an *internegative* is required. An internegative is a negative made from the transparency. A good quality internegative is essential if one expects to make a black-and-white print with satisfactory tone reproduction. One of the problems commonly encountered in making a black-and-white print from a transparency is excess contrast. Color transparencies typically have a density range as high as 3.00. Black-and-white photographic paper is capable of producing a density range of about 2.00—the exact value depends on the paper and paper surface. As a result it is necessary to compress the tonal range of the subject when converting from a transparency to a print. One factor affecting quality of the print is how the tonal compression was accomplished. A print that exhibits poor tonal compression as the result of a poor internegative will have poor highlight separation and will show a loss of shadow detail.

There are several different ways to make internegatives. The following is a discussion of a variety of techniques for different user requirements.

Bellows and Extension Tube Method: This is a quick and easy method for making black-and-white internegatives of a large number of transparencies. A small format camera is used with extension tubes or auxiliary bellows to increase magnification. A light box or slide copying apparatus (see illustration on page 95) is used as a light source. The same procedure that is used for slide duplication is used except that black-and-white film is exposed in the camera instead of color reversal film. KODAK PLUS-X Pan Film is a good choice for this purpose. It is available in most small-format sizes, has medium speed, fine grain, and the resultant internegative produces acceptable tone reproduction for many purposes. KODAK Developer D-76 diluted 1:1 works well for this method. The table below gives suggested developing times to be used as a starting point for making internegatives with this method.

Processing Black-and-White Internegatives Exposed on KODAK PLUS-X Pan Film in Bellows Slide Copier, and Developed in KODAK Developer D-76 (1:1)

KODAK Film Type Original Slide	Enlarger Type to be used	Small Tank Development Time at 68°F (20°C)
KODACHROME	Condenser	6 minutes
EKTACHROME	Condenser	8 minutes
KODACHROME	Diffusion	8½ minutes
EKTACHROME	Diffusion	10 minutes

KODAK Technical Pan Film 2415 can also be used to make black-and-white internatives from slides. It is sharper and finer grained than KODAK PLUS-X Pan Film, but it is slower, and extra care must be taken with agitation to insure even development (see page 60). KODAK Technical Pan Film also has extended red sensitivity which will make red tones appear lighter in the final print than with a normal panchromatic film. Use of a KODAK WRATTEN Filter No. 38 gives a corrected panchromatic tone rendition.

Duplicate negative by Tony Mercadol

This illustration was made from a color print made from a duplicate color negative. The duplicate negative was made on KODAK EKTACHROME Duplicating Film 6121 by the method described starting on page 101.

This series of illustrations was made to show the use of KODAK PLUS-X Pan Film to make black-and-white negatives from slides. All slides were on KODACHROME Film. Above is a normal contrast, normal exposure slide.

An underexposed slide.

This is a print from an internegative on KODAK PLUS-X Pan Film. The negative was made with a slide copier and accessory bellows attached to a 35-mm single-lens reflex camera. Development was in KODAK D-76 Developer (1:1) for 6 minutes in a small tank at 68°F.

The black-and-white internegative was given one stop more exposure than the normal slide. It was given the same development (6 minutes).

An overexposed slide.

A reproduction of a low contrast slide.

The black-and-white internegative was given one stop less exposure than the normal slide. It was given the same development (6 minutes).

This print was made from an internegative on PLUS-X Pan Film exposed the same as the normal slide, but given a longer developing time (10 minutes) to increase the contrast. Internegatives made from slides on EKTACHROME Film require slightly more development. See the table in the text.

105

The above illustration was made from a high contrast slide.

The internegative from this slide was given the same exposure as the normal slide, but was given less development (5 minutes) to lower the contrast. All the black-and-white negatives were enlarged with a condenser enlarger.

Small Tank Development of Technical Pan Film

KODAK Film Original Slide	Enlarger Type to be used	Starting Times at 68° (20°C)	
		TECHNIDOL LC Developer (powdered)	TECHNIDOL Liquid Developer
KODACHROME	Condenser	11 min.	7 min.
EKTACHROME	Condenser	14 min.	9 min.
KODACHROME	Diffusion	15 min.	9 min.
EKTACHROME	Diffusion	18 min.	11 min.

Note: If the contrast is too low, increase the developing time; if it is too high, decrease the developing time.

One of the biggest advantages of this method is that the internegative can be enlarged in any small-format enlarger. Another advantage is that a large number of slides can be converted to black-and-white with each roll of 35 mm film.

Contact Method: The contact method is a simple method requiring little equipment and is especially useful for making internegatives of sheet-film transparencies. All that is needed to expose the internegative is a piece of clear glass or a contact frame and a light source. An enlarger (without a negative in it) or a safelight (with the filter removed) can be used as the light source. The light source should be connected to a timer for consistency and repeatability.

The procedure is simple. In the dark, the transparency is placed in contact with a piece of film of appropriate size. The emulsion of the transparency should face the emulsion of the film. This combination is put in a contact frame or under a sheet of glass and exposed to the light source. A piece of black paper should be put on the bottom to minimize the amount of light reflected back through the film base. A diagram of the arrangement of the elements is shown in the illustration. After exposure

the film is developed with shortened developing times. Suggested developing times are given in the table for KODAK SUPER XX Pan Film developed in KODAK Developer D-76 1:1. The times are given as starting points from which the proper developing time for your own circumstances and equipment can be determined. In general, for a high contrast transparency the exposure should be increased slightly and development reduced. A low contrast transparency will produce a better internegative if it is given slightly less exposure and more development.

As mentioned above, this method is especially useful for large-format transparencies. It provides higher quality images than lens-imaging methods because it keeps image degrading flare to a minimum. It also requires little or no special equipment.

Exposing B/W Internegatives by Contact

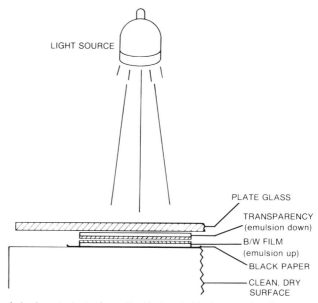

A simple contact setup for making black-and-white internegatives from large transparencies.

Starting Development Times for Internegatives on KODAK SUPER-XX Pan Film (ESTAR Thick Base) KODAK D-76 Developer (1:1)

Method of Exposing Internegative	Developing Method	Enlarger to be Used in Printing	Development Time at 68°F (20°C)	
			Original EKTACHROME	Original KODACHROME
Contact	Tank	Condenser	6 minutes	5 minutes
Contact	Tank	Diffusion	8 minutes	6½ minutes
Contact	Tray	Condenser	4 minutes	3¼ minutes
Contact	Tray	Diffusion	5½ minutes	4½ minutes
Enlarger	Tank	Condenser	7 minutes	5½ minutes
Enlarger	Tank	Diffusion	9 minutes	7 minutes
Enlarger	Tray	Condenser	5 minutes	4 minutes
Enlarger	Tray	Diffusion	6½ minutes	5¼ minutes

A disadvantage of this system is that dust elimination can be difficult when handling the transparency and film in the dark. Dust is most troublesome with small format transparencies, which are more often enlarged when making internegatives.

Enlarger Method: This method is one of the most commonly used methods for exposing internegatives. It is convenient because the same tools used for enlarging can be used for making internegatives. For small format transparencies there is an additional advantage gained by the use of larger film sizes for the internegative. A 35 mm or 2¼ transparency can be enlarged onto a 4 x 5 or 8 x 10 sheet of film thereby minimizing the grain of the intermediate negative. Enlarging the transparency also offers the advantage of being able to clean the transparency under the illumination of the enlarger light source. This minimizes the possibility of getting dust on the transparency once it has been cleaned because the carrier is placed in the enlarger as soon as the transparency is cleaned.

The enlarger is usually connected to a timer and a voltage regulator. An easel is used to hold the film to be exposed. Black paper should be put over the surface of the easel to prevent light from reflecting back through the base of the film. Either a condenser or a diffusion enlarger can be used to make the internegative. However, a diffusion enlarger will tend to reduce the effects of dust or dirt on the transparency. As with other types of enlarging, burning-in and dodging can be used for local tone control. It must be remembered that burning-in will lighten the areas in the final print and dodging will darken areas in the final print.

The procedure of making an enlarged internegative is simple to one familiar with basic enlarging techniques. The transparency is placed in a negative carrier (this usually requires unmounting the transparency) and the negative carrier is put in the enlarger. As mentioned above, with some types of enlargers it is convenient at this point to clean the transparency under the illumination of the enlarger light source with compressed air or an anti-static brush. The transparency is usually oriented with the emulsion side up in the enlarger so that the resulting internegative is right-reading through the base of the film. This is so that internegatives made by contact and by projection will have the same orientation. The image is sized on the easel and focused. The size of the internegative is determined by the method with which the internegative will be printed. If the internegatives are to be contact printed they will be enlarged to the size of the final print. If they are to be printed in an enlarger they will all be made to the maximum size of the enlarger format. Large-format transparencies as well as small format transparencies can be exposed by this method with an appropriate enlarger.

The exposed negative is then developed in the normal manner. Suggested starting times for this method are also included in the chart above.

Color Internegative Method: Color internegatives can also be used to make black-and-white prints from color transparencies. A color internegative is convenient to have because both color and black-and-white prints can be made from it. A panchromatic black-and-white paper must be used for printing, however, such as KODAK PANALURE Paper, KODAK PANALURE II RC Paper, and KODAK PANALURE II Repro RC Paper.

The black-and-white print quality can be very good when internegatives are made on one of the KODAK VERICOLOR Internegative Films. These internegative films have a characteristic curve shape that increases highlight contrast, helping to prevent muddy highlights. The procedure for making color internegatives is described in the section starting on page 110.

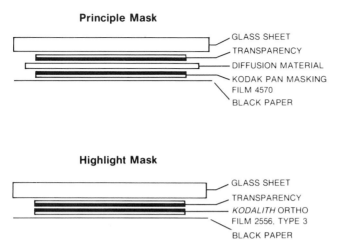

Principle Mask

GLASS SHEET
TRANSPARENCY
DIFFUSION MATERIAL
KODAK PAN MASKING FILM 4570
BLACK PAPER

Highlight Mask

GLASS SHEET
TRANSPARENCY
KODALITH ORTHO FILM 2556, TYPE 3
BLACK PAPER

The arrangements for making contact principal masks and highlight masks using the contact set-up shown on page 106.

Masking Methods for Use With B/W Camera Films

The highest quality black-and-white print is possible by using one or more masks in addition to the camera film. Using a mask is a way to alter the tone reproduction of the final print in a fashion not possible by using a camera-film internegative alone. Masking techniques for internegatives usually lower overall contrast and increase highlight contrast.

The simplest masking technique is to use a negative highlight mask taped in register with the internegative to make the black-and-white print. The black-and-white internegative is made in the normal fashion (either by contact or with an enlarger). Then a mask is made from the transparency exactly the same size as the internegative. KODALITH Ortho Film, Type 3 or KODALITH Pan Film can be used to make the mask (developed in Developer D-11 for 1-2 minutes in a tray). The mask should be a very low density record of the highlight areas of the transparency. This mask can then be taped in register on top of the internegative and printed in the normal manner. The mask will add contrast to the highlight areas of the reproduction.

A more sophisticated approach is to mask the transparency before exposing the internegative. One or two masks can be used. A contrast-reducing mask can be used alone or a contrast-reducing mask can be used with a highlight mask. A contrast reducing mask is made from the transparency on KODAK Pan Masking Film. This must be done by contact printing the transparency onto the masking film through diffusion sheeting. The diagram shows the position of the elements during this step. Diffusion sheeting is used to make an unsharp mask. An unsharp mask is necessary to minimize registration problems and to enhance the contrast of fine detail. The mask can be developed in KODAK HC-110 Developer (dilution F) in a tray for about three minutes.

Exact exposure and development can be determined by experience. As a general guide the density range of the mask should be about 20–30 percent of the density range of the transparency. If the transparency density range is 3.00, the mask density range would be about 0.75. The finished mask is taped in register with the transparency and used to expose the internegative. Because the contrast of the transparency has been reduced with the mask the developing time of the internegative can be increased slightly.

In addition to the contrast-reducing mask a highlight mask can be used to increase tonal separation in the highlight areas of the copy. To use a highlight mask with a contrast-reducing mask, the highlight mask must be made and placed in register with the transparency before the contrast-reducing mask and the internegative are made. The highlight mask is made in the same fashion as when it is used directly with the internegative except that it should have slightly more density. A summary of the three masking methods is provided below:

1. **Highlight Mask on Internegative:**

   a) Highlight Mask—Made from the transparency on KODALITH Ortho Film, Type 3, developed in KODAK Developer D-11. Very low density image.

   b) Internegative—Made from the transparency on KODAK SUPER-XX Pan Film developed in KODAK Developer D-76 1:1. The mask is attached in register to the internegative to make the black-and-white print.

2. **Single Mask on Transparency:**

   a) A contrast-reducing mask is made from the transparency on KODAK Pan Masking Film (with diffusion sheeting) and developed in KODAK HC-110 Developer dilution F. The mask is then taped in register to the transparency and the internegative is exposed from this combination.

3. **Two Masks and Transparency:**

   a) A highlight mask is made from the transparency on KODALITH Ortho Film, Type 3, developed in KODAK Developer D-11. This mask is placed in register with the transparency and used to expose the next mask.

   b) A contrast-reducing mask is made from the highlight mask and transparency combination on KODAK Pan Masking Film (with diffusion) and developed in KODAK HC-110 Developer Dilution F. This mask is then taped in register to the transparency and the highlight mask removed. This combination is used to expose the internegative.

Photo by Tom Benson

The original transparency. Illustration made directly from the transparency.

Internegative by Dennis Thompson

Black-and-white print made from internegative.

Internegative by Wanda Radke

Black-and-white print made on KODAK PANALURE II RC Paper from color internegative made from the transparency. Note the good highlight tone separation.

Mask by Dennis Thompson

Black-and-white print made from masked black-and-white internegative. Note the good highlight tone separation.

Making Color Internegatives From Color Transparencies with KODAK VERICOLOR Internegative Films

Color negatives, or internegatives, are often made from color transparencies so that color prints can be made. While other color negative films are sometimes successfully used to make color copy negatives from color prints and other reflection originals, KODAK VERICOLOR Internegative Films are almost always used in making color internegatives from transparencies.

All three KODAK VERICOLOR Internegative Films (4112, 4114 and 6011) are used to make internegatives from color transparencies. KODAK VERICOLOR Internegative Films 4112 and 6011 are recommeded for making internegatives from a variety of original transparencies and for use in making color negatives from colored relection originals. The new film, KODAK VERICOLOR Internegative Film 4114 Type 2 is designed specifically for making internegatives from slides made on KODAK EKTACHROME and KODACHROME Films.

Three methods are generally used to make color internegatives from transparencies.

1. Contact printing the transparency on VERICOLOR Internegative Film.

2. Placing the transparency on an illuminator and copying it with a camera onto the internegative film.

3. Projecting the image of a transparency onto the internegative film with an enlarger.

Contact Printing Internegatives: The advantages of contact printing to make internegatives from transparencies are: better shadow tone reproduction and better sharpness because there are no lens flare or resolving-power problems to contend with. Disadvantages are: the internegative is always the same size as the transparency, more difficulty with dust, and the potential for Newton's-ring images on the internegative. If the original transparencies are small, there is likely to be a higher graininess level on enlarged prints made from contact internegatives than if the internegatives had been enlarged. If slides are being used, they must be removed from the mounts.

The contact printing can be done with either a spring-tension or a vacuum printing frame. The glass surface is next to the base side of the transparency, which is usually quite smooth and glossy. This can easily lead to Newton's rings which will show in the internegative. Using anti-Newton's-ring glass or lithographer's offset powder (see page 91) almost entirely eliminates this problem.

Although several types of 3200 K light sources can be used to expose the internegative, a dichroic color enlarger is an excellent source because color balance of the light can be controlled by dialing in filter correction. Also, color enlargers are generally equipped with constant voltage regulators which keep both the intensity and color temperature of the light reasonably constant. With enlargers that do not have dial filtration, KODAK Color Compensating or Color Printing Filters can be used.

Sharpness

A. For maximum sharpness in contact printing, the emulsion of the transparency should face the emulsion of the internegative film. This means internegatives will be in a reversed orientation compared with camera negatives.

B. For consistency, the projection of internegatives should also be made in this reverse disfiguration. This is achieved by aligning the support side of the transparency in the holder and facing the emulsion side of the internegative.

C. For printing internegatives in a reversed configuration, remember you are printing through the base and, therefore, the image is in a different focal plane. On automatic printers, a separate lens focused on the internegative emulsion is required.

D. Dismounting of slides and the use of glass carriers will minimize buckling that may be present in the mounted slide and eliminate popping or slide movement during the exposure of the internegative.

E. Use a good-quality lens.

Copying Color Transparencies: Copying transparencies with a copy camera is a common method used to make internegatives. The transparencies are placed on an illuminator with 3200 K lights in it, and copied in a manner similar to copying a print. The internegative can be made larger or smaller than the transparency, or the same size. Care is used to minimize flare in the same ways discussed in copying prints. The most important factor is to mask off all the illuminator area except for the transparency opening.

Copying is often the only practical way of making an internegative from a very large color transparency. It is a useful way to convert transparencies with a variety of sizes to a standard size internegatives. Once a standard filter balance is found for a given type of transparency, a group of transparencies, either ganged or in sequence, can quickly be copied on internegative film.

The copying procedure is the same as conventional copying, except that the transparencies are placed on an illuminator in place of the copyboard,

**Schematic Diagram of
KODAK VERICOLOR Internegative Film 4112**

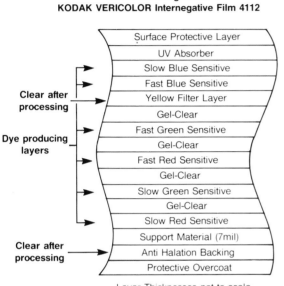

Layer Thicknesses not to scale

and completely masked with black paper. The illuminator should have a 3200 K balance. Fluorescent lamps are generally unsuitable sources for color applications, and are not recommended.

A particular problem can be reflections off the surface of the transparencies. This can be controlled by turning off all the room illumination, and by using a deep black mask of cardboard covered with black velvet in front of the camera. A circular hole is cut in the mask for the camera lens.

It is usually important to get the highest degree of sharpness possible in the copy internegatives. A magnifier should be used when focusing with a ground glass. The best aperture of the copy lens should be used. This usually is a middle aperture. Larger apertures (lower f-numbers) may not give maximum aberration correction and limit depth of field which can lead to focus errors. Using smaller apertures (higher f-numbers) introduces diffraction, which lowers sharpness. Keeping the copy lens clean aids both sharpness and tone reproduction.

Photographic step tablets are used to monitor the making of internegatives by all three methods. KODAK Photographic Step Tablets No. 2 and No. 3 are recommended for large transparency reproduc-tion, while the smaller No. 1A can be cut and mounted in a slide mount to monitor the reproduction of slides. Photographic step tablet No. 2 can be cut and realigned when internegatives are being made from intermediate-size transparencies (6 x 4.5 to 6 x 7 transparencies). The illustration shows how this is done. In addition to making the step tablet a convenient size, this realignment procedure helps to reduce the effect of nonuniform illumination on the test exposures.

It is also useful to make a test transparency using a 35 mm camera with a metering system by copying a gray scale and color patches on KODACHROME or EKTACHROME Film as a visual check. Reproducing this via internegative film gives a visual check as described on page 72 for making copy negatives from color prints.

Making Internegatives with an Enlarger: Using the enlarger to make internegatives is quite a common practice because all of the equipment for the procedure is usually in place for making color prints. It offers the opportunity to make almost any size internegative, as well. A color enlarger with dial filtration is a most convenient method, and the same on-easel color densitometry can be adapted for exposure and color balance control. If care is taken, there is somewhat less of a problem with dust than with contact printing because, if a glassless carrier is used, there are fewer surfaces to keep clean and dirt free.

The basic procedure is the same as making a color print. The transparency is placed in the enlarger and the image sized and focused on the easel. If the transparency is placed emulsion side up, the negative image will have the correct orientation. However, because contact internegatives have reversed images, they must be printed reversed, as well. A grain focuser is a help in achieving exact focus. The enlarger lens is stopped down to its sharpest aperture—usually $f/11$ or $f/8$. The internegative film is placed on the easel for the exposure (in total darkness, of course).

Controlling the Internegative: KODAK VERICOLOR Internegative Film 4114, Type 2 is a new film designed specifically for making internegatives from transparencies made on EKTACHROME and KODACHROME Films or other films with similar dyes. It is available in 4 x 5-inch, 5 x 7-inch and 8 x 10-inch sheets. If internegatives are being made of transparencies with roll film cameras, KODAK VERICOLOR Internegative Film 6011 is recommended. KODAK VERICOLOR Internegative Film 4112, a sheet film, can also be used. These latter two films require a different filter pack when the original is a transparency on EKTACHROME Film than when the original is on KODACHROME Film.

The following instructions are basically for the use of the 4114 film. Please refer to the instruction sheets packaged with the film for balancing instructions.

The recommended basic exposure time for VERICOLOR Internegative 4114 Film is 10 seconds. The illumination at the exposure plane should be about 0.75 footcandles for this exposure time.

To determine this level for contact printing, or enlarging, place a piece of white paper in the exposing plane (on the enlarging easel) and adjust the light level by raising and lowering the enlarger and adjusting the f-number until reflection exposure meter reading of $1/8$ sec at $f/5.6$ is achieved with the film speed setting placed at ISO 400. There should be no filtration of the light when this measurement is made. This indicates an illuminance of 3 footcandles. Stop the lens down two stops to obtain an illuminance of 0.75 footcandles.

The enlarger, illuminator, or other exposure lamp should be equipped with a heat absorbing glass and a UV filter such as the KODAK WRATTEN Filter No. 2B. The starting filter pack recommendations call for a filtration of 30M + 30Y, either as a setting on the enlarger dial or with CP or CC filters.

The recommended exposure time for KODAK VERICOLOR Internegative Film 4114, Type 2 is 10 seconds. Because of changes in the speed in the three dye image layers that results from exposure time changes due to the reciprocity characteristics of the film, it is advisable to keep the exposure time as close to 10 seconds as practical. Changes in exposure time may require changes in color balance for optimum internegatives. With contact printing, this is usually no problem. When an enlarger is used as a light source, changing the enlarger height and the lens f-number can almost always provide the right level of illumination to give a 10-second exposure time. With an exposure lamp, raising and lowering the lamp adjusts the illumination level.

However, when using the copying techniques with an illuminator, changing the illumination level to attain a 10-second exposure at the sharpest f-number of the copying lens may be difficult. A variable transformer cannot be used with the illuminator lamps to change the light intensity because changing the voltage changes the color temperature, which must remain constant. One solution is to use higher or lower wattage bulbs to shorten or lengthen the exposure time to 10 seconds. In the extreme, more bulbs can be added to the illuminator or subtracted from it to obtain the correct exposure time. Sheets of KODAK WRATTEN Neutral Density Filter No. 96 in varying densities can be used to lower the light level. Each 0.10 density lowers the exposure by $1/3$ stop. A 0.30 filter lowers the exposure by 1 stop. Sheets of KODAK Neutral Density Filter are catalog listed up to 125 mm (5 inches) square, and can be special ordered up to 350 mm (14 inches) square. Once the exposure time of 10 seconds is achieved, however, it should become a constant for all transparencies. Slight changes in aperture are used to compensate for light and dark transparencies.

Making the Exposure: In making a test, the film step tablet chosen earlier is imaged on the film. In contact printing, the step tablet is placed in contact with the internegative film. In copying, the step tablet is placed on the illuminator and masked with black paper. In enlarging, the step tablet is placed in the negative carrier and completely masked.

Place the starting filter pack in place in the enlarger (or dial it in), on the copy lens, or on the exposure lamp. Place a sheet of KODAK VERICOLOR Internegative Film 4114, Type 2, in place and give it a 10 second exposure. Process the film in a well-controlled Process C-41.

KODAK Photographic Step Tablets

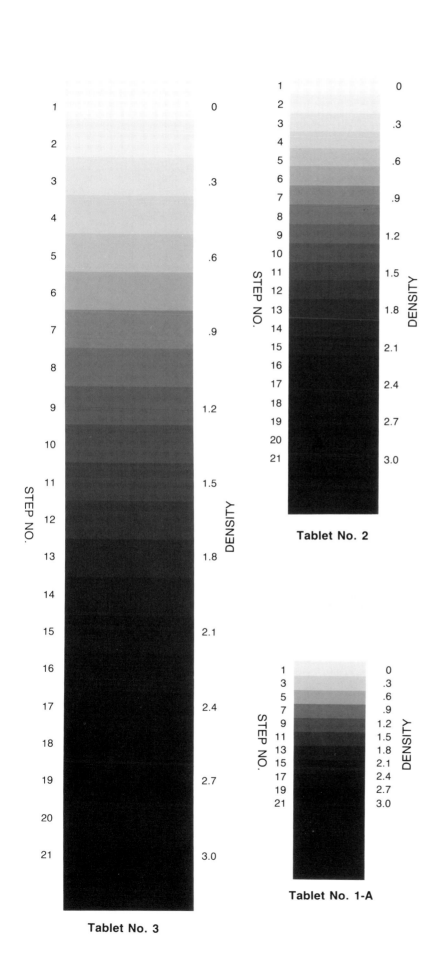

Tablet No. 3

Tablet No. 2

Tablet No. 1-A

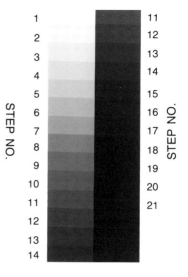

Tablet No.2
Cut and realigned to reduce effect of non-uniformity of illuminant

Note that some steps are duplicated in order to closely align steps 3 with 13, 5 with 15, etc. Closely aligning the pairs of steps is recommended in order to place them in the same area of illumination.

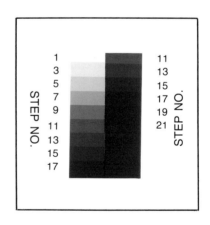

Tablet No. 1-A
Mounted with steps paired to reduce effect of non-uniformity of the illuminant

Controlling the Internegative

As mentioned earlier in connection with making copy internegatives of reflection originals, there are several methods of controlling the reproduction by the internegative film. The first to be discussed is the density-difference method.

Density-Difference Balancing Method

As with making copy internegatives of color prints, the density-difference method of balancing requires less time, but may not give as much information as the curve comparison method.

This method can be used for balancing the 4112, 4114, and 6011 films when using the appropriate density-difference tables. For detailed instruction for the density-difference procedure, please refer to the balancing procedures given in KODAK Data Release E-24S, *Interim Balancing Procedure for KODAK VERICOLOR Internegative Films 4112 (ESTAR Thick Base)* and 6011, and KODAK Data Release E-24T, *Balancing Procedure for KODAK VERICOLOR Internegative Film 4114, Type 2*.

When the film is dry, measure the red, green and blue densities of the number 3 step as imaged on the film. (See illustration for locating the steps.)

The densities of step 3 should not exceed these values.

Red Filter   1.50 (Cyan Emulsion Layer)
Green Filter 1.90 (Magenta Emulsion Layer)
Blue Filter   2.30 (Yellow Emulsion Layer)

If any of the densities exceeds these values, measure the No. 5 step. Note that only the odd-numbered steps are used. These are 0.30 or 1 stop apart on the original step tablet. Usually the No. 3 or No. 5 steps will meet the criteria. If not, make a new test film giving it 2 stops less exposure.

You have now located a step where the red, green, and blue densities do not exceed the values shown above. Count to a step number that is 10 greater than this step. If it is No. 3, count to Step No. 13. If it is No. 5, count to Step No. 15.

Measure the densities of this step.

With a 21 step tablet, you will end up with the densities of a pair of steps that are 10 steps apart such as 3 and 13 or 5 and 15. With an 11 step tablet, the pair of steps will be 5 steps apart, although the numbers will be 10 apart because the steps are all odd numbered.

Finding the Density Differences: Density difference is simply the difference in density between two values. It is found by subtracting the smaller value from the larger value. As an example, let us use the density values shown above for steps No. 3 and No. 13. The density difference calculation is shown.

Example Density-Difference Calculations

Density	R	G	B
Step 3	1.10	1.50	2.11
Step 13	0.51	0.90	1.27
DD Values	0.59	0.60	0.84

Aim Density Differences: With KODAK VERICOLOR Internegative Film 4114, Type 2, the aim density differences are as shown below:

Density Difference Aims for 4114 Film

Red DD	Green DD	Blue DD
0.66 + .03	0.68 + .03	0.79 + .03

Aims for 4112 and 6011 Film

Red DD	Green DD	Blue DD
0.63 ± .03	0.73 ± .03	0.79 ± .03

Note that the aim density differences are not the same for the three layers.

The reason for these differences is that the transmissions of the status M filters used to measure the color densities do not exactly match the color sensitivities of the paper layers on which the negatives are printed. The DD aims given are status M aims that match the contrast as the paper sees the dyes in the color film. This situation is not limited to color internegative films, and is equally true with camera color negative films.

These density differences are designed to fit the averages of the three image layers of KODAK EKTACOLOR Paper. Aims may be different for other color print materials.

Also, the aims should be considered starting points that may have to be adjusted for any particular set of circumstances. When you have reached the aims with a test internegative, this negative should be printed, a neutral balance for the midtones should be achieved. If the highlight and shadow tones are also neutral, the DD aims are satisfactory for your conditions. If, however, there is a color shift from the highlights to the shadows, the aims need to be changed because the internegative is out of balance.

To correct the imbalance, subtract the color of the highlight tinge from the filter pack. If, for example, the highlights have a tinge of yellow, subtract yellow filtration from the pack. There is a discussion of this procedure on page 72 in the section entitled "Visual Check of Color Internegatives." The testing continues until a test print shows a neutral gray scale along its entire length. The density differences of this internegative becomes your new set of DD aims.

Finding a New Filter Pack for the Density Differences: The table on page 116 is used to find the filter pack changes required to bring the negative density differences close to the aim values on the next test internegative.

Look for the red, green, and blue density differences in the DD columns. The recommended filter change is found in the next column.

Where the red filter density is 0.59, as in our example, the recommended cyan filter change is − CC25. The recommended filter changes are added to the original filter pack, which was 30M + 30Y (the starting pack when you do not have other information). The following example is based on the use of KODAK VERICOLOR Internegative film, 4114.

Example of Filter Pack Correction

Status M Filter	DD	Filter Pack Change
Red	0.59	− 25 cyan
Green	0.60	− 18 magenta
Blue	0.84	+ 10 yellow

Note that when the change is minus (−), "adding" the change really means subtracting it from the pack value.

Filter Pack Calculation

	CYAN	MAGENTA	YELLOW
1. Starting Pack	0C	+ 30M	+ 30M
2. Filter Change from above	− 25C	− 18M	+ 10Y
3. Addition -	− 25C	+ 12M +	40Y
4. Neutral Density Elimination	+ 25C	+ 25M +	25Y
	0C	+ 37M +	65Y
5. New Filter Pack		37M +	65Y

In practice, the 37M could be rounded to 35M.

If CC filters are used over a lens, as when enlarging with a black-and-white enlarger, or when copying a transparency, as few filters as possible (not more than three) should be used to avoid possible loss of contrast and sharpness. The 35M + 65Y pack can be reduced by using red filters.

$$30Y + 30M = 30R$$
$$5Y + 5M = 5R$$

This gives 35M + 35Y. 30 additional yellow is required to make the 65Y filtration. The final pack can be

$$30R + 5R + 30Y,$$

which is the limit of three filters.

When using CP filters, it is not necessary to reduce the filter number. This problem does not arise with enlargers in which filtration is dialed.

Exposure-Change Table

For Plus Values		For Minus Values	
If the neutral density added in line 4 is:	Multiply the internegative exposure by:	If the neutral density subtracted in line 4 is:	Multiply the internegative exposure by:
0.00	1.00	− 0.00	1.00
+ 0.02 (no change)	1.06	− 0.02 (no change)	0.96
+ 0.04	1.12	− 0.04	0.92
+ 0.06	1.17	− 0.06	0.88
+ 0.08	1.23	− 0.08	0.84
+ 0.10 (+ 1/3 stop)	1.28	− 0.10 (− 1/3 stop)	0.80
+ 0.12	1.34	− 0.12	0.77
+ 0.14	1.40	− 0.14	0.73
+ 0.16	1.46	− 0.16	0.69
+ 0.18	1.51	− 0.18	0.65
+ 0.20 (+ 2/3 stops)	1.57	− 0.20 (− 2/3 stops)	0.61
+ 0.22	1.66	− 0.22	0.60
+ 0.24	1.74	− 0.24	0.58
+ 0.26	1.82	− 0.26	0.55
+ 0.28	1.90	− 0.28	0.53
+ 0.30 (+ 1 stop exposure)	2.00	− 0.30 (− 1 stop exposure)	0.50

Filter Changes Based on Density Differences of KODAK VERICOLOR Internegative Films 4112 Type 2, (ESTAR Thick Base) 4112, and 6011

Red DD	Cyan Filter Change	Green DD	Magenta Filter Change	Blue DD	Yellow Filter Change
		Under 0.60	−45	Under 0.66	−45
		0.60	−45	0.66	−45
		0.61	−40	0.67	−42
Under 0.53	−45	0.62	−36	0.68	−38
0.53	−45	0.63	−32	0.69	−34
0.54	−36	0.64	−28	0.70	−30
0.55	−30	0.65	−24	0.71	−26
0.56	−25	0.66	−21	0.72	−22
0.57	−21	0.67	−18	0.73	−18
0.58	−17	0.68	−15	0.74	−15
0.59	−13	0.69	−12	0.75	−12
0.60	−10	0.70	−09	0.76	−08
0.61	−07	0.71	−06	0.77	−05
0.62	−04	0.72	−03	0.78	−03
AIM: 0.63	00	0.73	00	0.79	00
0.64	+02	0.74	+02	0.80	+02
0.65	+05	0.75	+05	0.81	+04
0.66	+08	0.76	+07	0.82	+06
0.67	+11	0.77	+10	0.83	+08
0.68	+13	0.78	+13	0.84	+10
0.69	+15	0.79	+15	0.85	+12
0.70	+17	0.80	+17	0.86	+14
0.71	+19	0.81	+19	0.87	+16
0.72	+21	0.82	+21	0.88	+18
0.73	+23	0.83	+23	0.89	+20
0.74	+25	0.84	+25	0.90	+22
0.75	+27	0.85	+27	0.91	+24
0.76	+29	0.86	+29	0.92	+26
0.77	+31	0.87	+31	0.93	+28
0.78	+33	0.88	+33	0.94	+29
0.79	+35	0.89	+35	0.95	+31
0.80	+37	0.90	+36	0.96	+33
0.81	+38	0.91	+38	0.97	+34
0.82	+40	0.92	+40	0.98	+36
0.83	+42	0.93	+42	0.99	+37
0.84	+44	0.94	+43	1.00	+39
0.85	+45	0.95	+45	1.01	+41
Over 0.85	+45	Over 0.95	+45	1.02	+42
				1.03	+44
				1.04	+45
				Over 1.04	+45

Filter Changes Based on Density Differences of KODAK VERICOLOR Internegative Film 4114, Type 2

Red DD	Cyan Filter Change	Green DD	Magenta Filter Change	Blue DD	Yellow Filter Change
		Under 0.54	−35	Under 0.66	−45
		0.55	−32	0.66	−45
		0.56	−29	0.67	−42
Under 0.56	−45	0.57	−27	0.68	−38
0.56	−45	0.58	−24	0.69	−34
0.57	−36	0.59	−21	0.70	−30
0.58	−30	0.60	−18	0.71	−26
0.59	−25	0.61	−16	0.72	−22
0.60	−21	0.62	−14	0.73	−18
0.61	−17	0.63	−12	0.74	−15
0.62	−13	0.64	−10	0.75	−12
0.63	−10	0.65	−08	0.76	−08
0.64	−07	0.66	−06	0.77	−05
0.65	−04	0.67	−03	0.78	−03
AIM: 0.66	0	0.68	0	0.79	0
0.67	+02	0.69	+01	0.80	+02
0.68	+05	0.70	+03	0.81	+04
0.69	+08	0.71	+05	0.82	+06
0.70	+11	0.72	+07	0.83	+08
0.71	+13	0.73	+09	0.84	+10
0.72	+15	0.74	+10	0.85	+12
0.73	+17	0.75	+12	0.86	+14
0.74	+19	0.76	+14	0.87	+16
0.75	+21	0.77	+16	0.88	+18
0.76	+23	0.78	+18	0.89	+20
0.77	+25	0.79	+20	0.90	+22
0.78	+27	0.80	+21	0.91	+24
0.79	+29	0.81	+22	0.92	+26
0.80	+31	0.82	+23	0.93	+28
0.81	+33	0.83	+26	0.94	+29
0.82	+35	0.84	+28	0.95	+31
0.83	+37	0.85	+29	0.96	+33
0.84	+38	0.86	+31	0.97	+34
0.85	+40	0.87	+33	0.98	+36
0.86	+42	0.88	+34	0.99	+37
0.87	+44	0.89	+36	1.00	+39
0.88	+45	0.90	+37	1.01	+41
Over 0.88	+45	0.91	+38	1.02	+42
		0.92	+40	1.03	+44
		0.93	+42	1.04	+45
		0.94	+44	Over 1.04	+45
		Over 0.94	+45		

Calculating Exposure Changes for the New Pack:
The amount of exposure change is determined by how much the neutral density is changed in the calculations above. If neutral density is added, as in our example, the exposure must be increased for the next exposure on the internegative film. If neutral density is subtracted, the exposure is decreased.

The table on page 115 can be used to calculate the amount of exposure change. Look up the + or − neutral density change in the proper column, and note the exposure change in stops or in a factor by which to change the exposure time.

In our example, the neutral density change was + 0.25, so the left columns are used. The value shows a change of + 1 stop, which means opening up the lens by one stop, or multiplying the exposure time by a factor of between 1.74 and 1.82, or 1.78. If the original time is 10 seconds, the changed time would be 18 seconds. The aperture change is preferable because 18 seconds is nearly twice the preferred 10-second exposure.

If the neutral density change value had been a − 0.10, for example, then the lens is stopped down by $\frac{1}{3}$ stop or the exposure time is multiplied by 0.80. The 10-second exposure would become 10 x 0.80 = 8 seconds.

In practice when copying or enlarging, it is wise to adjust in such a way that the exposure time stays as near to 10 seconds as practical, and the lens stays in its middle f-number range for maximum sharpness.

The scale shown on the top of page 118 displays a $\frac{1}{6}$-stop increment f-number series. Each $\frac{1}{6}$ stop is equivalent to a 0.05 neutral density change.

Partial stop aperture changes are equivalent to the following exposure time factor changes:

Stops Change	
Increase	*Exposure Time Factor*
$\frac{1}{6}$ Stop	1.12X
$\frac{1}{3}$ Stop	1.26X
$\frac{1}{2}$ Stop	1.41X
1 Stop	2.00X
Decrease	
$\frac{1}{6}$ Stop	0.89X
$\frac{1}{3}$ Stop	0.79X
$\frac{1}{2}$ Stop	0.71X
1 Stop	0.50X

Internegatives made by contact should be enlarged with the base side toward the lens to obtain the correct image orientation in the print.

Making a Print: When the internegative meets the aims, a test print is made that is balanced to the middle gray. If the gray scale is neutral, a balance has been achieved.

If the highlights have a tinge of color, a correction needs to be made. The same procedure of correcting is used as if making a copy internegative of a color print. See the discussion on page 70.

It should be noted that a print of the step scale that is neutral from black to white does not necessarily mean the internegatives are exactly balanced. The step scale is a black-and-white silver image while the transparency is a dye image, and the two image materials do not always reproduce exactly the same. The final judgement must therefore be made on the print reproduction of the transparency.

There are several reasons why you may need slightly different density-difference aims than those given above. One is flare. If lens coatings cause "colored" flare, then the image formed by that lens may have a different exposure range in one color than another. If a transparency has predominance of one strong color, the flare will be colored. This causes the same effect. Another reason is that paper may vary slightly, box to box, and a slight shift in the aims may be needed to adjust for normal manufacturing tolerance. Yet another reason is that color processes are not identical, and adjustment must be made for the particular process being used. Print viewing and evaluation will indicate the need for aim changes.

If a transparency is very contrasty or very low in contrast, all three aims can be lowered or raised to obtain a normal contrast internegative. A test can be run using a $\frac{1}{2}$-stop change in exposure to find how much the aims need to be changed.

Curve-Plotting Method of Internegative Control

Editor's Note:

> The following section is a description of the curve-plotting method of controlling exposure and color balance of internegatives made from transparencies. We do not include the detailed instructions for this method. To do so would increase the cost of this publication, and we expect that only a small percentage of the users of this book would want to pay this extra cost. However, for those that conclude, on the basis of the following description, that they do need the details, we include a coupon at the end of the book which can be mailed to Eastman Kodak Company. On receipt of this coupon we will send a complimentary copy of the appropriate publication for the film specified.

Curve plotting is an alternative method of controlling the balance and exposure of color internegatives made from transparencies. This method takes

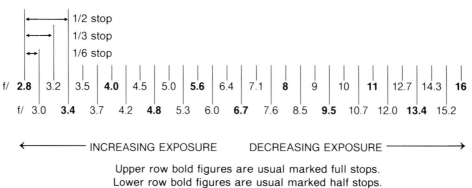

Change in Exposure by Aperture (f-Number)

1/2 stop
1/3 stop
1/6 stop

| f/ | **2.8** | 3.2 | 3.5 | **4.0** | 4.5 | 5.0 | **5.6** | 6.4 | 7.1 | **8** | 9 | 10 | **11** | 12.7 | 14.3 | **16** |

| f/ | 3.0 | **3.4** | 3.7 | 4.2 | **4.8** | 5.3 | 6.0 | **6.7** | 7.6 | 8.5 | **9.5** | 10.7 | 12.0 | **13.4** | 15.2 |

←———————— INCREASING EXPOSURE   DECREASING EXPOSURE ————————→

Upper row bold figures are usual marked full stops.
Lower row bold figures are usual marked half stops.

longer than the density-difference method, but provides the user with more detailed information about the contrast relationships between the individual red-, green-, and blue-sensitive emulsion layers of the internegative film. A description of the curve-plotting method of internegative control follows.

Overview: The internegative film is exposed to a photographic step tablet as described on page 112. The 1-A step tablet may be cut and mounted in a standard 35 mm slide mount as described in publication E-24S and E-24T. The expsoure conditions are the same as for the density-difference method, and are described on page 114. After exposure, the internegative is processed in a well controlled process C-41.

Measuring the Internegative: Once the transparency is processed, the red-, green-, and blue-status M densities of the 21 steps of the exposed silver tablet are measured and recorded. The measured densities of the individual steps are needed for the balancing step, and status M densitometry is required.

Plotting: The status M densities recored earlier are then plotted on *KODAK Curve-Plotting Graph Paper*, Publication No. E-64. The plotted curves are then compared to the reference curves plotted on the

same paper in E-24S and in E-24T. This paper is thin and transluscent for easy comparison on an illuminator.

The density of each step is plotted as a point above the appropriate step number in Scale A on the plotting paper. When all the steps are plotted, each curve is drawn by connecting the plotted points of each color. The three connecting lines can be drawn with a French curve to provide a smoothed curve, as the illustration shows, three curves result. The lower curve is the red curve, the middle curve, the green, and the upper curve is the blue.

Note that each of the curves should have a straight-line section to the left, and an upward sweep to the right. It is this upward sweep that provides the highlight tone separation needed for the best tone reproduction. (See page 4.)

Interpreting the Curves: The curves from the status M densities are then compared to the reference curves published in E-24S or E-24T, depending on the film being used. The comparing is done by superimposing the red, green, and blue curves, respectively, on top of the reference curves. Filter pack and exposure data are then determined by shifting each internegative curve to obtain the best possible match with the appropriate reference curve. An internegative is correctly balanced and

KODAK Curve Plotting Graph Paper

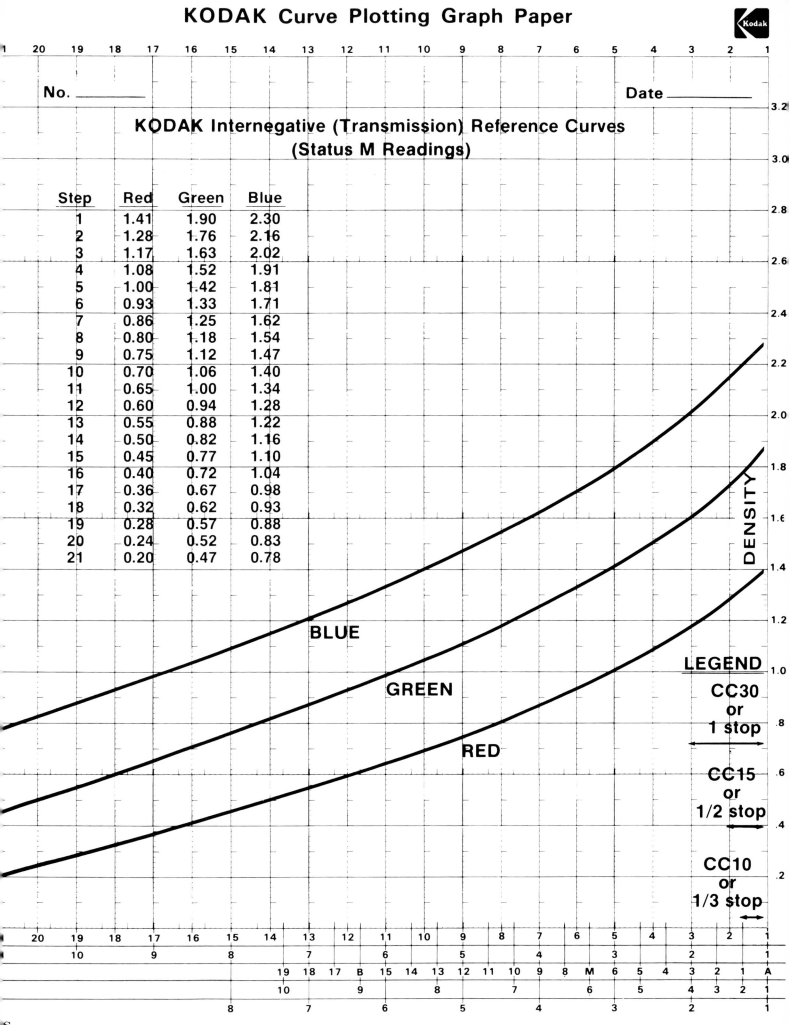

KODAK Internegative (Transmission) Reference Curves
(Status M Readings)

Step	Red	Green	Blue
1	1.41	1.90	2.30
2	1.28	1.76	2.16
3	1.17	1.63	2.02
4	1.08	1.52	1.91
5	1.00	1.42	1.81
6	0.93	1.33	1.71
7	0.86	1.25	1.62
8	0.80	1.18	1.54
9	0.75	1.12	1.47
10	0.70	1.06	1.40
11	0.65	1.00	1.34
12	0.60	0.94	1.28
13	0.55	0.88	1.22
14	0.50	0.82	1.16
15	0.45	0.77	1.10
16	0.40	0.72	1.04
17	0.36	0.67	0.98
18	0.32	0.62	0.93
19	0.28	0.57	0.88
20	0.24	0.52	0.83
21	0.20	0.47	0.78

No. _____

Date _____

BLUE

GREEN

RED

DENSITY

LEGEND

CC30
or
1 stop

CC15
or
1/2 stop

CC10
or
1/3 stop

exposed when the red, green, and blue curves match the appropriate reference curves.

What the Curves Tell You: A properly exposed and balanced internegative will make a print with a gray scale which is balanced for color along its entire tonal scale, and which has proper tone separation in the highlight steps. A balanced but overexposed negative will print a balanced gray scale, but will have too much highlight tone separation and too little shadow tone separation. Conversely, an underexposed internegative will have too little highlight separation, and will give a generally low contrast print.

Any out-of-balance in the internegative is indicated by difficulty in printing a gray scale that is neutral from highlight to shadow. If a middle tone is balanced, the highlight tones will have a color cast of one color, and the shadow tones will have a cast of the complimentary color.

Because the photographic step tablet being used in this procedure is made of a photographic silver image, while the transparencies from which the internegatives are being made have dye images, a print from an internegative that has a perfectly neutral gray scale may not be perfectly balanced for the transparency. This can be corrected by optimizing the internegative filter pack based on typical production transparencies.

General Comments: The curves for KODAK VERICOLOR Internegative films 4112 and 6011 are identical. Detailed instructions for comparing test curves with a set of reference curves and interpreting differences in terms of correcting filtration and exposure are given in Publication No. E-24S, *Interim Balancing Procedure for KODAK VERICOLOR Internegative Films 4112 (ESTAR Thick Base) and 6011.* The curves for the 4114 film are slightly different and require a different set of reference curves. These, along with detailed introductions are given in Publication No. E-24T, *Balancing Procedure for KODAK VERICOLOR Internegative Film 4114, Type 2.* As indicated above, a coupon for obtaining these publications can be found at the back of the book.

Making Color Transparencies from Color Negatives

There are often requirements for color transparencies when the original is an internegative or an original camera negative.

KODAK VERICOLOR Print Film 4111 (ESTAR Thick Base) is made for this purpose. It is available in sheet sizes from 4 x 5 inches up to 30 x 40 inches.

It is designed for exposure times of 10 to 120 seconds, and balanced for 3200 K tungsten illumination. It is processed using KODAK FLEXICOLOR Chemicals (Process C-41 or C-41V). (KODAK VERICOLOR Slide Film 5072 and SO-279 are available in 35 mm width for making color slides from color negatives and is discussed on page 123.)

Details are given in KODAK Publication No. E-24, *Using KODAK VERICOLOR Slide and Print Films.*

Except for processing, this film is printed in a manner similar to that for KODAK EKTACOLOR Paper. An approximate starting filter pack for negatives on Kodak Internegative Film would be about 60M + 50Y. Starting packs for other Kodak color negative films are given in the publication mentioned above.

A typical exposure of 10 to 20 seconds is usually about right when the illumination at the printing surface is 2 footcandles. With a white piece of paper on the enlarger easel, 2 footcandles is achieved when a reflection exposure meter reads $1/8$ sec at $f/6.7$ (halfway between $f/8$ and $f/5.6$) when the meter is set at a speed of ISO 400.

A visual method of controlling color balance is usually adequate.

Make a test strip, giving a series of exposures such as 5, 7, 10, 14 and 20 seconds. Look at the color balance of the correctly exposed area. If the color balance is off in one direction, add that color filtration to the pack. If, for example, the test print is too yellow, add yellow filtration. Judge the test on an illuminator with a color temperature that matches the illuminator on which the transparency will be displayed. To find how much filtration to change, use viewing filters that are complementary to the color cast. If the cast is yellow, use blue viewing filters. Look at the middle tones. When you find how much blue viewing filter is required, add *half* that amount of yellow to the pack:

Example:

Original Color Cast	Yellow
Viewing Filter that corrects—CC20B	
Add to pack	CC10Y

If color paper prints are regularly made with on-easel densitometry, the densitometry can be calibrated for VERICOLOR Print Film, which is likely to

The upper illustration was made directly from an original color transparency. The lower illustration was made from a two-step duplicate transparency. A color internegative was made of the original on KODAK VERICOLOR Internegative Film 4114, Type II. The internegative was printed on KODAK VERICOLOR Print Film to make the duplicate transparency.

Printing from Color Negatives

Starting Filter Packs for Printing KODAK Color Negative Films onto KODAK VERICOLOR Print Film 4111

KODAK Films	Exposed to	Enlargers Using Dichroic Filters with Tungsten-Halogen Lamps	Enlargers Using KODAK CC Filters with Tungsten Lamps No. 212 or 302
VERICOLOR III	Electronic Flash or Daylight	20M + 25Y	40M + 35Y
VERICOLOR II Professional, Type S	Electronic Flash or Daylight	25M + 20Y	50M + 30Y
KODACOLOR VR 100, 200, 400	Electronic Flash or Daylight	20M + 30Y	45M + 35Y
KODACOLOR VR 1000	Electronic Flash or Daylight	25M + 15Y	50M + 20Y
KODACOLOR VR 400	Tungsten	50M + 60Y	75M + 70Y
KODACOLOR VR 400	Flourescent	30M + 70Y	44M + 80Y

have a different balance than EKTACOLOR Paper. The same techniques are used, however.

As indicated above, the film is processed in KODAK FLEXICOLOR Chemicals (Process C-41 or C-41V). For small-scale production, a tank process can be used. Roller-transport processors are made that process sizes (sheets or rolls) up to about 50 inches in width. Drum-type processors are made to process sheets up to about 16 x 20-inches in size. These produce large size transparencies for display purposes.

For a small-scale tank process, replenishers can be added manually based on tables. For large scale production, Process C-41 monitoring strips are generally used to monitor the process. Replenishers are added automatically.

The following Kodak publications cover the various aspects of processing with the Process C-41.

Publication No.	Publication Name
E-24	*Using KODAK VERICOLOR Slide and Print Films*
E-36	*KODAK Color Films for Process C-41*
E-58	*Preparing Large Transparencies for Display*
E-66	*Printing Color Negatives*
J-3	*Introduction to Color Photographic Processing*
R-19	*KODAK Color Darkroom DATAGUIDE*
R-25	*KODAK Color Print Viewing Filter Kit*
Z-99	*Introduction to Color Process Monitoring*
Z-121	*Using Process C-41*

A Two-Step Color Duplicating Process

The normal method of duplicating transparencies is to use KODAK EKTACHROME Duplicating Film 6121 and use a one-step duplicating procedure. (See page 93). In cases where the original has delicate highlights it may be difficult to reproduce these with the one-step process.

A two-step duplication can be used to obtain improved highlight tone reproduction. An internegative is made from the transparency and the internegative is printed on VERICOLOR Print Film. Properly exposed, the internegative corrects for the compression of highlight tones in the transparency, and gives highlight tones in the transparency print that show less compression. With two-step duplication, care must be taken at each step to minimize any loss in quality such as a loss of sharpness.

Duplicating Faded Transparencies

The method of making color internegatives from transparencies on one of KODAK VERICOLOR Internegative Films can be used to "restore" faded transparencies.

Overall contrast (density range) is increased by increasing the overall exposure. Where one dye layer has faded more than the others, this layer is given additional exposure by changing the filter pack. The internegative can then be used to print a new transparency on KODAK VERICOLOR Print Film. It can also be used to make color prints on one of the KODAK EKTACOLOR Papers.

Detailed instructions for this restoration procedure are given in the KODAK *Current Information Summary CIS-28*. A copy may be obtained on request from:

> Dept. 412-L
> Eastman Kodak Company
> 343 State Street
> Rochester, New York 14650

KODAK VERICOLOR Slide Film 5072 and SO-279

This slide film is a 35 mm and long roll-film version of VERICOLOR Print Film. The 5072 film is available in long rolls, while the SO-279 film is available in the 135-36 magazine format, as CAT No. 167 2364. It is printed in a similar manner. The film is designed for exposures from $1/4$ to 8 seconds with a 3200 K tungsten source.

This film is usually used to make slides from color negatives and internegatives using professional optical printers. It can be used, however, in a 35 mm copy set up when the negative is placed in an illuminator, and "copied" on the VERICOLOR Slide film placed in the camera. It is rarely printed with an enlarger or contact printed. Details are given in KODAK Publication No. E-24, *Using KODAK VERICOLOR Slide and Print Films*.

KODAK DURATRANS Display Material

This material is essentially a slightly denser color paper emulsion coated on a translucent film base. It is designed to make large display transparencies (color positives).

It is printed from color negatives and internegatives in the same manner as KODAK EKTACOLOR Papers, and processed in EKTAPRINT 2 chemicals using a 6-minute developing time.

While small transparencies can be processed in small drum processors or trays, most professional work is processed in the same roller transport processors used to process EKTACOLOR Paper.

DURATRANS Material is not designed to make transparencies for half-tone reproduction. However, it offers a less costly method of making color positives for display.

Making B/W Interpositives and B/W Duplicate Negatives

A black-and-white duplicate negative can be made in one step using KODAK Professional B/W Duplicating Film as described previously. It can also be made in two steps using an intermediate called an interpositive or a diapositive. The reason that you might want to create a duplicate negative in two steps instead of one is that you can exercise more control over the quality of the duplicate negative in two steps than in one. In fact, the amount of control is so great that workers sometimes make a corrected diapositive and a duplicate negative for printing in preference to printing the original negative. The extra step makes more retouching possible (the diapositive can be enlarged) and eliminates the risk associated with retouching an original negative. There are also more opportunities to manipulate local tone control through dodging, burning-in, intensification, dyeing, and chemical reduction.

The format (size) of the film that you use to make the interpositive and negative depends upon the equipment available and upon the method of printing that is preferred. The best quality is produced by using a large format film for the interpositive and duplicate negative. If a large format enlarger is not available to print the negatives, they can be contact printed. Local treatment (retouching, dyeing, intensification or reduction) is made easier by the use of a large format internegative and duplicate negative.

Interpositives can be made on KODAK SUPER-XX Pan Film 4142 or on KODAK Commercial Film 4127 (ESTAR Base) or 6127 (acetate base). SUPER-XX Pan Film has a long straight-line characteristic curve which makes it well-suited for this application. It is especially useful when duplicating negatives that have a long density range or high contrast such as old glass plates that were made to be printed on albumen paper. Contrast can be reduced by moderately overexposing and shortening the developing time.

KODAK Commercial Film is easier to handle in the darkroom. Because it is a blue-sensitive film, it can be handled under safelight conditions normally used only for printing. KODAK Commercial Film is also a finer grain film than KODAK SUPER-XX Pan Film. This may be important if the final negative is to be enlarged. The interpositive can be exposed with an enlarger or by contact. When exposing with an enlarger the original negative should be oriented in the negative carrier the same as it would be for making a print (emulsion down). The film for the diapositive is held down on an easel covered with black paper. It is inserted emulsion side up. Because film is more sensitive to light than paper, when exposing film under an enlarger, care must be

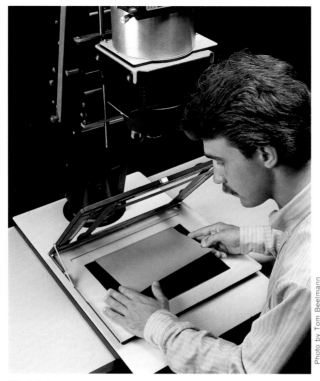
Film is being placed on the easel to make an enlarged interpositive from a black-and-white negative. This is done in the dark when panchromatic film is being used, or under a red safelight when the film is orthochromatic.

Photo by Tom Beelmann

taken to avoid fogging. Light leaks from the enlarger bouncing against a light-colored wall can create a substantial amount of image degrading fog. Dirty lenses can be a source of flare, which can also degrade the image quality.

When the interpositive is being exposed, dodging and burning-in can be done as if a print were being made. Only dark-colored tools should be used, but dodging tools can be white on top for easier visiblity during the exposure.

It is important to make the interpositive with enough exposure so that highlight detail is recorded above the toe of the characteristic curve. This will help preserve highlight tonal separation. The appearance of the interpositive should be darker than a transparency that has good density for viewing. Diffuse highlight density should be at least 0.30.

The duplicate negative is usually contact printed from the interpositive. This reduces the possiblity of flare and sharpness loss due to enlarger optics.

Contact exposures of both the interpositive and the duplicate negative can be made in a contact frame, or under a heavy sheet of glass. Black paper should be used as a backing to prevent halation. The original negative is placed emulsion-to-emulsion on top of the unexposed interpositive film or an interpositive is placed emulsion-to-emulsion with the unexposed duplicate negative film. The enlarger light or a small bare bulb can be used to expose the film.

The same film that is used to make the interpositive can be used to make the duplicate negative. Suggested developing times for two different films and developers are listed below. These are starting points from which one can establish more precise times for a particular set of circumstances. The developing times are for tray development at 68°F (20°C).

KODAK Films and Developers

Interpositive	Duplicate Negative
SUPER-XX Pan Film—	SUPER-XX Pan Film—
7 min. DK-50	8 min. DK-50
Commercial Film—	Commercial Film—
4 min. HC110-B	7 min. HC110-B

To make duplicate negatives that have good printing characteristics it is important that the density range of the duplicate negative matches the density range required for the photographic paper and printing system that will be used to print the negative. Because original negatives do not always have a density range that matches the printing system, it is very practical to alter the density range or contrast when making the duplicate so that it is close to the density range required for that particular printing system.

To do this visually is difficult, but not impossible. The experienced printer can tell by looking at a negative whether it is excessively contrasty or extremely flat. The printer can usually tell by observation whether a negative has a density range suitable to print on a paper grade close to normal with a particular enlarger or contact printer. The experienced worker can thus determine if the original negative is high or low in contrast and make the appropriate exposure and development modifications when making the interpositive and duplicate negative. Most of the contrast adjustments are made when making the duplicate negative rather than the interpositive, because visually it is easier to judge contrast when the original is a negative. Negative contrast is reduced by overexposing and underdeveloping. Contrast is increased by slightly underexposing and overdeveloping.

With a densitometer it is possible to make accurate density range measurements. Negatives to be printed on a condenser enlarger with a Grade 2 paper usually require a density range of 0.80 to 0.90.* Negatives to be printed on a diffusion enlarger will require a density range of 1.00 to 1.10 with a grade 2 paper. More often the upper part of these ranges are used rather than the lower part. The

*For a more detailed discussion of density range see KODAK Publication No. F-5, KODAK *Professional Black-and-White Films.*

The upper illustration is from a print that was made from the original negative.

The lower illustration is from a print made from a duplicate negative produced by the 2-step procedure.

negative density range required will vary because of a number of factors that influence the system such as: the brand of photographic paper, the enlarger, the lens, the amount of flare from surfaces in the darkroom, paper developer, and personal preference in print quality. To determine the required negative density range for a particular set of circumstances choose a negative that prints well on a Grade 2 photographic paper. Read the density of a diffuse highlight (an area that prints just darker than white) and read a shadow tone that prints just lighter than the darkest part of the print. The difference between the shadow and highlight densities is the required negative density range for that enlarger (or contact printer) using the same photographic paper and developer.

Once the required negative density range is determined, the density range of duplicate negatives can be aimed at this range. To do this, first measure the density range of the original negative. If the density range is longer (indicating higher contrast), then the duplicate negative should be overexposed and underdeveloped. The amount of overexposure and underdevelopment for a given density change must be determined by trial and error. Keep records of the amounts of density changes that occur with different development times for future reference.

The interpositive is usually made so that it reproduces the density range of the original negative and contrast changes are usually made when the duplicate negative is made. However, if the difference between the original negative density range and the required density range is large (0.40 or more) the contrast can be reduced in the interpositive step also, so that development times remain of reasonable length.

To increase the contrast of a low-contrast original *slight* underexposure and longer development times are required. Again, contrast is usually increased in the last step but if the density range of the original is a great deal lower than the required negative density range then the contrast can be increased in both the interpositive and the duplicate negative.

Making B/W Negatives from Color Negatives

A black-and-white negative can be made from a color negative in much the same way as a black-and-white negative is duplicated in two steps. The significant difference is the choice of films and developers.

Interpositives can be made on several KODAK Films. EKTAPAN Film 4162, Separation Negative Film 4131, Type 1, or other general purpose medium contrast films. The film/developer combination should produce an interpositive that is close in density range to the final negative and slightly dark for viewing. The film/developer combination will need to be higher contrast than would be used for black-and-white duplicate negatives because black-and-white negative films generally yield low contrast when exposed to color negatives.

The black-and-white negative can be made on either KODAK Commercial Film 4127 or KODAK Technical Pan Film 2415.

Two suggested film/developer combinations for producing black-and-white negatives from color negatives are given below. The developing times are starting points for workers using a condenser enlarger to print the final negative. The interpositives and the negatives were exposed by contact. The density range of the final negative should match the required density range for the printing system being used (see previous section).

	Interpositive	B/W Negative
Method A	Separation Negative Film 4131 Type 1 HC-110, developer (dilution B)— 6½ minutes tray development)	Technical Pan Film 2415 HC-110, developer (dilution B)—5 minutes (tray development)
Method B	EKTAPAN Film 4162 HC-110, developer (dilution B)—7 minutes (tray development)	Commercial Film 4127 HC-110, developer (dilution B)—8 minutes (tray development)

This black-and-white print was made from a black-and-white negative that was made from an original color negative by the 2-step duplication process.

Making Title Slides

Attractive title slides can be made fast and easily with a minimum of equipment employing basic copying techniques. Using a basic copy setup with a 35 mm camera, black-and-white artwork can be photographed to make the slides with either white letters on a colored background, or colored letters on a black background. Other more sophisticated techniques are also available for making title slides but are beyond the scope of this book.

Black-and-white artwork that is to be used for title slides can be made by using typeset copy, by applying presstype to clean white paper or board, or by using type from a typewriter with a carbon ribbon. If many title slides are to be made, it is convenient to have all the artwork made to the same size so that copying can be done at the same magnification and focus. See the upper left illustration on page 28 for an appropriate copying setup.

Usually it is necessary to have a macro lens or other close focusing method for the camera when the characters in the original copy are small. Otherwise the characters in the title slides will be hard to read when projected. Typewritten characters on a 3 x 5-inch card produce about the smallest text on a slide that can be easily read when the slide is projected.

Colored Letters/Black Background: To make slides with a black background and colored or clear letters the artwork is photographed with a high contrast black-and-white film such as KODALITH Ortho Film 6556, Type 3. This film is available for 35 mm in 100 ft rolls. It can be loaded into 135-size magazines with a bulk film loader using KODAK SNAP-CAP 135 Magazines. It is also available in 135-36 magazines under the name of KODAK EKTAGRAPHIC HC Slide Film.

KODALITH Ortho Film has an exposure index of 8. Light meter readings should be made with a KODAK Gray Card instead of the copy because the large white areas of the copy will cause the light meter to indicate less exposure than is necessary. KODALITH Ortho Film can be processed in KODALITH Developer with a light red safelight (KODAK 1A Safelight Filter). Developing times are provided in the Data Sheet on page DS-12.

KODAK Technical Pan Film 2415 can also be used for this purpose. KODAK Technical Pan Film is available in 135-36 exposure magazines and in 35 mm 150 ft rolls. For this application, KODAK Technical Pan Film should be exposed at EI 200 and developed in KODAK DEKTOL Developer for 3 minutes at 68°F (20°C) with agitation at 30-second intervals.

The processed films can be mounted and used as slides without adding color. They also can be dyed or sandwiched with filters to add color to the clear letters. Dying can be done by immersing the processed film in a liquid dye such as food coloring or transparent water colors. Felt tip markers that are fresh can also be used to add color to the slides.

COPYING and DUPLICATING
in Black-and-White and Color

A KODAK Data Book

A title slide made on an extremely high contrast black-and-white film such as one of the KODALITH Films, or KODAK Technical Pan Film developed for 3 minutes in KODAK DEKTOL Developer 1:2. The slide was placed in a yellow dye and rinsed before drying.

After the films are dried, imperfections can be retouched by applying opaque to slides made on KODALITH Film. Imperfections such as dirt, cut lines, or pinholes appear as clear white marks on the film. These marks are easily eliminated by painting them with KODAK Opaque (Black or Red) or by using a technical pen with black ink to cover them.

Clear Letters/Colored Background: A very attractive type of title slide can be created that has a bright, vivid background color with clear letters. The same-type original can be used for this technique: black letters with a white background. The only requirement that is different is that the originals must be clean and free of cut marks. Cut marks are the dark lines that are created when one piece of paper is pasted on top of another. They are common on "paste-up" artwork. Because the background will be photographed as a colored tone, there is no opportunity to opaque or retouch the marks.

If the original is a paste-up, copy it on a high contrast film as just described. Opaque the cut lines and make a B/W print from the opaqued negative. This copy print can be used as an original for the next step.

To make the slides, the artwork is photographed on a film such as KODAK VERICOLOR Slide Film 5072 or SO-279. These films are normally used for making slides from color negatives. KODAK VERICOLOR Slide Film 5072 is available in long rolls (35 mm x 100 ft). KODAK VERICOLOR Slide Film SO-279 is a similar film that is available in 35 mm, 36-exposure magazines. Both of these films are processed in KODAK FLEXICOLOR Chemicals (Processes C-41 and C-41V).

The exposure index for VERICOLOR Slide Film 5072 and SO-279 is 8.

The colors are produced by using filters over the lens while copying the artwork. Because the film is a negative/positive film a filter approximating the complement of the desired color must be used. Normally the film is used to make slides from color negatives that have an orange mask. As a result, the film will produce a dark red color if no filter at all is used. The table below lists some of the colors that are possible and the corresponding KODAK WRATTEN Filters that produce the colors. The table is based upon the use of a 3200 K tungsten light source. Exposure times should be kept between $1/10$ and 8 seconds for best results.

Background Color	KODAK WRATTEN Gelatin Filters	Exposure Increase (in stops)
Diazo Blue	12 or 15 (yellow) + 85B or 86 (orange)	+2
Cyan	29 (red)	+4
Green	34A (deep magenta)	+4
Red	38 (light blue)	+4
Orange	44 (cyan)	+4
Yellow	45 (deep blue-green)	+4
Magenta	61 (deep green)	+5
Yellow-Brown	47 (deep blue)	+4
Dark Red	No Filter	—

Colors may also be created by making the artwork with black letters on colored paper. This, however, reduces the flexibility to change colors if the color that is produced is not satisfactory.

For more information on making this type of title slides, see KODAK Publication S-26, *Reverse Text Slides*.

A reverse-text title slide made by copying a black-and-white original through a light blue filter (see table) on KODAK VERICOLOR Slide Film 5072 and processed as a color negative in Process C-41 with KODAK FLEXICOLOR Chemicals.

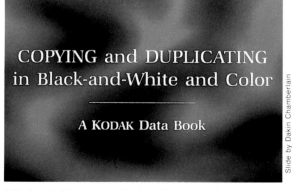

A black-and-white negative like the slide on the left was contact printed on KODALITH Film to make a title of black letters on a transparent background. This was placed in a raised position over a piece of artwork far enough below the title to be out-of-focus when copied. It was then copied through a yellow filter and processed as a color negative.

BLACK-AND-WHITE SLIDES

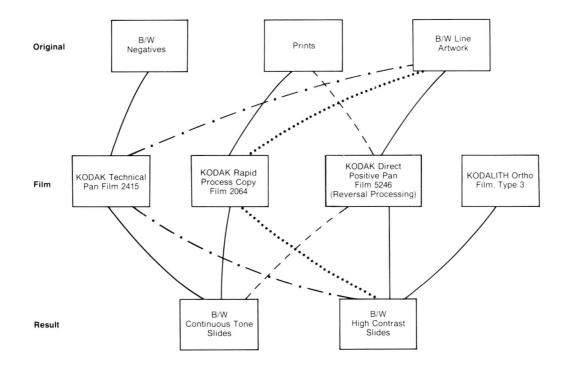

COLOR SLIDES

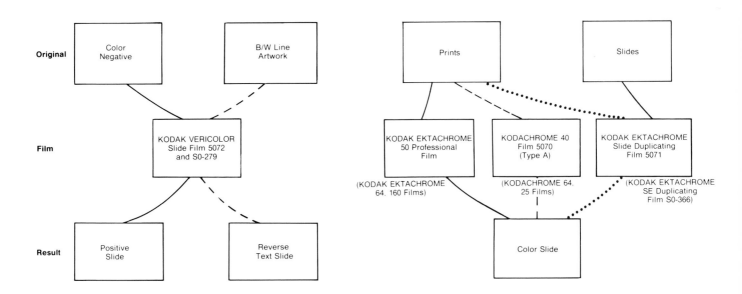

The schematic drawings on this page show a number of methods for making slides from a variety of originals using different films. All of the films shown are available in 35 mm format and can be used to make slides either by copying or duplicating.

APPENDIX

Copying and Duplicating Today

Because the KODAK Publication No. F-40, *Conservation of Photographs*, treats the subject in detail, little attention is given in this book to the stability of images created when copying or duplicating. Copying and duplicating procedures are used extensively in the conservation of photographic images. These procedures are mentioned in F-40, but the details are given in this publication. F-40 also shows how to maximize the stability of images being made today; this subject is not included in this publication. These two books supplement each other where photographic image stability is important.

Copying Colored Maps, Charts, and Drawings

Valuable colored maps and drawings can be preserved with photographic reductions. These maps, charts, and drawings, on the average, are from 12 x 18 inches to 40 x 60 inches. The proper reduction ratio depends upon the use of both the intermediate negatives and transparencies generated. The reduction ratio is the size relationship between the original and the smaller format produced. For example, if a 40 x 60-inch drawing is copied to 1/10 its size (4 x 6 inches) the reduction ratio is 10X.

Usually a small intermediate is desirable to provide greater convenience in filing and storing, especially when full-size reproductions of excellent quality can be made whenever needed. A practical size is the fiche format (4 1/8 x 5 7/8 inches) common in microfilming. Because of the very subtle colors that must be reproduced, the fiche must have excellent image quality and good image stability. Two color fiche methods are outlined in the chart and described below.

The films recommended for the production of color fiche for these methods provide excellent long-term keeping. These films have the following resolving power properties

KODAK EKTACHROME 64
   Professional Film 6117   —125 4 lines/mm
KODAK EKTACHROME Duplicating
   Film 6121   —125 4 lines/mm
EASTMAN Color Intermediate II
   Film 5243 (SO-420*)   —500 4 lines/mm
EASTMAN Color Print
   Film 5384 (SO-396*)   —630 4 lines/mm

---

*These motion picture films are available on 4.7 mil ESTAR Base as SO-420 and SO-396 in 105 mm width.

The optimum reduction ratios for Methods I and II are respectively 6X and 10X. Either system can be used at greater reduction but only with a loss in image quality. Method I is preferred for reduction ratios up to 6X. At this reduction, the reversal color film products, KODAK EKTACHROME 64 Professional Film 6117 and KODAK EKTACHROME Duplicating Film 6121, provide sharp fiche and enlargements. However, since the resolving power of these films is less than that of the Method II film, they will not provide as sharp enlargements when used at reductions greater than 6X. Originals up to 24 x 34 1/2 inches will fit onto a fiche when copied at 6X reduction.

Method II should be used for copying larger size originals up to 40 x 60 inches. The speed of the film used in Method II, EASTMAN Color Intermediate II Film 5243 (SO-420), is much lower than those in Method I. This film requires exposure conditions approximating two 2400 watt-second strobe lights at a 45° angle and at a distance of 6 to 9 feet with a lens aperture of f/5. Because of the greater reduction, more camera precision is required. The camera equipment must be vibration-free, provide the shortest exposure time possible, and allow "blow-back" or enlargement to original size through the same optical system. More complicated processing is also involved.

Typical process cameras suitable for this work include an air-mounted HLC Dekanon Precision Camera or an Opticopy Camera—both equipped with a vacuum board and film holder.

Some process lenses suitable for this high quality reduction copying include a 19-inch APO-Nikkor Lens or a 19-inch Schneider Lens at about f/8.0 for 6X reduction. A 210 mm APO-EL Nikkor Lens at f/6.3 to f/8.0 or equivalent is required for 10X reduction.

As indicated in the chart, the positive color fiche images can be viewed in a fiche reader or they can be enlarged to partial or full size onto KODAK EKTACHROME 22 Paper. Similarly the EASTMAN Color Intermediate II Film 5243 can be enlarged onto KODAK EKTACOLOR Professional Paper.

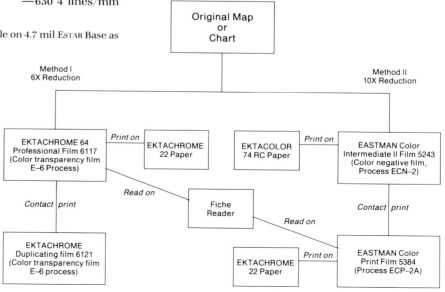

Data Sheets

KODAK Films for B/W Copying and Duplicating

Immediately following is a Summary Usage Chart, that suggests which black-and-white films can be used to copy different types of originals. Following the summary chart are Data Sheets for the Kodak films recommended in the text for black-and-white copying. These Data Sheets contain the pertinent information about the films as they are used in copying. Some of the films are general-purpose films, and general-purpose data about them can be found in the Data Sheets in KODAK Publication No. F-5, KODAK *Professional Black-and-White Films*.

The data provided in this section represent current product that has been stored, exposed, and processed according to the recommendations given in these Data Sheets and in the text. The data are averages of a number of production runs, and do not necessarily apply to each package of product because of manufacturing variations, the effects of storage conditions, and different usage conditions. The data do not represent standards or specifications which must be met by Eastman Kodak Company. General purpose films are not regularly tested for copying purposes. The Company reserves the right to change and improve product characteristics at any time.

Note: The following abbreviations are used in the table above.

ETB–ESTAR Thick Base
EB–ESTAR Base

Summary of Films, Developers, and Filters for B/W Copying

Type of Original	KODAK Film	KODAK Developer	KODAK WRATTEN Filter	Remarks
Continuous Tone B/W	Professional Copy EKTAPAN PLUS-X Pan (35 mm)	HC-110 or D-76		Various dilutions of HC-110 developer concentrate can be used to obtain different contrasts.
B/W Prints with faded yellow/brown area in dark tones.	EKTAPAN PLUS-X Pan (35 mm) Technical Pan (increased contrast)	DK-50 or HC-110B HC-110 (various dilutions) or D-76 TECHNIDOL for Technical Pan	Blue (47B)	Strength of developer dilution depends upon the degree of fading of the original.
B/W Prints faded to Yellow	Commercial Contrast Process Ortho or Pan Technical Pan	D-11 or D-19 DEKTOL HC-110	Blue (47B)	
B/W Prints with Yellow or Reddish Brown Stains	PLUS-X Pan EKTAPAN Technical Pan (increased contrast)	HC-110E HC-110E HC-110 (various dilutions) or D-76	Red (25)	
B/W Prints with Colored Stain from ink or dye	PLUS-X Pan EKTAPAN Technical Pan (increased contrast)	HC-110E HC-110E HC-110 (various dilutions) or D-76 TECHNIDOL for Technical Pan	Use filter of same color as stain	
Brown Toned B/W Prints	EKTAPAN Professional Copy Film Technical Pan Film (increased contrast)	HC-110-E HC-110-E HC-110 (various dilutions) or D-76 TECHNIDOL for Technical Pan		
Hand Colored B/W Prints	EKTAPAN Technical Pan Film (increased contrast)	HC-110 (various dilutions) or D-76	CC50C to start	
Ambrotypes/Tintypes	Professional Copy Film SUPER-XX Pan Technical Pan	HC-110 or D-76		Strength of developer dilution depends upon the degree of fading of the original. (See text.)

Type of Original	KODAK Film	KODAK Developer	KODAK WRATTEN Filter	Remarks
Daguerreotypes	Professional Copy Film PLUS-X Pan Technical Pan	HC-110 or D-76		Strength of developer dilution depends upon the degree of fading of the original. (See text).
B/W Halftone Reproductions	Professional Copy Film EKTAPAN	HC-110-E HC-110-E		
B/W Line (includes printed matter & drawings with solid black lines)	KODALITH ORTHO Type 3 Technical Pan	KODALITH D-19 DEKTOL		
Colored Line	KODALITH Pan Technical Pan Contrast Process Pan	KODALITH KODALITH D-8	Use a complementary filter to darken lines	
Handwritten Manuscripts	Contrast Process Pan or Ortho Technical Pan	D-19 or HC-110-B	For blue ink use yellow filter	For lower contrast use HC-110-B
Documents on Yellowed Paper	Contrast Process Pan Technical Pan	D-8 or D-19	Yellow (8 or 9)	When writing is faint, develop for higher contrast
Oil Paintings	EKTAPAN SUPER-XX Pan PLUS-X Pan	HC-110-B	Polarizing filter	See text
Watercolors	EKTAPAN SUPER-XX Pan PLUS-X Pan Prof.	HC-110-B		See text
Blueprints	Contrast Process Pan Technical Pan KODALITH Pan	D-8 or KODALITH	Red (25)	
Drawings with dark gray lines	Commercial or Contrast Process Pan/Ortho Technical Pan	HC-110-B HC-110-E		Develop for medium contrast
Pencil Drawings	Commercial or Contrast Process Pan/Ortho Technical Pan	HC-110-B D-8 HC-110-E		Develop for medium contrast
Etchings	Commercial or Contrast Process Pan/Ortho Technical Pan	D-11 or D-19		Develop for medium contrast
Tapestry & Textiles	SUPER-XX Pan EKTAPAN PLUS-X Pan	HC-110-B		Develop for Medium contrast

Summary of Films and Developers
for Black-and-White Duplicating

Type of Original	Purpose	KODAK Film	KODAK Developer	Remarks
B/W Negatives	Duplicate B/W negatives	Professional B/W Duplicating or Rapid Process Copy Film	DK-50 or DK-50 1:1	One-step duplication
B/W Negatives	Duplicate B/W negatives in two steps	SUPER-XX Pan-Interpositive SUPER-XX Pan-Duplicate Negative	DK-50 DK-50	See text for additional recommendations
B/W Line Negatives	High Contrast positives	KODALITH Ortho, Type 3	KODALITH Developer	Gives extremely high contrast
B/W Line Negatives	Duplicate negatives	PRECISION LINE Film LPD4	DEKTOL or D-11	Available from graphics arts dealers
Color Transparencies	B/W negatives for prints	SUPER-XX Pan PLUS-X Pan Technical Pan	D-76 1:1 D-76 1:1 Technidol	Large format internegative Small format internegative
Color Negatives	B/W negatives	EKTAPAN-Interpositive Commercial-Duplicate Negative	HC-110B HC-110B	See text for additional recommendations

Dilutions of KODAK HC-110 Developer:

Prepare a stock solution by diluting 1 part of the developer concentrate with 3 parts of water. The following table shows various working solution dilutions.

HC-110 Working Solution	Parts Stock Solution	Parts Water
Dilution A	1	3
Dilution B	1	7
Dilution C	1	4
Dilution D	1	9
Dilution E	1	11
Dilution F	1	19

KODAK Commercial Film 6127 and 4127 (ESTAR Thick Base)

These medium-speed, blue-sensitive films yield moderately high contrast and are used for copying continuous-tone, black-and-white prints and other reflection originals. They are also useful for making both the interpositives and final duplicate negatives in the two-step duplication of black-and-white negatives. Because of their blue sensitivity, these films can be processed with a red safelight; they can be developed by inspection.

Forms Available: Sheets only. The 6127 film has an acetate base, while the 4127 film has a .007 inch ESTAR base.

Speeds: Daylight—EI 50
Tungsten—EI 8
White-Flame Arc—EI 20
Quartz Iodine—EI 8

Emulsion Characteristics: Grain—Very Fine

Resolving Power { High Contrast—100 lines/mm (High)
Low Contrast— 40 lines/mm

Color Sensitivity—Blue

Safelight: KODAK Safelight Filter No. 1 (red) in a suitable safelight lamp with a 15-watt bulb. Keep safelight at least 4 feet from the film.

Development: The development times given in the following table are for negatives with moderately high contrast. To raise contrast, increase the developing time; to lower contrast, decrease the developing time.

Trial Developing Times for Moderately High Contrast

KODAK Developer	Developing Times in Minutes				
	Tray (Continuous Agitation)				
	65°F (18°C)	**68°F (20°C)**	70°F (21°C)	72°F (22°C)	75°F (24°C)
DK-50	2½	**2**	2	1¾	1¾
DK-50 (1:1)	4	**3¼**	3¼	2½	2½
HC-110 (Dil B)	2¾	**2¼**	2¼	2	1¾
HC-110 (Dil D)	4¾	**4½**	4¼	4	3¾
D-11*	9	**8**	7	6½	5½
	Tank (Agitation at 1-Minute intervals)				
	65°F (18°C)	**68°F (20°C)**	70°F (21°C)	75°F (22°C)	(24°C)
DK-50	—	**—**	—	—	—
DK-50 (1:1)	5¼	**4½**	4½	—	—
HC-110 (Dil B)	—	**—**	—	—	—
HC-110 (Dil D)	6	**5¾**	5¼	5	4¾
D-11*	12	**10**	9	8½	7

*For very high contrast

Note: Tank developing times less than 5 minutes can result in unsatisfactory uniformity.

Characteristic Curves

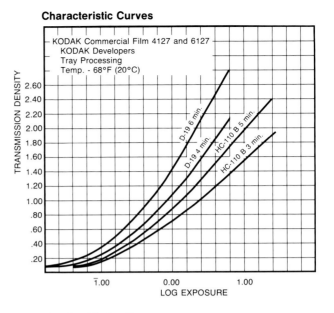

KODAK Commercial Film 4127 and 6127
KODAK Developers
Tray Processing
Temp. - 68°F (20°C)

Contrast Index Curves

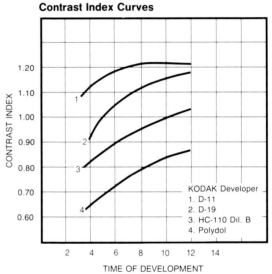

KODAK Developer
1. D-11
2. D-19
3. HC-110 Dil. B
4. Polydol

TIME OF DEVELOPMENT

Reciprocity Curve

KODAK Commercial Film 4127 and 6127

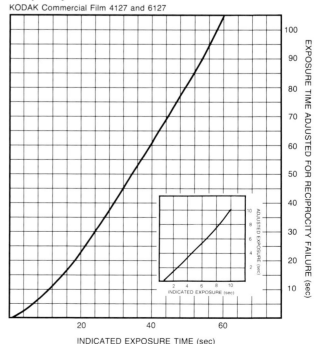

INDICATED EXPOSURE TIME (sec)

Note: Film speed is based upon an exposure of 10 sec.
Indicated exposures shorter than 10 sec. will require
a decrease in exposure.

KODAK Contrast Process Ortho Film 4154 (ESTAR Thick Base)

This is a very-high contrast, fine-grain, orthochromatic film with very high resolving power. It is recommended for making copies of printed material on white, blue, blue-green, green and yellow paper. It is not suitable for making copies of originals on orange or red paper. When developed to a moderately high contrast, this film records the intermediate tones of etchings and handwritten materials while maintaining a good background white. It can also be used to copy faded, continuous-tone photographs that are low in contrast.

Form Available: Sheets

Speed: White-Flame Arc—EI 100
Pulsed-Xenon—EI 100
Tungsten—EI 50
Quartz Iodine—EI 50

The above exposure index values are for use with meters marked with ISO or ———ASA speeds. The pulsed-xenon arc speed is for light-integrating meters. Meter readings should be considered the basis for trial exposures. See the text for information on making lens-extension and reciprocity exposure corrections.

Emulsion Characteristics: Grain—Fine

Resolving Power $\left\{\begin{array}{l}\text{High Contrast—200 lines/mm (Very High)}\\\text{Low Contrast — 50 lines/mm}\end{array}\right.$

Color Sensitivity—Orthochromatic

Safelight: KODAK Safelight No. 1 (red) in a suitable safelight lamp with a 15-watt bulb. Keep film at least 4-feet away from lamp.

Filter Factors: Multiply the unfiltered exposure time by the filter factor given below:

KODAK WRATTEN Filter	Filter Factors							
	No. 6	No. 8	No. 9	No. 15	No. 58	No. 47	No.47B	Polarizing Filter
Tungsten	1.5	1.5	2	3	3	10	16	2.5
Quartz Iodine	1.2	1.5	2	2.5	3	10	16	2.5
White-Flame Arc*	2	2.5	3	5	6	6	8	2.5
Pulsed-Xenon	2.5	3	4	6	5	6	10	2.5

*With the positive carbon in the lower position for direct current lamps.

Development: Develop at approximate times and temperatures given below. Increase developing times to raise contrast; decrease developing times to lower contrast.

KODAK Developer	Developing Time in Minutes									
	Tray (Continuous Agitation)					Tank (Agitation at 1—minute Intervals)				
	65°F (18°C)	**68°F (20°C)**	70°F (21°C)	72°F (22°C)	75°F (24°C)	65°F (18°C)	**68°F (20°C)**	70°F (21°C)	72°F (22°C)	75°F (24°C)
D-8 (2:1) Max. Contrast	4½	**4**	3¾	3¼	2¾	6	**5¼**	4¾*	—	—
D-11						6	**5**	4½*	—	—
High Contrast HC-110	4¾	**4**	3½	3	2½					
(Dil B) High Contrast	6	**5**	4½	4	3¾	7½	**6½**	6	5½	4¾*

*Tank developing times shorter than 5 minutes can result in unsatisfactory uniformity.

Characteristic Curves

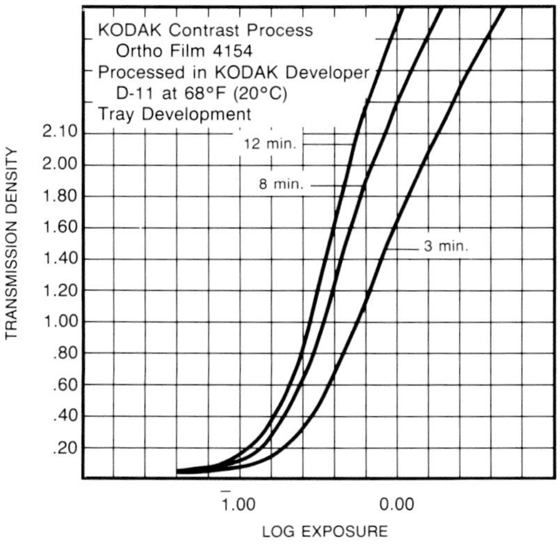

Contrast Index Curves

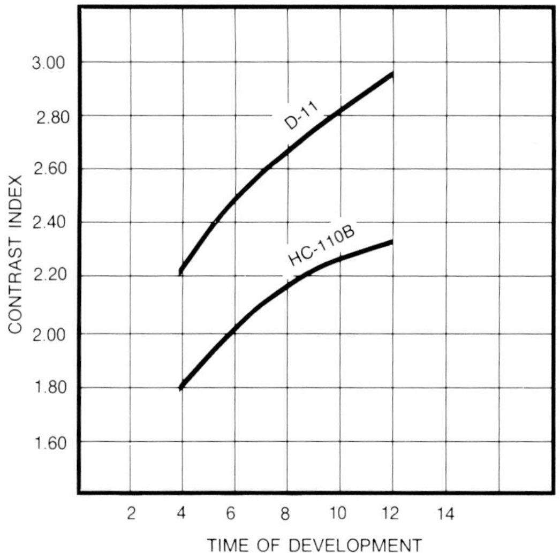

KODAK
Contrast Process Pan Film 4155
(ESTAR Thick Base)

Characteristic Curves

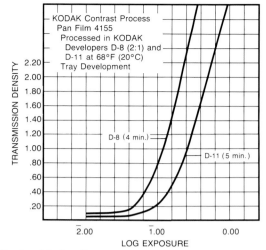

Contrast-Index Curve

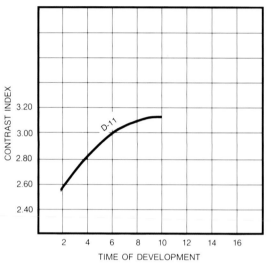

KODAK Contrast Process Pan film is a panchromatic version of Contrast Process Ortho film. Like the Ortho film, it is a very-high contrast, fine-grain film with high resolving power. It is suitable for making copies of printed material on any color paper. When developed to a moderately high contrast, this film can be used to copy colored art originals such as etchings, aquatints, mezzotints etc., and will reproduce the intermediate tones as well as the darker tones. Various colors can be lightened or darkened by the use of filters. It can also be used to copy faded, continuous-tone photographs of low contrast. Stains can be minimized or eliminated by copying on this film through appropriate filters.

Form Available: Sheets

Speed: White-Flame Arc—100   Tungsten 80
           Pulsed-Xenon—100   Quartz Iodine 80

    Settings are for meters marked for ASA or ISO speeds. Pulsed-xenon illumination should be measured with a light integrating meter.

Emulsion Characteristics: Grain—Very Fine

Resolving Power $\begin{cases} \text{High Contrast—160 lines/mm (Very High)} \\ \text{Low Contrast — 50 lines/mm} \end{cases}$

Color Sensitivity—Panchromatic

Filter Factors—Multiply the normal exposure by the filter factor given below:

KODAK WRATTEN Filter	No. 8	No. 9	No. 15	No. 29	No. 25	No. 58	No. 47	No. 47B	Polarizing Filter
Tungsten	1.2	1.5	1.5	6	3	4	12	20	2.5
Quartz Iodine	1.2	1.5	1.5	10	5	6	20	25	2.5
White-Flame Arc	2	2.5	2.5	25	10	8	6	8	2.5
Pulsed-Xenon Arc	1.5	2	2	16	6	6	8	12	2.5

Development: Develop at approximate times and temperatures given below. Increase developing time to increase contrast; decrease developing times to decrease contrast.

KODAK Developer	Developing Time in Minutes									
	Tray (Continuous Agitation)					Tank (Agitation at 1—minute Intervals)				
	65°F	68°F	70°F	72°F	75°F	65°F	68°F	70°F	72°F	75°F
D-8 (2:1) (Max. Contrast)	2¼	2	1¾	1½	—	NR	NR	NR	NR	NR
D-11 (High Contrast)	4¾	4	3½	3	2½	6	5	4½*	3¾*	3*

*Tank developing times less than 5 minutes can result in unsatisfactory uniformity of development.

DS-8

KODAK EKTAPAN Film 4162 (ESTAR Thick Base)

KODAK EKTAPAN Film is a medium speed camera film often used for making black-and-white copies of black-and-white and colored originals. It is a fine-grain, panchromatic, medium resolving-power film. Its panchromatic sensitivity makes it ideal for copying black-and-white originals that require red filtration. Its characteristic curve shape provides moderate highlight tone expansion. It can also be used to make intermediate positives from negatives as a first step in making black-and-white duplicate negatives.

Form Available: Sheets, 3½-inch and 70 mm long rolls.

Speed: ISO 100/21°

Filter Factors: See Color Filter Circle on page 35.

Emulsion Characteristics: Grain—Fine

Resolving Power { High Contrast—80 lines/mm (Medium)
{ Low Contrast —40 lines/mm

Sensitivity—Panchromatic

Safelight: Handle in total darkness

Development: Develop at approximate times and temperatures given below. Increase the developing time to increase contrast, decrease the developing time to decrease contrast. Use of KODAK MICRODOL-X and KODAK D-76 developers tends to shorten the toe and straighten the characteristic curve which reduces the highlight expansion in copy negatives. Use of KODAK HC-110 developer maintains the long toe characteristic curve.

Characteristic Curves

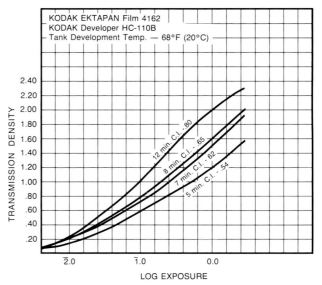

Contrast Index Curves

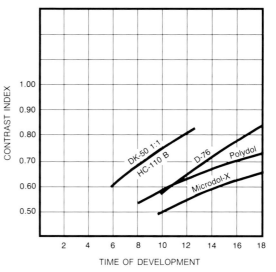

Reciprocity Characteristics: See general curves for black-and-white films on page 36.

KODAK Developer	Developing Time in Minutes									
	Tray (Continuous Agitation)					Tank (Agitation at 1—minute Intervals)				
	65°F	68°F	70°F	72°F	75°F	65°F	68°F	70°F	72°F	75°F
HC-110 (Dil A) 2¾*	3¼	3	2¾	2½	2¼	4*	3¾*	3¼*	3*	
HC-110 (Dil B)	5	4½	4¼	4	3½	7	6	5½	5	4¼*
DK-50 (1:1)	5	4½	4¼	4	3½	7	6	5½	5	4¼*
D-76	9	8	7	6½	5½	11	10	9	8½	7½
MICRODOL-X	12	10	9½	8	7	16	13	12	10	9

*Tank development times shorter than 5 minutes can lead to unsatisfactory uniformity.

KODAK High Speed Infrared Film 4143 (ESTAR Thick Base)
KODAK High Speed Infrared Film 2481

A high-speed, infrared-sensitive film used to make copies in investigative work to show characteristics of originals not visible in light, or in copies made with light. Two common uses are in copying altered or burned documents, and in copying paintings that have been overpainted to show the nature of the painting underneath. Because this film has sensitivity to light in addition to its infrared sensitivity, it is almost always used with a red or infrared filter to prevent the light from recording. Load 35-mm film in camera in dark to avoid fogging.

Forms Available: Sheets—KODAK High Speed Infrared Film 4143 (ESTAR Thick Base).

Film Code Letter Designation: HIE; 35-mm magazines and long rolls—KODAK High-Speed Infrared Film 2481.

Speed: The meter settings in the table below are for trial exposures based on measurements made with meters marked for ASA or ISO speeds, and are based on development in KODAK D-76 Developer.

KODAK WRATTEN Filters	Film Speeds	
	Tungsten and Quartz Iodine	White-Flame Arc and Pulsed-Xenon
Nos. 25, 29, 70, 89B	125	50
Nos. 87, 88A	64	25
No. 87C	25	10

Photolamp Exposure Table: Based on the use of two R2 reflector photolamps or two No. 2 Photolamps in 12 inch reflectors placed at 45° on each side of the copyboard.

Lamp Distance	3 ft	4½ ft	6½ ft
Lens Opening at ¹⁄₃₀-Second Shutter Speed	f/11	f/8	f/5.6

Use larger lens opening to correct underexposure; use smaller lens opening to correct overexposure.

Emulsion Characteristics: Grain—Medium

Resolving Power { High Contrast—80 lines/mm (Medium)
{ Low Contrast —32 lines/mm

Sensitivity—Infrared with proper filtration

Safelight: Handle in total darkness. When development is half complete, the film can be examined *for a few seconds* in the light from a suitable safelight lamp equipped with a KODAK Safelight Filter No. 3 (dark green) and a 15 watt bulb at a distance not closer than 4 feet from the film.

Development: Develop at approximate times and temperatures given below. Increase developing time to increase contrast; decrease developing time to lower contrast.

KODAK Developer	Developing Time in Minutes for 4143 (Sheets)									
	Tray (Continuous Agitation)					Tank (Intermittent Agitation)*				
	65°F	68°F	70°F	72°F	75°F	65°F	68°F	70°F	72°F	75°F
D-76 (Normal Contrast)	9	**8**	7½	7	6	12	**10**	9	8	7½
MICRODOL-X (Normal Contrast)	13	**11**	10	9	8	16	**14**	12	10	9
HC-110 (Dil B) High Contrast)	5	**4½**	4½	4¼	4	7	**6½**	6	5½	5
D-19 (Maximum Contrast)	13	**11**	10	9	8	16	**14**	12	10	9

*Agitation at 1-minute intervals.

KODAK Developer	Developing Times in Minutes for 35 mm Film 2481				
	Small Tank (Intermittent Agitation)*				
	65°F	68°F	70°F	72°F	75°F
D-76 (Normal Contrast)	13	**11**	10	9½	8
HC-110 (Dil B) (High Contrast)	7	**6**	6	5½	5
D-19 (Maximum Contrast)	7	**6**	5½	5½	4†

*Agitation at 30-second intervals

†Developing times shorter than 5 minutes can lead to unsatisfactory uniformity.

Reciprocity: This film varies little in speed from 10 seconds to ¹/₁₀₀₀ second, hence no correction for reciprocity is usually needed.

Characteristic Curves

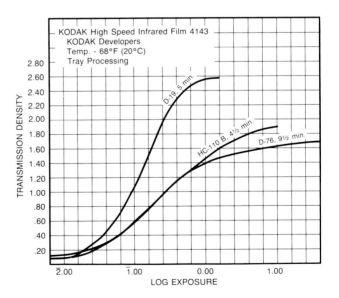

KODAK High Speed Infrared Film 4143
KODAK Developers
Temp. - 68°F (20°C)
Tray Processing

KODALITH Ortho Film 2556, Type 3 (ESTAR Base)
KODALITH Ortho Film 6556, Type 3 (Acetate Base)
KODALITH Ortho Film 8556, Type 3 (Thin Base)

These films are used extensively for copying line copy and text materials. Developed in the various KODALITH developers, they produce high-density blacks with low density lines. Developed in KODAK Developer D-11, KODALITH films are used for highlight masking to improve the separation of highlight tones when a transparency is being masked to reduce its density range.

Forms Available: 2556, Sheets
6556, Long rolls and sheets
8556, Sheets
135-36 as KODAK EKTAGRAPHIC Slide Film

The 2556 and 6556 versions are available from professional stockhouse dealers. Dealers who handle graphic-arts materials stock or can order all versions.

Base Thickness: 2556—.0053 inch
6556—.004 inch
8556—.0032 inch

Speed: For meters marked with ISO or ASA speeds.

KODALITH Developer		KODAK Developer D-11
White-Flame Arc	12	—
Tungsten	8	25

To obtain a trial exposure, take a reflected-light measurement from the gray (18% reflection) side of a KODAK Gray Card (Publication No. R-27) placed on the copyboard. If the white (90% reflection) side is used, multiply the exposure by 5. Measuring the actual drawing or printed material can give misleading results because of variations in the proportional areas of black-and-white. If the background density in the test negative is light, increase the exposure. If the lines or characters are filled in, decrease the exposure.

Sensitivity: Orthochromatic. Not suitable for making line negatives of originals printed on red or orange paper.

Safelight: Use a KODAK Safelight Filter No. 1A (light red) in a suitable safelight lamp with a 15-watt bulb placed 4 feet or farther from the film location.

Filter Factors: Multiply the normal exposure by the filter factors given below.

KODAK WRATTEN Filter	No. 8	No. 15	No. 47B	No. 58
White Flame Arc Photolamp (3400 K) or Other High-Efficiency	2.5	8	12	5
Tungsten lamp	1.5	3.5	20	3

Development: Tray develop at approximate times given below at a temperature of about 68°F (20°C).

KODAK Developer	Developing Time (Minutes)		Development Time Range
	Agitation	Line Negatives	(Minutes)
KODALITH Super RT	Continuous	2¾	2¼ to 3¼
KODALITH	Continuous	2¾	2¼ to 3¼
KODALITH Fine Line	See Note Below	2¾	—
KODALITH Liquid (1:3)	Continuous	2¾	2¼ to 3¼
KODAK Developer D-11	Continuous	2½*	2 to 3

Note: To develop in KODALITH Fine Line Developer agitate continuously for 45 seconds, then still develop for 2 minutes.

*For highlight masks, develop for 2 minutes. Expose and develop to obtain a density from 0.30 to 0.50 in areas corresponding to transparency diffuse highlights.

KODALITH Developers are available from dealers who handle graphic-arts materials.

Characteristic Curve

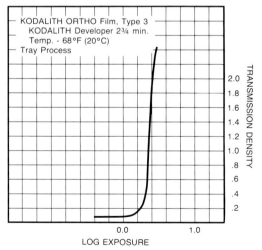

KODALITH ORTHO Film, Type 3
KODALITH Developer 2¾ min.
Temp. - 68°F (20°C)
Tray Process

TRANSMISSION DENSITY

2.0 1.8 1.6 1.4 1.2 1.0 .8 .6 .4 .2

0.0   1.0

LOG EXPOSURE

KODALITH Pan Film 2568 (ESTAR Base)

As a copy film, KODALITH Pan Film is very useful for producing extremely high contrast negatives from colored originals. By the use of filters, original colors with little tonal separation can be separated as black-and-white tones. It is also useful for copying line drawings or printed materials that are stained; use of the appropriate filter can often completely eliminate any evidence of the stain in the copy negative. It is also useful for making highlight masks for color duplicating, especially when highlight tones are pastel colored.

Form Available: Sheets

Speed: White-Flame Arc—40   Tungsten—32
for meters marked with ISO or ASA speeds.

These speeds are recommended for first trial exposures when copying, and are based on development in KODALITH Developer. See text on page 40 for instructions on the use of meters to find copy exposures.

Safelight: Use a KODAK Safelight Filter No. 3 (dark green) in a suitable safelight lamp with a 15-watt bulb at not less than 4 feet.

Sensitivity: Panchromatic (See spectral sensitivity curve below)

Filter Factors: When a filter is used, multiply the unfiltered exposure time by the factor for the particular KODAK WRATTEN Filter shown in the table below. Because of varying conditions, these factors are only approximate.

KODAK WRATTEN Filter	No. 8	No. 15	No. 25	No. 58	No. 47B
White-Flame Arc	2.5	2.5	5	15	15
Tungsten (3400 K)	1.8	1.5	3	12	36

Development: Tray develop at 68°F (20°C) for approximate times given below. As the characteristic curves below indicate, changing developing time changes the film speed so that, within limits, changing developing time can correct for exposure variations.

KODAK Developer	Developing Time (Minutes)	Range (Minutes)
KODALITH Developer	2½	2 to 3
KODALITH Super RT	2¾	2¼ to 3¼
KODAK Developer D-11	2*	—

Notes: KODALITH Liquid Developer is not recommended for this film.

*For highlight masks. Expose and develop to obtain a density from 0.30 to 0.50 in areas corresponding to transparency diffuse highlights.

Characteristic Curves

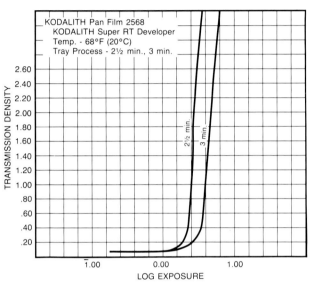

KODAK PLUS-X Pan Film 5062
KODAK PLUS-X Portrait Film 5068
KODAK PLUS-X Pan Professional Film

These films have similar emulsion characteristics, but are available in different roll-film formats. They are suitable both for continuous tone black-and-white copying and for making black-and-white negatives from transparencies. They have extremely fine grain, are medium speed, and have excellent sharpness. PLUS-X Pan Film is on a gray-dyed base. PLUS-X Pan Professional Film and PLUS-X Portrait Film 5068 are on a clear acetate bases with a retouching surface on the emulsion side.

Forms Available: KODAK PLUS-X Pan Film 5062 is available in 35-mm magazines, 35-mm and 70-mm long rolls. PLUS-X Portrait Film is available in 70-mm long rolls. PLUS-X Pan Professional is available in 120- and 220-roll film sizes.

Film Code Letter Designation: PX (35 mm), PXP (120 and 220)

Speed: ISO 125/22°

Emulsion Characteristics: Grain—Extremely Fine

Resolving Power $\begin{cases} \text{High Contrast—125 lines/mm (High)} \\ \text{Low Contrast — 50 lines/mm} \end{cases}$

Sensitivity—Panchromatic

Safelight: Handle in total darkness

Development: Develop at approximate times and temperatures given below for normal results. Recommended development times for special purposes are given in the text. KODAK Publication No. F-5, *KODAK Professional and Black-and-White Films* gives considerable information on changing developing times for particular results.

KODAK Developer	**Developing Time in Minutes***									
	SMALL Tank (Agitation at 30-Second Intervals					**LARGE Tank (Agitation at 1-Minute Intervals)**				
	65°F (18°C)	**68°F (20°C)**	70°F (21°C)	72°F (22°C)	75°F (24°C)	65°F (18°C)	**68°F (20°C)**	70°F (21°C)	72°F (22°C)	75°F (24°C)
HC-110 (Dil B)	6	**5**	4½	4	3½	6½	**5½**	5	4¾	4
D-76	6½	**5½**	5	4½	3¾		**7½**	6½	6	5½
4½										
D-76 (1:1)†	8	**7**	6½	6	5	10	**9**	8	7½	7
MICRODOL-X	8	**7**	6½	6	5	10	**9**	8	7½	7
MICRODOL-X (1:3)†	—	—	11	10	9½	—	—	14	13	11

*Tank developing times shorter than 5 minutes can lead to unsatisfactory uniformity.

†Dilute developers give slightly greater sharpness but slightly higher graininess levels than concentrated developers.

Note: Do not use developers containing thiocyanate silver-halide solvents such as KODAK DK-20 Developer.

Characteristic Curves

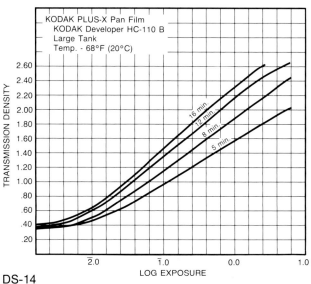

KODAK PLUS-X Pan Film
KODAK Developer HC-110 B
Large Tank
Temp. - 68°F (20°C)

TRANSMISSION DENSITY / LOG EXPOSURE

DS-14

**KODAK PLUS-X Pan Film
KODAK PLUS-X Portrait Film
KODAK PLUS-X Pan Professional Film** Large Tank

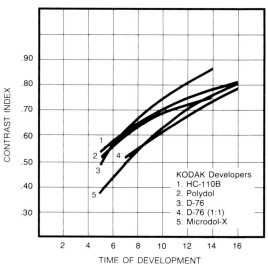

KODAK Developer
1. D-76
2. D-76 (1:1)
3. MICRODOL-X
4. MICRODOL-X (1:3) 75°F

TIME OF DEVELOPMENT (minutes)
20°C (68°F) Agitation at 30-second Intervals

Reciprocity: Use the general black-and-white reciprocity curve on page 36.

Contrast-Index Curves Small Tank

KODAK Developers
1. HC-110B
2. Polydol
3. D-76
4. D-76 (1:1)
5. Microdol-X

CONTRAST INDEX / TIME OF DEVELOPMENT

KODAK PLUS-X Pan Professional Film 2147 (ESTAR Base) 4147 (ESTAR Thick Base)

Developed in KODAK HC-110 Developer, these films produce a long toe characteristic curve which gives a degree of highlight tone expansion when used to copy black-and-white or colored reflection originals and transparencies. They are recommended for use in copying continuous-tone originals where the use of filters is required, either to minimize the effects of stains, or to provide needed color tone separation. 2147 is the long-roll version, while 4147 is the sheet version. Developed in KODAK D-76 or MICRODOL-X Developer, this film produces a short toe, long straight line characteristic curve suitable for making diapositives from black-and-white or color negatives using the two-step duplicating procedure.

Forms Available: KODAK PLUS-X Pan Professional Film 2147, (ESTAR base) is available as 35 mm, 46 mm and 70 mm long rolls. The 4147 film is available in sheet form and 3½ inch long rolls.

Speed: ISO 125/22°

Emulsion Characteristics: Grain—Very Fine

Resolving Power { High Contrast—125 lines/mm (High)
{ Low Contrast — 50 lines/mm

Color Sensitivity—Panchromatic

Safelight: Handle in complete darkness

Development: Develop at approximate times and temperatures shown below. Development is the main control of photographic contrast. To raise the contrast, increase the developing time; to lower the contrast, decrease the developing time. Some exposure compensation may be necessary.

KODAK Developer	Developing Time (in Minutes)									
	Tray (Continuous Agitation)					Large Tank (Intermittent Agitation)*				
	65°F (18°C)	68°F (20°C)	70°F (21°C)	72°F (22°C)	75°F (24°C)	65°F (18°C)	68°F (20°C)	70°F (21°C)	72°F (22°C)	75°F (24°C)
HC-110- (Dil B)	6	5	4¾	4½	4	8	7	6½	6	5½
DK-50 (1:1)	5	4½	4¼	4	3½	6½	6	5¾	5½	5
D-76	7	6	5½	5	4½	9	8	7½	7	6
MICRODOL-X	9	8	7½	7	6	11	10	9½	9	8

*Agitation at 1-minute intervals.

Reciprocity: Use the general black-and-white reciprocity curve on page 36.

Characteristic Curves

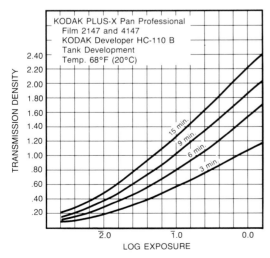

Contrast Index Curves

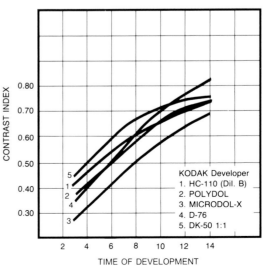

KODAK Professional Copy Film 4125 (ESTAR Thick Base)
KODAK Ortho Copy Film 5125

These are films designed specifically for copying black-and-white continuous-tone originals, especially photographs. The film characteristic curve has an upsweep in the highlight region that expands highlight tones. Highlight contrast is largely controlled by exposure: increased exposure increases highlight contrast (and negative density range) while decreased exposure reduces highlight contrast (and negative density range). Detailed instructions on the use of these films starts on page 37.

Forms Available: 4125, Sheets only
5125, 70 mm long roll, not perforated.

Speed: White-Flame Arc—EI 25
Tungsten and Quartz Iodine—EI 12
Pulsed-Xenon—EI 25

These speed are for use with meters marked for ASA or ISO speeds. The pulsed-xenon speed is for light integrating meters. All speeds are for trial exposures in copying. Directions for use of meters is given on page 32.

Emulsion Characteristics: Grain—Moderately Course

Resolving Power { High Contrast—80 lines/mm (Medium)
Low Contrast —40 lines/mm

Sensitivity—Orthochromatic

Development: For normal purposes, exposure and development should produce copy negatives with a density range of about 0.85 for condenser enlargers and 0.95 to 1.05 for diffusion enlargers. The following provides developing times for first trial negatives.

KODAK Developer at 68°F (20°C)	Developing Time	
	Tray— Continuous Agitation	Tank— Intermittent Agitation
HC-110 (Dil E)	4 minutes	5　minutes
DK-50 (1:1)	3 minutes	3½ minutes*

*Unsatisfactory uniformity may result with tank development times of less than 5 minutes.

Note: With these recommended developing times, exposure difference is used to achieve the aim density ranges given on page 37.

Characteristic Curves

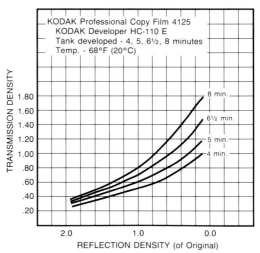

Reciprocity Curves

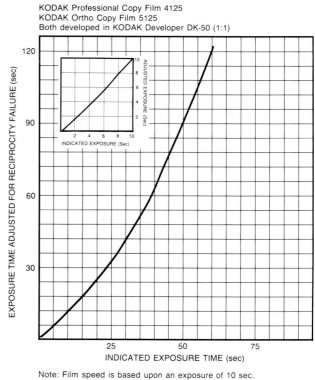

Note: Film speed is based upon an exposure of 10 sec. Indicated exposures shorter than 10 sec. will require a decrease in exposure.

KODAK Professional B/W Duplicating Film 4168 (ESTAR Thick Base)
KODAK Rapid Process Copy Film

KODAK Professional B/W Duplicating Film is designed to produce direct duplicates of black-and-white negatives with a standard photographic process. This means that a reversal process is not required. The film makes duplicates by contact printing, copying in a camera, or projection in an enlarger. The film is normally processed to a gamma of 1.0 for a one-to-one reproduction of the original, but the development can be changed to decrease or increase the density range of the original. KODAK Rapid Process Copy Film is a similar film but in 35 mm roll size on a bluish-colored film base.

Format Available: 4168 Film available in Sheets, 4 x 5-inch, 5 x 7-inch, 8 x 10-inch sheets; Rapid Process Copy Film available in 35 mm magazines and 35 mm 150 ft long rolls.

Film Code Letter Designation: RPC (35 mm)

Speed: The speed of this film is so low (approximately .01) for tungsten illumination that meters can only be used to compare originals once a basic exposure has been found. In making duplicates by projection, when the enlarger is set to produce 3 footcandles on the easel, a starting exposure time of 40 seconds can be tried. KODAK AZO or VELOX paper, F-1, may have a speed sufficiently close to Professional B/W Duplicating Film, so that tests made on the paper can be related to the film for exposure (of course, the paper will produce positive images, while the film produces negative images.) Because of the slow speed, a special metering technique is required. Set the meter dial at a speed of 100, measure the original with the meter, and multiply the indicated exposure time by 10,000. For example, if the meter indicates an exposure of $\frac{1}{100}$ second at f/11, try an exposure of

$$\frac{10,000}{100} = 100 \text{ seconds at f/11.}$$

KODAK Rapid Process Copy Film has about the same speed as KODAK Professional B/W Duplicating Film.

Sensitivity: Orthochromatic

Safelight: Use a KODAK Safelight Filter No. 1A (light red) in a suitable safelight lamp with a 15-watt bulb. Keep the film at least 4 feet from the safelamp.

Development: For approximately 1:1 tone reproduction (gamma of 1) develop as follows. To raise the contrast, increase developing time; to lower contrast, decrease the developing time. See table of developing times on page 92.

Characteristic Curves

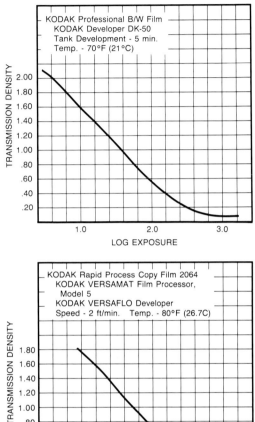

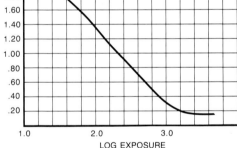

TIME-GAMMA CURVES
Professional B/W Duplicating Film

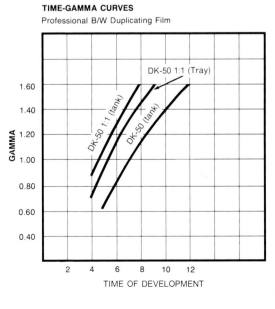

KODAK Developer	KODAK Film	Development Time at 70° (21°C)	
		Tray (Continuous Agitation)	Large Tank (Agitation at 1-min intervals)
DEKTOL (1:1)	Prof B/W	2¼ min	—
DK-50	Prof B/W	—	4¾
DK-50 (1:1)	Prof B/W	5¼ min	7
DK-50	Rapid Process	—	6½

KODAK Separation Negative Film 4131, Type 1 (ESTAR Thick Base)

A fine-grain, moderately fast panchromatic film designed for making color separation negatives with low to medium contrast. The emulsion surface is suitable for retouching. The characteristic curve has a long straight line so this film is suitable for making positive transparencies (inter-positives) from color negatives and for making black-and-white negatives from color transparencies.

Film Speeds: The following meter settings can be used with meters masked for ISO or ASA film speeds, and can be used as an aid to find trial exposures.

Pulsed Xenon*	ISO 125/22°
White-Flame Arc	ISO 125/22°
Tungsten	ISO 100/21°
Quartz Iodide	ISO 100/21°

*Measured by a light integrator

Sensitivity: Panchromatic

Filter Factors: Multiply the unfiltered exposure time by the following factors. These factors are approximate because of variations in lighting conditions.

Safelight: Handle in complete darkness. After development is half complete, the developing film can be examined for a few seconds by the light of a KODAK Safelight filter No. 3 (dark green) in a suitable safelight lamp with a 15-watt bulb at a distance not less than 4 feet.

Development: Starting development times for tray development at 68°F (20°C) for two KODAK Developers are given in the following table. To raise contrast, increase the developing time; to lower contrast, decrease developing time.

KODAK Developer	Developing Time
DK-50	4 minutes
HC-110 (Dil C)	4 minutes

Light Source	KODAK WRATTEN Filter Number								
	23A	25	29	33	47	47B	49	58	61
Pulsed-Xenon Arc	6	10	20	20	15	20	25	12	20
White-Flame Arc	6	10	25	20	6	8	20	10	15
Tungsten	4	6	12	15	30	36	72	12	18
Quartz Iodine	4	6	12	15	30	36	72	12	18

Characteristic Curves

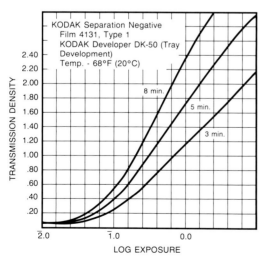

Contrast Index Curves

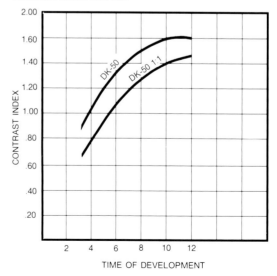

KODAK SUPER-XX Pan Film 4142 (ESTAR Thick Base)

A moderately high-speed, panchromatic, general purpose film with a straight-line characteristic curve, used for making black-and-white negatives from color transparencies or black-and-white interpositives from color negatives. It can also be used to make black-and-white copy negatives of color prints and other reflection color originals.

Form Available: Sheets

Speed: ISO 200/24°

Emulsion Characteristics: Grain—Fine

Resolving Power { High Contrast—100 lines/mm (High)
{ Low Contrast — 40 lines/mm

Color Sensitivity—Panchromatic

Safelight: Handle in complete darkness. After development is half completed, the film can be examined for a few seconds only in the light of a KODAK Safelight filter No. 3 (dark green) in a suitable safelight lamp with a 15-watt bulb no closer than 4 feet from the film.

Filter Factors: Use color filter circle on page 35.

Development: Develop at approximate times and temperatures given in the table below. To raise contrast, increase the developing times; to lower contrast, decrease the developing times.

Characteristic Curves

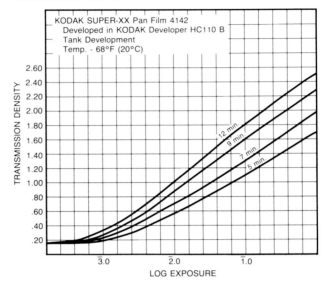

Contrast Index Curves

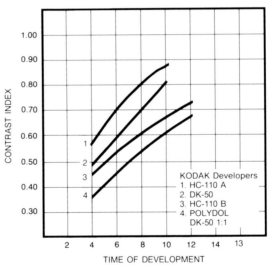

Reciprocity Adjustment: Use general graph for black-and-white films on page 36.

KODAK Developer	Developing Time in Minutes									
	Continuous Agitation (Tray)					Intermittent Agitation* (Tank)				
	65°F (18°C)	68°F (20°C)	70°F (21°C)	72°F (22°C)	75°F (24°C)	65°F (18°C)	68°F (20°C)	70°F (21°C)	72°F (22°C)	75°F (24°C)
HC-110 (Dil A)	4½	4	3¾	3½	3	6	5	4½†	4¼†	3½†
HC-110 (Dil B)	8	7	6½	6	5	11	9	8	7	6
DK-50	5½	5	4¾	4½	4	8	7	6½	6	5
DK-50 (1:1)	9	8	7½	7	6	11	10	9½	9	8

*Agitation at 1-minute intervals during development.

†Development times of less than 5 minutes in a tank may produce poor uniformity and should be avoided.

KODAK Technical Pan Film 2415 and 6415

A relatively slow-speed, extremely-fine grain and extremely-high resolving power panchromatic film with extended red sensitivity. A very wide range of contrast is possible with this film, depending on the developer and degree of development. It is this characteristic that makes this film an extremely versatile film for copying. Developed in a very high contrast developer such as KODALITH or DEKTOL Developers it can be used to copy type or linework. Low contrast originals can be copied on Technical Pan Film and developed in a moderate-contrast developer for increased contrast. When KODAK HC-110 Developer is chosen various developer dilutions and changing developing times can be used to control contrast. When being developed for normal contrast, the 35 mm Technical Pan Film 2415 can be developed in either KODAK TECHNIDOL LC or TECHNIDOL Liquid Developer. The 120-size Technical Pan Film 6415, however, should only be developed in TECHNIDOL Liquid Developer, otherwise nonuniform densities may occur. Development of sheet film for normal contrast is not recommended because nonuniform densities will result. This film is very useful as a copy film of both black-and-white and colored originals. It can also be used to make interpositives and duplicate negatives by the two-step process.

Forms Available: 2415 film: sheets, 135-36 magazines, and 150-ft. rolls. 6415 film: 120-size rolls.

Film Code Letter Designation: TP

Speed: Varies with the developer and development. Typical exposure indexes of from 25 to 200 can be seen in the contrast-index curves below.

Emulsion Characteristics: Grain—Extremely Fine Grain

Resolving Power (with KODAK HC-110 Developer)
High Contrast—320 lines/mm
Low Contrast —125 lines/mm

(with KODAK TECHNIDOL LC and TECHNIDOL Liquid Developer)
High Contrast—320 lines/mm
Low Contrast —125 lines/mm

Sensitivity—Panchromatic with extended red sensitivity.

Filter Factors: Multiply unfiltered exposure time by filter factors shown below:

Safelight: Handle in complete darkness. After development is half complete, developing film can be examined for a few seconds only in the light of a KODAK Safelight filter No. 3 (dark green) in a suitable safelight lamp with a 15-watt bulb at a distance no less than 4 feet from the film.

Development: Many developers can be used to develop Technical Pan Film for different degrees of contrast.

Contrast	KODAK Developer
Extremely High High Contrast Moderate Contrast	KODALITH, D-19, DEKTOL HC-110 (Dil B) HC-110 (Dil D, Dil F) D-76, MICRODOL-X
Normal Contrast 35 mm Film	TECHNIDOL LC or Liquid
Normal Contrast 120 Film	TECHNIDOL Liquid

The curves are for small tank development of 35 mm Technical Pan Film. Reduce the times slightly for tray development of Technical Pan Film in sheets.

KODAK WRATTEN Filter Numbers

Illumination	8	11	12	13	15	25	38	47	58
Tungsten	1.2	5	1.2	6	1.2	3.0	—	25	12
Daylight Balance	1.5	—	—	—	2.0	3.0	3.0	—	—

—Means only that a filter factor has not been determined.

Characteristic Curves

Contrast Index Curve

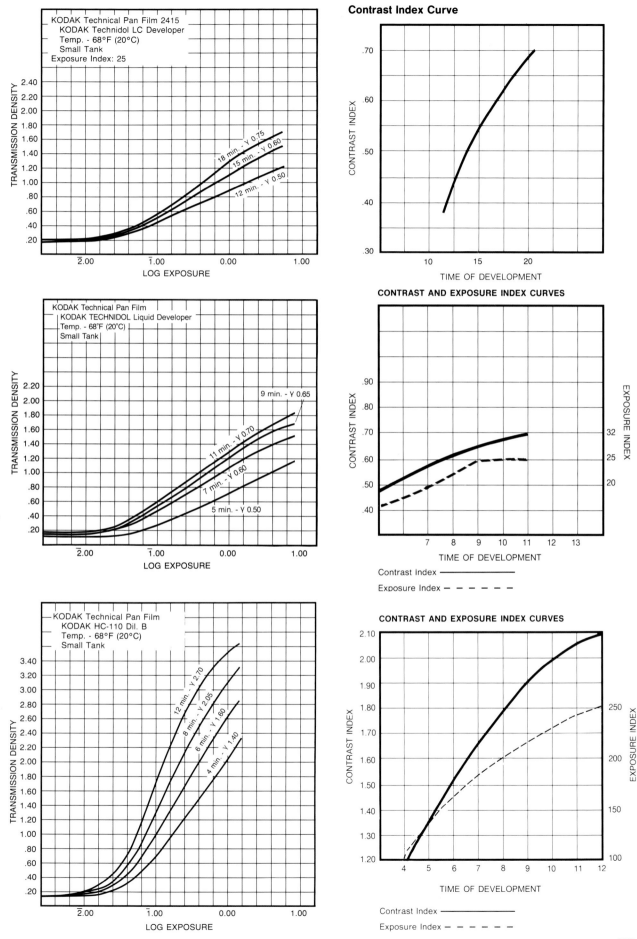

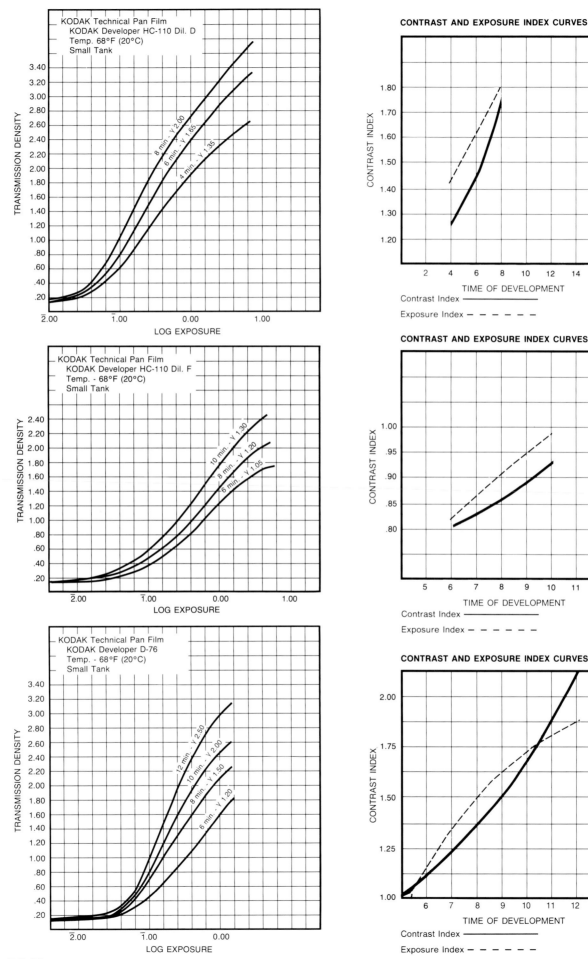

KODAK Technical Pan Film
KODAK Developer HC-110 Dil. D
Temp. 68°F (20°C)
Small Tank

8 min. - γ 2.00
6 min. - γ 1.65
4 min. - γ 1.35

TRANSMISSION DENSITY

LOG EXPOSURE

CONTRAST AND EXPOSURE INDEX CURVES

CONTRAST INDEX

EXPOSURE INDEX

TIME OF DEVELOPMENT
Contrast Index ——————
Exposure Index — — — — — —

KODAK Technical Pan Film
KODAK Developer HC-110 Dil. F
Temp. - 68°F (20°C)
Small Tank

10 min. - γ 1.30
8 min. - γ 1.20
6 min. - γ 1.05

TRANSMISSION DENSITY

LOG EXPOSURE

CONTRAST AND EXPOSURE INDEX CURVES

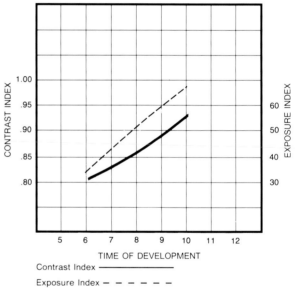

CONTRAST INDEX

EXPOSURE INDEX

TIME OF DEVELOPMENT
Contrast Index ——————
Exposure Index — — — — — —

KODAK Technical Pan Film
KODAK Developer D-76
Temp. - 68°F (20°C)
Small Tank

12 min. - γ 2.50
10 min. - γ 2.00
8 min. - γ 1.50
6 min. - γ 1.20

TRANSMISSION DENSITY

LOG EXPOSURE

CONTRAST AND EXPOSURE INDEX CURVES

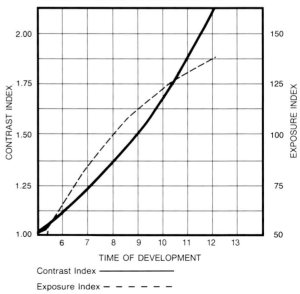

CONTRAST INDEX

EXPOSURE INDEX

TIME OF DEVELOPMENT
Contrast Index ——————
Exposure Index — — — — — —

DS-22

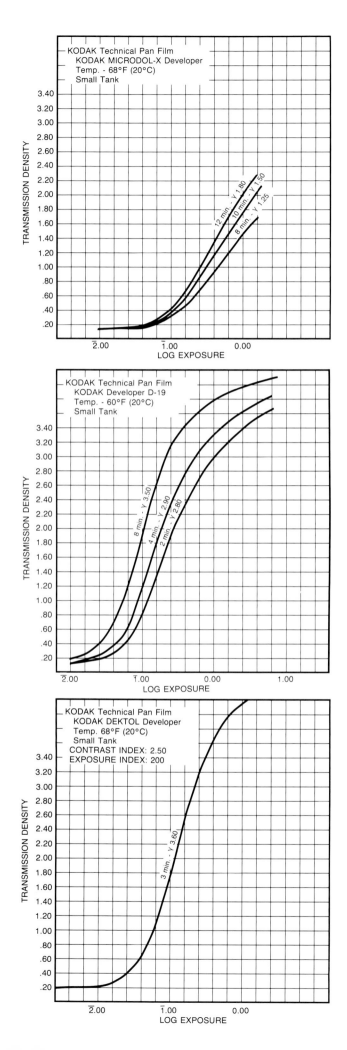

KODAK Technical Pan Film
KODAK MICRODOL-X Developer
Temp. - 68°F (20°C)
Small Tank

12 min - γ 1.80
10 min - γ 1.50
8 min - γ 1.25

TRANSMISSION DENSITY

LOG EXPOSURE

KODAK Technical Pan Film
KODAK Developer D-19
Temp. - 60°F (20°C)
Small Tank

8 min - γ 3.50
4 min - γ 2.90
2 min - γ 2.80

TRANSMISSION DENSITY

LOG EXPOSURE

KODAK Technical Pan Film
KODAK DEKTOL Developer
Temp. 68°F (20°C)
Small Tank
CONTRAST INDEX: 2.50
EXPOSURE INDEX: 200

3 min - γ 3.60

TRANSMISSION DENSITY

LOG EXPOSURE

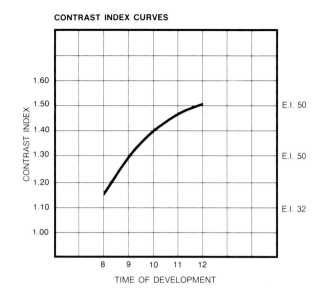

CONTRAST INDEX CURVES

CONTRAST INDEX

E.I. 50

E.I. 50

E.I. 32

TIME OF DEVELOPMENT

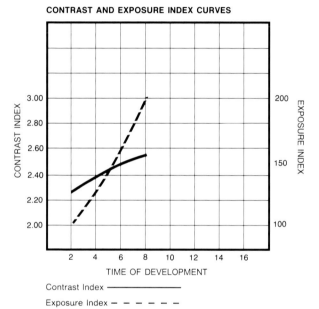

CONTRAST AND EXPOSURE INDEX CURVES

CONTRAST INDEX

EXPOSURE INDEX

TIME OF DEVELOPMENT

Contrast Index ————
Exposure Index — — — — —

Reciprocity Curve

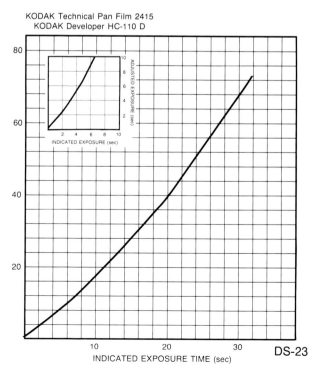

KODAK Technical Pan Film 2415
KODAK Developer HC-110 D

ADJUSTED EXPOSURE (sec)

INDICATED EXPOSURE (sec)

INDICATED EXPOSURE TIME (sec)

DS-23

KODAK ULTRATEC UGF Film 2583

A moderately fast, extremely high-contrast, Orthrochromatic film for making line negatives of line originals. The line-copy results are similar to the results with KODALITH Ortho film, Type 3. KODAK ULTRATEC Tray Developer and Replenisher is used for this film in machine processors, and KODAK ULTRATEC Tray Developer is used for tray development. KODALITH Developers *must not be used*. The ULTRATEC Developer is quite stable; it can be used for 8 hrs. of tray developing under normal conditions.

Available: Sheets, 8 x 10-inch to 30 x 40-inch
Long Rolls, 6″ wide to 52″ wide.

Base: .004-inch ESTAR

Speed: The following exposure indexes can be used with exposure meters to establish trial exposures. When using pulsed-xenon arc lights, use a light integrator to measure.

Pulsed-Xenon arc	E.I. 10/11°
Tungsten or Quartz Iodine	E.I. 10/11°

Sensitivity: Orthochromatic.

Safelight: Use a KODAK 1A Safelight Filter (light red) with a 15-watt bulb placed 4 feet or farther from the film location.

Filter Factors: Multiply the normal exposure by the filter factor given below.

Light Source:	No. 8	No. 15	No. 30	No. 47B	No. 58
Pulsed-Xenon arc	1.5	2.5	10	10	4
Tungsten or Quartz-Iodine	1.5	2.0	12	16	8

Process: Develop in KODAK ULTRATEC Tray Developer using continuous agitation.

Temperature (F)	Recommended Time	Useful Range
65	3½ min	3–3½ min
68	2¾ min	2½–3½ min
70	2¾ min	2½–3½ min
75	2½ min	2–3 min
80	1¾ min	1½–2½ min

Stop in acid stop bath for 10–15 sec. Fix in KODAK ULTRATEC Fixer & Replenisher for 1–2 minutes. Do not use hardener in fixer. Wash 10–15 minutes and dry.

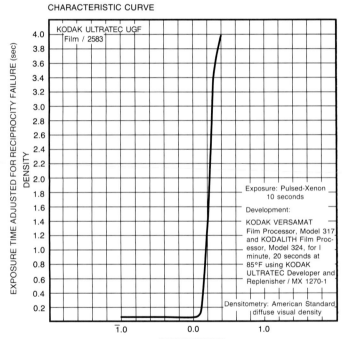

CHARACTERISTIC CURVE

KODAK ULTRATEC UGF Film / 2583

Exposure: Pulsed-Xenon 10 seconds

Development:
KODAK VERSAMAT Film Processor, Model 317 and KODALITH Film Processor, Model 324, for I minute, 20 seconds at 85°F using KODAK ULTRATEC Developer and Replenisher / MX 1270-1

Densitometry: American Standard diffuse visual density

KODAK Films for Color Copying and Duplicating

The Summary Usage Chart for color films which follows, suggests which color films can be used to copy or duplicate various color originals.

Following the Summary Chart are Data Sheets for the KODAK color films commonly used in the copying and duplicating procedures. The Data Sheets contain the pertinent information about the color films as they are used for these purposes. Some of the films are general-purpose camera films, and the general data about them can be found in KODAK Publication No. E-77, *KODAK Color Films* and in No. AF-1, *KODAK Films, Color and Black-and-White*.

The data provided in this section represents current product that has been stored, exposed and processed according to Kodak recommendations. The data are averages of a number of production coatings, and do not necessarily apply to each package of product because of manufacturing variations, the effects of storage conditions, and different usage conditions. The data do not represent standards or specifications which must be met by Eastman Kodak Company. General purpose films are not regularly tested for copying purposes. The company reserves the right to change and improve product characteristics at any time.

Certain KODAK EKTACHROME Films are made in both a professional version and a version intended for general use. The characteristics of the two films are nearly identical. The difference is in the original color balance and recommended storage. Professional EKTACHROME Films are shipped with a final color balance, and should be stored refrigerated 50°F (10°C) or lower to maintain the optimum balance at the time of shipment. Those EKTACHROME films without the word "Professional" in the name are made for general picture taking by non-professionals, and should be stored at normal room temperature. All films should be protected from excessive heat such as can occur inside automobiles parked in the sun, or in tropical areas without air conditioning.

Generally speaking, the "Professional" films can be expected to be manufactured very uniformly and can be expected to yield optimum quality results close to the time of manufacture.

Aside from these differences, the data characteristics of the Professional and general-purpose EKTACHROME Films are the same.

Product	Page

Summary of Films and Processes for Color Copying and Duplicating

Type of Original	Purpose	KODAK Film	Process	Remarks
Color prints Color paintings Color halftones illustrations	Color negatives for prints or transparencies	VERICOLOR Internegative 4112, 6011	C–41	Highest potential quality. Requires densitometry for control. Requires careful color balancing.
		VERICOLOR Type L and Type S	C–41	Requires flashing to lower contrast.
Color prints Color paintings Color halftones illustrations	Transparencies and Slides	EKTACHROME and KODACHROME Camera Films	E–6 K–14	May require flashing.
		EKTACHROME Duplicating Film, EKTACHROME Slide Duplicating Films	E–6 E–6	Contrast about right without flashing.
Color Transparencies and Slides	Color negatives for prints	VERICOLOR Internegative 4114, 4112, 6011	C–41	Highest potential quality, requires densitometry.
		VERICOLOR Camera Films		Requires flashing to lower contrast.
Color Transparencies	Duplicates	EKTACHROME Duplicating 6121	E–6	Highest potential quality.

Type of Original	Purpose	KODAK Film	Process	Remarks
Color Slides	Duplicates	EKTACHROME Slide Duplicating, 5071	E–6	For duplicating with tungsten light.
		EKTACHROME SE Duplicating, SO–366		For duplicating with electronic flash.
Color Negatives	Duplicate Color Negatives	EKTACHROME Duplicating Film 6121, EKTACHROME Slide Duplicating Film 5071 or EKTACHROME SE Duplicating Film SO–366	E–6	For duplicating with tungsten light. For duplicating with electronic flash.
Color Negatives	Color Transparencies	VERICOLOR Slide Film 5072 or SO–279, VERICOLOR Print Film 4111	C–41	For printing with tungsten light.
B/W Line Artwork	Reverse Text Slides	VERICOLOR Slide Film 5072 or SO–279	C–41	Use tungsten light and strong colored filters.
Faded Color Prints	Color Negatives for Prints	VERICOLOR Internegative 4112, 6011	C–41	Use special filtering technique.
Faded Color Transparencies	Color Negatives for Transparencies	VERICOLOR Internegative 4112, 6011	C–41	Use special filtering technique.
Colored Maps	Color Micofiche Copying for color Negatives or Transparencies	See page 88 for special information.		

KODAK EKTACHROME Duplicating Film 6121

A laboratory color–reversal sheet film for making duplicate color transparencies and for copying color reflective originals when a lower contrast is desired. It produces color transparencies for direct viewing or for halftone reproduction. Both surfaces are suitable for retouching. Its contrast is lower than that of camera films and is designed to produce duplicates of proper contrast from normal transparencies. An exposure time of 10 seconds is considered normal for this film. Exposure by fluorescent lamps or electronic flash is **not** recommended. Tungsten bulbs, such as normal enlarging bulbs, and tungsten–halogen bulbs are the light–sources for which the film is balanced. An ultraviolet filter such as the KODAK WRATTEN Filter No. 2B should be used over the light source(s). A heat absorbing glass should always be used when an enlarger is used to expose the duplicate. Exact color balance is controlled with color compensating or color printing filters, or with the dichroic filters built into modern color printing enlargers. See page 93 in the text for instructions on making duplicate transparencies. This film can also be used to make duplicate color negatives; see page 105. KODAK E–6 Transparency Dyes are recommended for retouching both original transparencies and duplicate transparencies.

Forms Available: Sheets

Speeds: There is no official film speed for this material because it is primarily exposed by contact or projection. If exposures are being made in a camera, with tungsten illumination, use a starting exposure index of 4. If exposure times are shorter than 10 seconds, use neutral density filters to bring the exposure time to 10 seconds. Meter the transparency with color correcting filters in place.

Emulsion Characteristics: Grain—Extremely Fine

Resolving Power { High Contrast—125 lines/mm (High)
{ Low Contrast — 63 lines/mm

Balance: Tungsten 3000 to 3200 K. Use the filter pack given on the instruction sheet packaged with the film as a starting pack and adjust the pack based on results. See page 93 in the text for details on the use of this film. Refrigerate unused film at 55°F (13°C) or lower to minimize emulsion changes. Warm up to room temperature before opening packaging.

Process: Use Process E–6. For transparencies to be displayed, use KODAK EKTACOLOR Print Film Stabilizer and Replenisher in place of the usual KODAK Stabilizer, Process E–6. However, for transparencies to be stored, the Process E–6 stabilizer provides superior dark storage.

Characteristic Curves

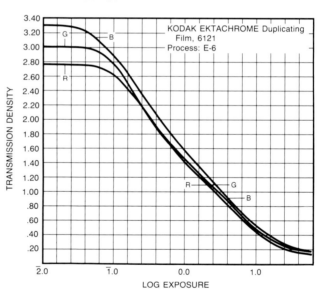

KODAK EKTACHROME 50 Professional Film (Tungsten)
KODAK EKTACHROME 50 Professional Film 5018 (Tungsten)

A slow–to–moderate speed camera color reversal film balanced for tungsten illumination (3200 K). It is balanced for an exposure time of 1/10 second and has an intended exposure range of 1/100 to 1 second. It can be used to copy colored reflection originals primarily for the purpose of making slides for projection, but it can also be used for photomechanical reproduction. It has very fine grain, very high sharpness and high resolving power.

Forms Available: EKTACHROME 50 Professional Film (Tungsten), 5018, 35 mm magazines. EKTACHROME 50 Professional Film 5018 (Tungsten), long rolls. EKTACHROME 50 Professional Film (Tungsten) 6018, 120 rolls.

Film Code Letter Designation: EPY

Speed: The nominal speed at 1/10 second and 3200 K is ISO 50. The instruction sheet in each film package specifies the speed of the film in that package. The comparative speeds with three light sources and appropriate filters are as follows:

Light Source	KODAK WRATTEN Filter	Nominal Speed
Tungsten 3200 K	None	ISO 50/18°
Photolamp 3400 K	81A	ISO 40/17°
Daylight	85B	ISO 32/16°

For blue flash or electronic flash, calculate the guide number on the basis of the daylight speed, and use the 85B filter. Refrigerate at 55°F (13°C) or below to minimize emulsion changes.

The speed and color balance of KODAK Professional color films is designed to be nominal when purchased, and the film should be stored under refrigeration at about 55°F (13°C) or lower, and warmed-up to room temperature before opening.

Emulsion Characteristics: Grain—Very Fine

Resolving Power { High Contrast—125 lines/mm (High)
{ Low Contrast — 50 lines/mm

Sharpness—Very High

Balance: 3200 K (Tungsten) at 1/10 sec exposure time.

Process: Use Process E–6

Characteristic Curves

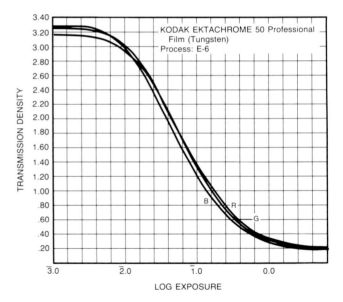

KODAK EKTACHROME 64 Professional Film (Daylight)
KODAK EKTACHROME 64 Professional Film 5017 (Daylight)
KODAK EKTACHROME 64 Professional Film 6117 (Daylight)

These are moderate speed, daylight balance, color reversal films with very fine grain, very high sharpness and high resolving power designed for professional use. They can be used to copy color reflection originals (color prints, paintings, etc.) when color transparencies or slides are needed and when the light source is electronic flash, daylight, blue flashlamps or other daylight balanced sources. These films are designed for professional camera photography of normal subjects, and the contrast may be too high for some originals. See page 79 in the text for a method of flashing to reduce contrast.

Forms Available: EKTACHROME 64 Professional-35 mm magazines, 120 and 220 rolls. 5017—Long Rolls. 6117—Sheets

Film Code Letter Designation: EPR

Speed:

Light Source	KODAK WRATTEN Filter	Nominal Speed
Daylight	None	ISO 64/19°
Photolamp (3400 K)	80B	ISO 20/14°
Tungsten (3200 K)	80A	ISO 16/13°

The specific speeds of each roll of film are printed on the instruction sheet enclosed.

For electronic flash or blue flash, calculate guide numbers on the basis of the daylight speed. The speed and color balance of KODAK Professional films is designed to be nominal when purchased, and the film should be stored under refrigeration at about 55°F (13°C) or lower, and warmed up to room temperature before opening.

Emulsion Characteristics: Grain—Very Fine

Resolving Power { High Contrast—125 lines/mm (High)
Low Contrast— 50 lines/mm

Sharpness—Very High

Balance: Daylight at 1/50 second. Exposure range 1/1000 to 1/10 second. See reciprocity curve for filter and exposure corrections beyond this range.

Process: Use Process E–6

Characteristic Curves

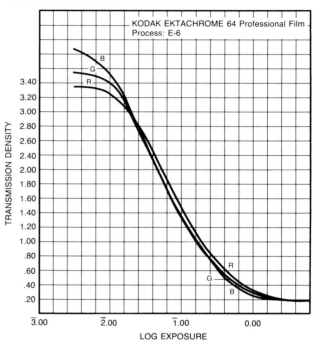

Reciprocity Curve

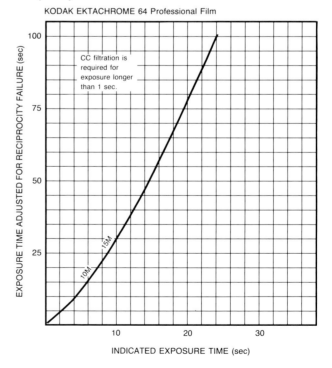

KODAK EKTACHROME 100 Film 5039 (Daylight)
KODAK EKTACHROME 100 Professional Film 6012 (Daylight)
KODAK EKTACHROME 100 Professional Film 6122 (Daylight)

These are moderate speed, daylight balance, color reversal films with very fine grain, very high sharpness, and high resolving power. They can be used to copy color reflection originals (color prints, paintings, etc.) when color slides or transparencies are required, and when the light source is electronic flash, daylight, blue flashlamps, or other daylight-balanced sources. These films have shorter red sensitivity to enable more accurate reproduction of far red reflecting objects. These films are designed for general camera photography of normal subjects, and the contrast may be too high for some copy originals. See page 79 in the text for a method of flashing to reduce contrast.

Forms Available: 5039—35 mm magazines. 6012—120 rolls. 6122—sheets.

Film Code Letter Designation: EN

Speeds:

KODAK WRATTEN Light Source	KODAK WRATTEN Filter	Speed
Daylight	None	ISO 100/21°
Photolamps (3400 K)	80B	ISO 32/16°
Tungsten (3200 K)	80A	ISO 25/15°

The specific speed of each roll of EKTACHROME 100 Professional Film is printed on the instruction sheet enclosed.

For electronic flash or blue flash, calculate guide number on the basis of the daylight speed.

The speed and color balance of KODAK Professional films is designed to be nominal when purchased, and the film should be stored under refrigeration at about 55°F (13°C) or lower, and warmed up to room temperature before opening. Store EKTACHROME 100 Film 5039 in a cool, dry place.

Emulsion Characteristics: Grain—Very Fine

Resolving Power { High Contrast—100 lines/mm (High)
{ Low Contrast — 50 lines/mm

Sharpness—Very High

Balance: Daylight with an intended exposure range of 1/10 second to 1/10,000 second.

Process: Use Process E–6

Reciprocity: Exposure times 1 second and longer are not recommended.

Characteristic Curves

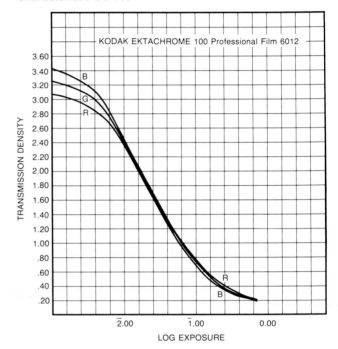

KODAK EKTACHROME 160 Professional Film 5037 (Tungsten)
KODAK EKTACHROME 160 Professional Film 6037 (Tungsten)

A high–speed tungsten balance (3200 K) color reversal film with very fine grain, high sharpness, and high resolving power. It is color balanced for an exposure time of 1/25 second, with an exposure time range of 1/1000 second to 1/10 second. These films can be used to copy reflection originals when color slides or transparencies are required, and when the light source is tungsten or photolamp. Because these films are designed for professional camera photography, the contrast may be too high for some copy originals. See page 79 in the text for a method of flashing to reduce contrast.

Forms Available: 35 mm magazines long rolls (5037)
120 roll film (6037)

Film Code Letter Designation: EPT

Nominal Speeds:

Light Source	KODAK WRATTEN Filter	Nominal Speed
Tungsten (3200 K)	None	160/23°
Photolamp (3400 K)	81A	125/22°
Daylight	85B	100/21°

Use the daylight speed for calculating electronic flash or blue flash guide numbers. Expose with an 85B filter. The speeds of each roll of film are enclosed in the package.

The speed and balance of KODAK Professional films are designed to be nominal at the time of purchase. They should be stored under refrigeration at about 55° (13°C) or lower, to minimize changes, and then warmed up to room temperature before opening.

Emulsion Characteristics: Grain—Very Fine

Resolving Power { High Contrast—125 lines/mm (High)
Low Contrast — 50 lines/mm

Balance: Balanced for tungsten (3200 K) at 1/25 second and have an intended range of 1/10 to 1/1000 second.

Process: Use Process E–6

Characteristic Curves

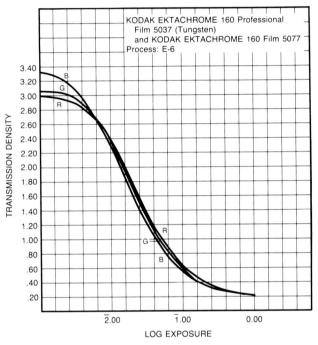

Reciprocity Curve

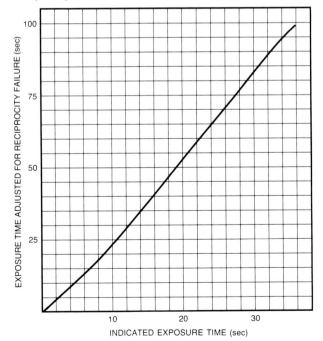

KODAK EKTACHROME 160 Film (Tungsten) 5077

Like the KODAK EKTACHROME 160 Professional Films (Tungsten) this film is a high–speed, tungsten balance (3200 K) color–reversal film with very–fine grain, high sharpness, and high resolving power. It has an intended exposure time range of 1/1000 to 1/10 second; but can be used up to an exposure times of up to 10 seconds with adjustments for reciprocity. KODAK EKTACHROME 160 Film (Tungsten) can be used to copy reflection originals when color slides are required, and when the light source is tungsten or photolamp. Because this film is designed for general camera photography, the contrast may be too high for some copy originals. See page 79 in the text for a method of flashing to reduce contrast.

Available: 35 mm magazines

Film Code Letter Designation: ET

Speeds:

Light Source	KODAK WRATTEN Filter	Speed
Tungsten (3200 K)	None	ISO 160/23°
Photolamp (3400 K)	81A	ISO 125/22°
Daylight	85B	ISO 100/21°

Use the daylight speed for calculating electronic flash or blue flash guide numbers. Expose with an 85B filter. Store in a cool, dry place.

Emulsion Characteristics: Grain—Very Fine

Resolving Power { High Contrast—125 lines/mm (High)
{ Low Contrast — 50 lines/mm

Sharpness—High

Balance: Balanced for tungsten (3200 K). See speed section above for filters to use with other light sources.

Process: Use Process E–6

Characteristic Curves

Same as curve for KODAK EKTACHROME 160 Professional Film.

KODAK EKTACHROME 200 Professional Film (Daylight) 5036
KODAK EKTACHROME 200 Professional Film (Daylight) 6036
KODAK EKTACHROME 200 Professional Film (Daylight) 6176

These are high–speed, daylight balanced, color reversal films with very fine grain, high sharpness, and high resolving power. They are color balanced for exposure at 1/100 second, and have an intended exposure range of 1/1000 to 1/10 second. However, they can be exposed with exposure times as short as 1/50,000 second and as long as 1 second with appropriate exposure adjustment and filtration. They are designed to produce color transparencies and slides for direct viewing, projection, and halftone reproduction. They are especially useful for copying color originals in museums where there is a low level of daylight balance or fluorescent illumination. Because these films are designed for professional camera photography, the contrast may be too high for some originals being copied. See page 79 in the text for a method of flashing to reduce contrast.

Characteristic Curves

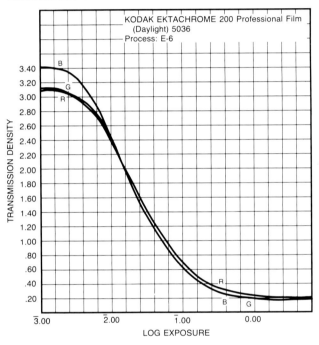

Forms Available: 35 mm and long rolls (5036)
120 and 220 rolls (6036)
Sheets (6176)

Light Source	KODAK WRATTEN Filter	Speed
Daylight	None	ISO 200/24°
Photolamp (3400 K)	80B	ISO 64/19°
Tungsten (3200 K)	80A	ISO 50/18°

Use the daylight speed for calculating guide numbers for electronic flash and blue flashlamps.

The speed and balance of KODAK Professional Color Films are designed to be nominal at the time of purchase. They should be stored under refrigeration at about 55°F (13°C), or lower, to minimize changes, and then warmed up to room temperature before opening.

Emulsion Characteristics: Grain—Very Fine

Resolving Power { High Contrast—125 lines/mm (High)
{ Low Contrast — 50 lines/mm

Sharpness—High

Balance: Daylight (at 1/100 second).

Process: Use Process E–6

KODAK EKTACHROME 200 Film (Daylight) 5076

This is a high–speed, daylight balanced, color reversal film with very fine grain, high sharpness and high resolving power. It is balanced for an exposure time range of 1/1000 to 1/10 second. However, it can be exposed with exposure times as short as 1/10,000 second or as long as 1 second. This film is designed to produce slides for projection and halftone reproduction. Because of its balance and speed, this film is especially useful for copying color originals in museums where there is a low level of daylight or fluorescent illumination. Because this film is designed for general camera photography, the contrast may be too high for some originals being copied. See page 79 in the text for a method of flashing to reduce contrast.

Forms Available: 35 mm magazines and long rolls.

Film Code Letter Designation: ED

Light Source	KODAK WRATTEN Filter	Speed
Daylight	None	ISO 200/24°
Photolamp (3400 K)	80B	ISO 64/19°
Tungsten (3200 K)	80A	ISO 50/18°

Use the daylight speed for calculating guide numbers for electronic flash and blue flashlamps. Store in a cool, dry place.

Emulsion Characteristics: Grain—Very Fine

Resolving Power { High Contrast—125 lines/mm (High)
{ Low Contrast — 50 lines/mm

Sharpness—High

Balance: Daylight

Process: Use Process E–6

Characteristic Curve

Same as curve for EKTACHROME 200 Professional Film.

KODAK EKTACHROME 400 Film (Daylight) 5074, 6074

A very high speed, daylight balanced, color–reversal film with fine grain, high sharpness and medium resolving power. It is balanced for an exposing time range of 1/1000 second to 1/10 second, but can be exposed for exposure times as short as 1/10,000 second or as long as 100 seconds if the appropriate exposure time and filter adjustments are made. (See reciprocity adjustment curves below). This film is designed to produce color transparencies and slides for direct viewing, projection, and halftone reproduction. Because of its balance and speed, this film is especially useful for copying color originals in locations that are dimly lit with daylight or fluorescent illumination. Because this film is designed for general camera photography, its contrast may be too high for some originals being copied. See page 79 in the text for a method of flashing to reduce contrast.

Forms Available: 35 mm magazines (5074) and 120 rolls (6074)

Film Code Letter Designation: EL

Light Source	KODAK WRATTEN Filter	Speed
Daylight	None	ISO 200/24°
Photolamp (3400 K)	80B	ISO 64/19°
Tungsten (3200 K)	80A	ISO 50/18°

Use daylight speed to find guide numbers for electronic flash and blue flashlamps.

Emulsion Characteristics: Grain—Fine

Resolving Power { High Contrast—80 lines/mm (Medium)
{ Low Contrast —50 lines/mm

Sharpness—High

Balance: Daylight

Process: Use Process E–6

Characteristic Curves

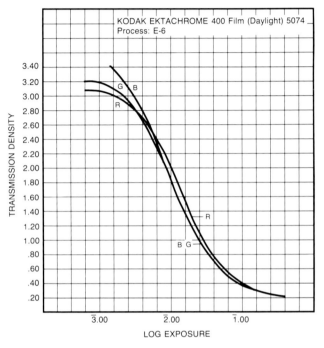

Reciprocity Curves

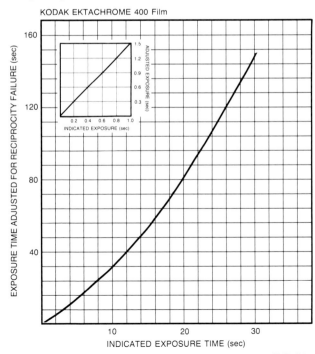

KODAK EKTACHROME Slide Duplicating Film 5071

A color–reversal, tungsten–balanced 35 mm and 46 mm film designed for making duplicate slides from original slides in the laboratory. It is balanced for exposure times of about 1 second. The recommended methods of duplicating are by projection printing with optical printers, contact printing, and duplicating with a camera.

Illuminating the original slide with diffuse light offers the least difficulty with scratches and dust. An ultraviolet absorbing filter such as the KODAK WRATTEN Filter No. 2B should always be used along with the other filters used for color correction. Use of a KODAK Infrared Cutoff Filter No. 304 is recommended when duplicating intermixed types of color slides with the same filtration. Directions for making duplicate slides with this film are given on page 94 in the text.

EKTACHROME Slide Duplicating Film 5071 is also recommended for making copy slides of color reflection originals, especially when the originals are high in contrast. See page 68 in the text.

Forms Available: 35 mm magazines and 46 mm long rolls.

Speed: There is no official film speed for this film, but an exposure index of 12 can be used to find trial starting exposures with an exposure meter when duplicating with a camera. Some meters do not have a 12 setting on the dial, so measure with a speed setting of 25 and give 1 stop more exposure than that indicated by the meter. This speed is based on an exposure time of 1 second, and applies to both tungsten and daylight illumination, filtered as shown below. Shorter exposure times are likely to give yellow highlights. Exposure and filter ring–arounds are recommended for finding proper exposures because the speed and balance can be different, carton to carton.

Emulsion Characteristics: Grain—Extremely Fine

Resolving Power $\begin{cases} \text{High Contrast—125 lines/mm (High)} \\ \text{Low Contrast — 63 lines/mm} \end{cases}$

These apply to the duplicating film only. Duplicate slides will have image characteristics formed by the original slide, the duplicating film, and the duplicating procedure and equipment.

Balance: Tungsten, 3000 to 3200 K. Use the following starting filter packs when using optical printers to duplicate the type of originals shown in the first column.

KODAK Film Originals	Filter Pack (1 sec @ f/5.6 to 11)
EKTACHROME E–6 KODACHROME (K–12) KODACHROME (K–14) (Separately or Intermixed)	KODAK Filter No. 2B + CC 35Y + CC 35C
EKTACHROME (E–4)	KODAK Filter No. 2B + CC 30Y + CC 20Y
EKTACHROME (E–4) intermixed with any of the following EKTACHROME (E–6) KODACHROME (K–12) KODACHROME (K–14)	KODAK Infrared Cutoff Filter No. 304 + KODAK Filter No. 2B + CC 15M + CC 50Y

When using a camera to make duplicate slides, use the following starting filtration. Use a KODAK WRATTEN Filter No. 2B in all situations.

KODAK Film Originals	Light Source		Daylight
	3200°K	5000°K	
EKTACHROME (E–4)	CC 30G + CC 20Y	CC 55Y	CC 10G + CC 45Y
EKTACHROME (E–6) KODACHROME (K–12)	CC 40G + CC 10Y	CC 55Y + 10R	CC 20G + CC 35Y
KODACHROME (K–14)	CC50G	CC 55Y	CC30G + CC 25Y

Refrigerate unused film at 55°F (13°C) or lower to minimize emulsion changes. Warm up to room temperature before opening packaging.

Process: Use Process E–6. Duplicating film can usually be processed along with camera films without adjustment of process.

Characteristic Curves

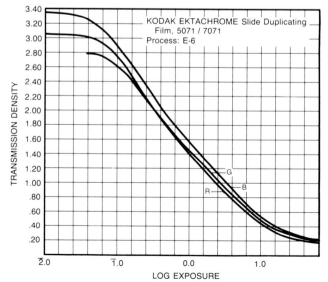

KODAK EKTACHROME SE Duplicating Film (SO–366)

A laboratory color reversal film for making duplicate color transparencies with electronic flash or daylight with exposure times 1/10 second and shorter. The recommended method of duplicating is with a camera or with an optical printer equipped with electronic flash.

Illuminating the original slide with diffuse light offers the least difficulty with scratches and dust. An ultraviolet absorbing filter such as the KODAK WRATTEN Filter No. 2B should always be used along with the other filters used for color correction. Use of a KODAK Infrared Cutoff Filter No. 304 is recommended when duplicating intermixed types of color slides with the same filtration. Directions for making duplicate slides with this film are given on page 94 in the text.

EKTACHROME SE Duplicating Film (SO–366) is also recommended for making copy slides of color reflection originals with electronic flash illumination, especially when the originals are high in contrast. See page 68 in the text.

Forms Available: 35 mm magazines (CAT 159 0223)
35 mm and 46 mm long rolls

Speed: As with the EKTACHROME Slide Duplicating Film 5071, there is no official film speed for this film, but an exposure index of 12 can be used to find starting trial exposures for duplicating and trial guide numbers for electronic flash when this film is used for copying. Exposure and filter ring arounds are almost a necessity for finding proper exposures because of the difficulty measuring electronic flash illumination and because the speed of this film can vary, carton to carton.

Emulsion Characteristic: Grain—Extremely Fine

Resolving Power $\begin{cases} \text{High Contrast—125 lines/mm (High)} \\ \text{Low Contrast— 63 lines/mm} \end{cases}$

These apply to the duplicating film only. Duplicate slides will have image characteristics formed by the original slide, the duplicating film, and the duplicating procedure and equipment.

Balance: Use the following starting filter packs when duplicating the type of originals shown in the first column.

KODAK Film Originals to be Duplicated	SE Film SO–366 Electronic Flash (5600 K)
EKTACHROME E–6 KODACHROME K-12 KODACHROME K–14 (Separately or intermixed)	KODAK WRATTEN Filter 2B + CC 90Y + CC 15 C
EKTACHROME E–4	KODAK WRATTEN Filter 2B + CC 90 + CC 05C
EKTACHROME E–4 intermixed with any of the following: EKTACHROME E–6 KODACHROME K–12 KODACHROME K–14	KODAK WRATTEN Filter KODAK Infrared Cutoff Filter No. 304 + CC 125Y + CC 40M

When using the film to copy color reflection originals, use the following starting filter pack. KODAK WRATTEN Filter 2B + CC 90Y + CC 10C. Run an exposure and filter ring around to find a suitable pack for your conditions. Because of the relatively slow speed of this film with the heavy filtration, relatively large output flash units may be required for larger sized originals. In some cases, the camera can be set on bulb, and several flashes given to obtain adequate exposure.

Refrigerate unused film at 55°F (13°C) or lower to minimize emulsion changes. Warm up to room temperature before opening packaging.

Process: Use Process E–6. Duplicating film can usually be processed along with camera films with no adjustment of process.

Characteristic Curves

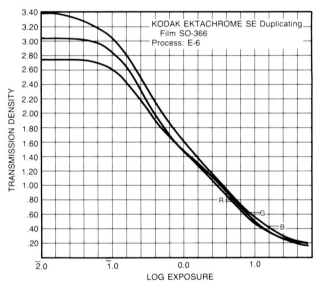

KODAK EKTACHROME Professional Film 6118 (Tungsten)

A slow–to–moderate, tungsten (3200 K) balanced color reversal sheet film with very high sharpness, very fine grain, and high resolving power. It is color balanced for exposures at 5 seconds, with an intended exposure range of 2 to 10 seconds without filtration and 1/10 to 100 seconds with filtration and exposure adjustment. It can also be exposed using photolamps (3400 K) daylight, electronic flash or flash bulbs with suitable filtration.

This film is useful for making color copy transparencies of color reflective originals. They are used for direct viewing with 5000 K illumination and for making halftone reproductions. It may have excessive contrast for copying some originals. The contrast can be lowered by flashing; see page 100 in the text for directions.

Forms Available: Sheets

Speed: The nominal speed at a 5–second exposure time is EI 32. However, being a professional color film, the measured speed for each package of film is given in the instruction sheet included, as well as speeds and color correction for 1/2, 30, and 100 second exposure times.

Example:

Exposure Time	Effective Speed	KODAK WRATTEN Correction Filter
1/2 sec	40	CC05G
30 sec	20	CC05B
100 sec	12	CC10B

With other light sources, the nominal speed and filtration are as follows:

Speeds:

Light Source	KODAK WRATTEN Filter	Speed
Tungsten (3200 K)	None	32 (5 sec exp. time)
Photolamp (3400 K)	81A	25 (5 sec exp. time)
Daylight	85B + CC10G	20 (1/2 sec exp. time)

Speeds given are for meters marked for ISO or ASA speeds.

Balance: Tungsten, 3200 K at 5 second exposure time. See above tables and graph below for use with other light sources and for other exposure times.

The speed and balance of KODAK Professional color films are designed to be nominal at the time of purchase, and they should be stored under refrigeration at about 55°F (13°C) or lower, and warmed up to room temperature before opening.

Emulsion Characteristics:

Resolving Power { High Contrast—125 lines/mm (High)
{ Low Contrast — 50 lines/mm

Sharpness—Very High

Process: Use Process E–6

Characteristic Curves

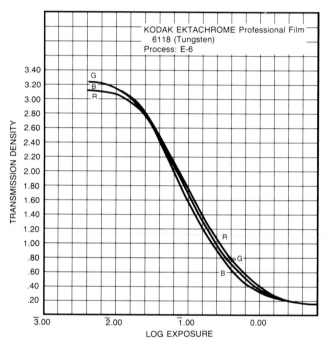

Reciprocity Curves

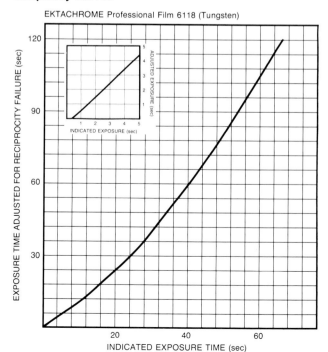

KODACHROME 25 Professional Film (Daylight)

A slow–to–moderate speed, daylight balanced, color slide film with extremely fine grain, extremely high sharpness, and high resolving power. It is balanced for short exposure times of 1/10,000 to 1/10 second, but with adjustment for exposure and appropriate filtration, it can be exposed up to exposure times of 100 seconds.

This is a camera film for general slide photography, it is particularly well suited for making duplicates and copies at a wide range of exposure times. The contrast may be too high for some originals, but can be lowered by flashing. See directions on page 100. This film has excellent dark keeping qualities, and, combined with its grain and sharpness characteristics, makes it a favorite 35-mm general purpose film for making duplicates. Duplicate and copy transparencies are for projection and halftone reproduction.

Form Available: 35 mm magazines

Film Code Letter Designation: KPM

Speeds:

Light Source	KODAK WRATTEN Filter	Speed
Daylight	None	ISO 25/15°
Photolamp (3400 K)	80B	ISO 8/10°
Tungsten (3200 K)	80A	ISO 6/9°

Emulsion Characteristics: Grain—Extremely Fine

Resolving Power { High Contrast—100 lines/mm (High) / Low Contrast — 63 lines/mm

Sharpness—Extremely High

Balance: Daylight. Designed for exposure times 1/1000 to 1/10 second. However, it can be used at exposure times of 1/10,000 second with no correction, and for exposure times as long as 100 seconds with exposure adjustment and proper filtration. See reciprocity curve below. Store in a cool, dry place to minimize emulsion changes.

Process: The K–14 process for KODACHROME films is complex and requires special equipment. KODAK and some other firms are equipped to process KODACHROME film.

Characteristic Curves

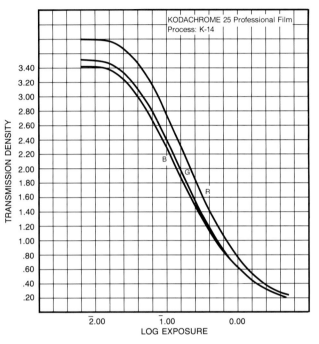

Reciprocity Curves

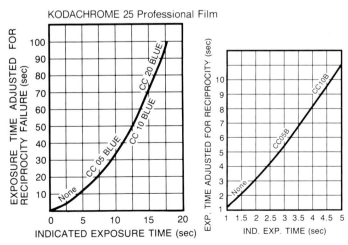

KODACHROME 64 Professional Film (Daylight)

A moderate speed, daylight balanced color slide film with extremely fine grain, extremely high sharpness and high resolving power. It is balanced for exposures of 1/10,000 to 1/10 second, but with adjustment for exposure and appropriate filtration, it can be exposed for exposure times up to 1 second. (See reciprocity curves below).

This is a camera film for general slide photography, but can be used for making duplicate and copy slides with moderate to short exposure times. The contrast may be too high for some originals, but can be lowered by flashing. See directions on page 100. Duplicate and copy transparencies are used primarily for projection and halftone reproduction. Like the other KODACHROME films, this film has excellent dark storage qualities.

Form Available: 35-mm magazines and 126 cartridges.

Film Code Letter Designation: KPR

Speeds:

Light Source	KODAK WRATTEN Filter	Speed
Daylight	None	ISO 64/19°
Photolamp (3400 K)	80B	ISO 20/14°
Tungsten (3200 K)	80A	ISO 16/13°

Emulsion Characteristics: Grain—Extremely Fine

Resolving Power { High Contrast—100 lines/mm (High)
Low Contrast — 63 lines/mm

Sharpness—Extremely High

Balance: Daylight. Designed for exposure time of 1/1000 to 1/10 second, but can be used for exposure times as short as 1/10,000 with no correction, and for exposure times as long as 1 second with exposure adjustment and proper filtration. See reciprocity curve below. Store in a cool, dry place to minimize emulsion changes.

Process: Send exposed film to a laboratory to have the film processed by the K–14 process.

Characteristic Curves

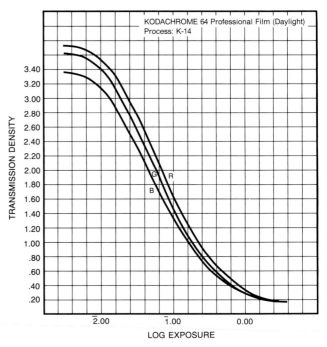

Reciprocity Curve

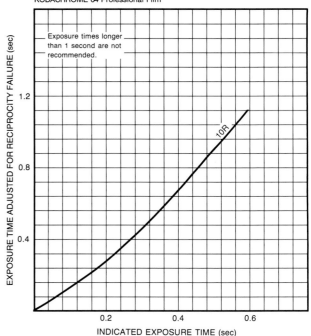

KODACHROME 40 Film 5070 (Type A)

A slow–to–moderate speed color slide film with extremely fine grain, extremely high sharpness, and high resolving power. It is balanced for use with photolamps (3400 K), but with filtration and exposure adjustment, can be used with tungsten lamps (3200 K), flashlamps, electronic flash and daylight. It is balanced for exposure times of 1/1000 to 1/10 second, but can be exposed at times as short as 1/10,000 without adjustment and as long as 5 seconds with proper exposure adjustment and filtration (see reciprocity curves below).

This is a camera film for general photolamp photography, but can be used for making duplicate and copy slides with moderate to short exposure times. The contrast may be too high for some originals, but can be lowered by flashing. See directions on page 100. Duplicate and copy transparencies are used primarily for projection and for halftone reproduction. Like the other KODACHROME films, this film has excellent dark storage qualities.

Form Available: 35 mm magazine

Film Code Letter Designation: KPA

Speeds:

Light Source	KODAK WRATTEN Filter	Speed
Photolamp (3400 K)	None	ISO 40/17°
Tungsten (3200 K)	82A	ISO 32/16°
Daylight	85	ISO 25/15°
Electronic Flash		
Blue Flash		

Emulsion Characteristics: Grain—Extremely Fine

Resolving Power { High Contrast—100 lines/mm (High)
{ Low Contrast— 63 lines/mm

Sharpness—Extremely High

Balance: Type A Photolamp (Photoflood), 3400 K. Designed for exposure times of 1/1000 to 1/10 second can be used for exposure times as short as 1/10,000 second with no correction, and for exposure times as long as 5 seconds with proper exposure adjustment. See reciprocity curve below. Store in a cool dry place to minimize emulsion changes.

Process: Send exposed film to a laboratory to have the film processed by the K–14 process.

Characteristic Curves

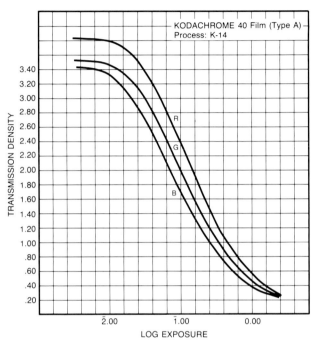

Reciprocity Curves

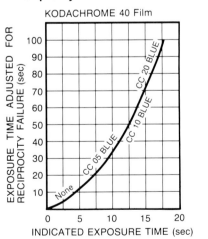

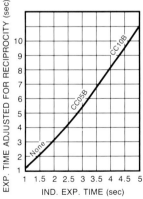

KODACOLOR VR 100 Film

A moderate–speed daylight balanced color negative film with extremely fine grain, very high sharpness, and a high resolving power. It is designed for short exposure times of 1/10,000 to 1/10 second, but can be used with exposure times up to 10 seconds with proper filtration and exposure time adjustment. It can be exposed to other light sources without filtration, but special printing will be required. Proper filtration will result in color negatives with consistent printing balance, thus making printing easier.

This film is designed to produce color negatives to be printed on color papers such as KODAK EKTACOLOR Papers, as well as KODAK VERICOLOR Slide and Print Films (and KODAK DURATRANS Display Films). Color negatives can also be printed on a panchromatic black–and–white paper such as one of the KODAK PANALURE Papers.

This film is designed for general camera photography, but can be used to make copy negatives of color reflection originals, especially when using electronic flash as light sources. Because it is the sharpest, finest grain KODAK color negative film, it is especially useful when copying with small format films such as 35 mm. See page 79 for a method of flashing to lower the contrast of color copy negatives.

Forms Available: 35 mm magazines

Film Code Letter Designation: CP

Speeds:

Light Source	Speed Without Filtration	KODAK WRATTEN Filter	Speed with Filtration
Daylight Electronic Flash	ISO 100/21°	None	ISO 100/21°
Photolamp (3400 K)	ISO 100/21°	80B	ISO 32/16°
Tungsten (3200 K)	ISO 100/21°	80A	ISO 25/15°

These speeds for exposure times 1/10,000 to 1/10 second. See reciprocity curve at right for exposure time adjustments and filtration for longer exposure times. These speeds are for use with meters marked for ISO or ASA speeds.

Balance: Daylight. Balanced for exposure times 1/10,000 to 1/10 second. See table above for filtration and speeds for other light sources, and reciprocity curve at right for exposure time adjustment and filtration for longer exposure times. Store in a cool dry place to minimize emulsion changes.

Emulsion Characteristics: Grain—Extremely Fine

Resolving Power { High Contrast—100 lines/mm (High)
Low Contrast — 50 lines/mm

Sharpness—Very High

Process: Use Process C–41 with KODAK FLEXICOLOR Chemicals.

Characteristic Curves

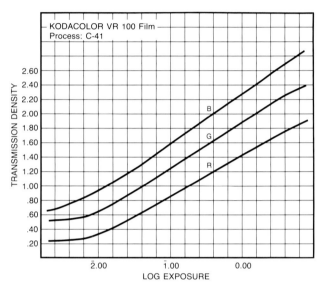

Reciprocity Curve

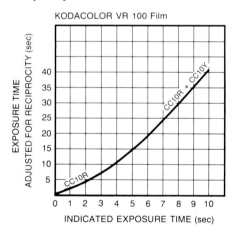

KODACOLOR VR 200 Film

A fast, daylight–balanced color negative film with extremely fine grain, high sharpness, and a high resolving power. It is designed for short exposure times of 1/10,000 to 1/10 second, but can be used with exposure times up to 10 seconds with proper filtration and exposure time adjustment. It can be exposed to other light sources without filtration, but special printing may be required. Proper filtration will result in negatives with consistent printing balance, thus making printing easier.

This film is designed to produce color negatives to be printed on color papers such as KODAK EKTACOLOR Papers, as well as KODAK VERICOLOR Print and Slide Films, and KODAK DURATRANS Display Films. Color negatives can also be printed on a panchromatic black–and–white paper such as one of the KODAK PANALURE Papers.

While designed for general camera photography, this film can be used to make copy negatives of color reflection originals, especially when using electronic flash as a light source. It can be used instead of KODACOLOR VR 100 Film when a higher speed film is needed. See page 79 for a flashing method to reduce the contrast of copy color negatives.

Forms Available: 35 mm magazines

Film Code Letter Designation: CL

Speeds:

Light Source	Speed Without Filtration	KODAK WRATTEN Filter	Speed with Filtration
Daylight } Electronic Flash }	ISO 200/24°	None	ISO 200/24°
Photolamp (3400 K)	ISO 200/24°	80B	ISO 64/19°
Tungsten (3200 K)	ISO 200/24°	80A	ISO 50/18°

These speeds are for exposure times 1/10,000 to 1/10 second. See reciprocity curve below for exposure time adjustments and filtration for longer exposure times. These speeds are for use with meters marked for ISO or ASA speeds.

Balance: Daylight. Balanced for exposure times 1/10,000 to 1/10 second. See table above for filtration and speeds for other light sources, and reciprocity curve at right for exposure time adjustment and filtration for longer exposure times. Store in a cool, dry place to minimize emulsion changes.

Emulsion Characteristics: Grain—Extremely Fine

Resolving Power { High Contrast—100 lines/mm (High) / Low Contrast— 50 lines/mm

Sharpness—High

Process: Use Process C–41 with KODAK FLEXICOLOR Chemicals.

Characteristic Curves

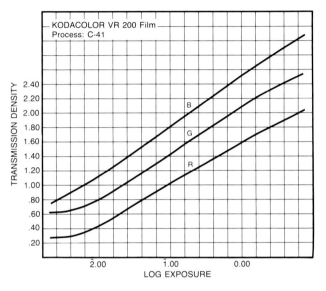

Reciprocity Curve

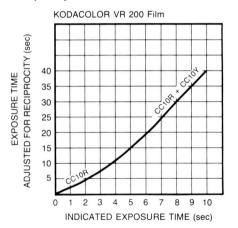

KODACOLOR 400 Film

A high-speed, daylight-balanced film with extremely fine grain, medium sharpness, and medium resolving power. It is designed for a wide range of exposure times of 1/10,000 to 100 seconds. From 1/10,000 second to 1/10 second, no exposure time adjustment is needed; from 1 second to 100 seconds, exposure time adjustment is required. No filtration is needed throughout the exposure time range.

It can be exposed to other light sources without filtration, but special printing will be required. Proper filtration will result in color negatives with consistent printing balance, thus making printing easier.

As with other color negative films, KODACOLOR VR 400 Film produces color negatives that are printed on color papers such as KODAK EKTACOLOR Papers, as well as KODAK VERICOLOR Slide and Print Films, and KODAK DURATRANS Display Film. Color negatives can also be printed on a black–and–white panchromatic paper such as one of the KODAK PANALURE Papers.

This film is designed for general camera photography of dimly illuminated subjects, or at high shutter speeds, but can be used to copy color-reflection originals. Because of its high speed, it should be used as a special-purpose copy film in situations where it is difficult, if not impossible, to use one of the slower KODACOLOR films which are sharper and somewhat finer grained. See page 79 for a flashing method to reduce the contrast of color copy negatives.

Forms Available: 35 mm magazines

Film Code Letter Designation: CM

Speeds:

Light Source	Speed Without Filtration	KODAK WRATTEN Filter	Speed with Filtration
Daylight } Electronic Flash }	ISO 400/27°	None	ISO 400/27°
Photolamp (3400 K)	ISO 400/27°	80B	ISO 125/22°
Tungsten (3200 K)	ISO 400/27°	80A	ISO 100/21°

These speeds are for exposure times 1/10,000 to 1/10 second. See reciprocity curve below for exposure time adjustments for longer exposure times. These speeds are for use with meters marked for ISO or ASA speeds.

Balance: Daylight. Balanced for exposure times of 1/10,000 to 1/10 second. See table above for filtration and speeds for other light sources, and the reciprocity curve below for exposure time adjustment and filtration for longer exposure times. Store in a cool, dry place to minimize emulsion changes.

Emulsion Characteristics: Grain—Extremely Fine

Resolving Power { High Contrast—80 lines/mm (Medium)
{ Low Contrast —40 lines/mm

Sharpness—Medium

Process: Use Process C–41 with KODAK FLEXICOLOR Chemicals.

Characteristic Curves

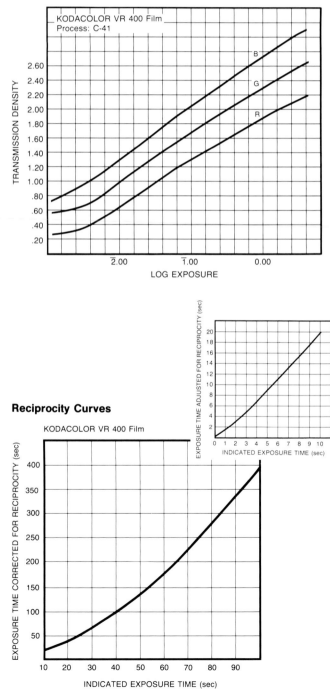

Reciprocity Curves

KODACOLOR VR 1000 Film

An extremely–fast, daylight-balanced, color negative film with very–fine grain, medium sharpness, and medium resolving power. It is designed for general photography of dimly lit subjects (existing–light photography) or for very high shutter speed photography of normally lit subjects (action photography). It should be considered a last resort copy film of colored reflection originals under very adverse lighting conditions.

This film is designed for a wide range of exposure times of 1/10,000 to 1/10 second, but can be used for exposure times up to 100 seconds if appropriate filtration and exposure time adjustment are used.

It can be exposed to other light sources without filtration, but special printing will be required. Proper filtration will result in color negatives with consistent printing balance, thus making printing easier. See page 79 for a method of flashing to reduce contrast for better copy negatives.

Forms Available: 35-mm magazines

Film Code Letter Designation: CF

Speeds:

Light Source	Speed Without Filtration	Kodak Wratten Filter	Speed with Filtration
Daylight } Electronic Flash }	ISO 1000/31°	None	ISO 1000/31°
Photolamp (3400 K)	ISO 1000/31°	80B	ISO 320/26°
Tungsten (3200 K)	ISO 1000/31°	80A	ISO 250/25°

These speeds are for exposure times 1/10,000 to 1/10 second. See reciprocity curve below for exposure time adjustment and filtration for longer exposure times. These speeds are for use with meters marked for ISO or ASA speeds.

Balance: Daylight. Balanced for exposure times of 1/10,000 to 1/10 second. See table above for filtration and speeds for other light sources, and the reciprocity curve at right for exposure time adjustment and filtration for longer exposure times. Store in a cool, dry place to minimize emulsion changes.

Emulsion Characteristic: Grain—Very Fine

Resolving Power { High Contrast—80 lines/mm (Medium)
Low Contrast —40 lines/mm

Sharpness—Medium

Process: Use Process C–41 with Kodak Flexicolor Chemicals.

Characteristic Curves

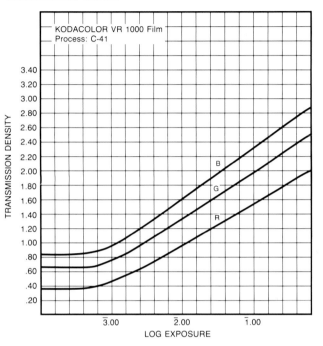

Reciprocity Curves

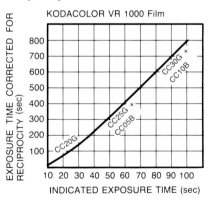

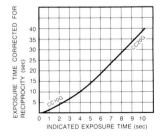

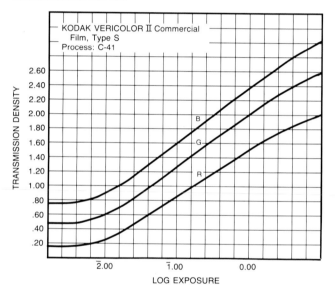

(old notch)   **(new notch)**

KODAK VERICOLOR II Commercial Film, Type S

A moderately-fast daylight-balanced, color-negative film with extremely fine grain, and high resolving power. It is designed for short exposure times of 1/10,000 to 1/10 second, and is not recommended for longer exposure times. It has slightly higher contrast and greater color saturation than many other color negative films. It can be exposed with other light sources without filtration, but special printing may be required. Proper filtration will result in color negatives with consistent color balance, thus making printing easier.

This film is designed to produce color negatives that are commonly printed on color papers such as KODAK EKTACOLOR Papers. They can also be printed on KODAK VERICOLOR Slide Film to make slides, and VERICOLOR Print Film to make color transparencies. Display transparencies can be made by printing color negatives on KODAK DURATRANS Display Film. Black–and–white prints can be made by printing color negatives on a panchromatic paper such as one of the KODAK PANALURE Papers.

VERICOLOR II Commercial Film can be used as a copy film when the reflection originals are low in contrast and when both color and contrast are to be enhanced by the copying procedure. For a method of flashing to reduce the contrast of copy negatives, see page 79.

Forms Available: 35-mm magazines, and 120 rolls. 4x5 and 8x10–inch sheets are available on special order (SO 472).

Film Code Letter Designation: VCS

Speeds:

Light Source	Speed Without Filtration	KODAK WRATTEN Filter	Speed with Filtration
Daylight } Electronic Flash }	ISO 100/21°	None	ISO 100/21°
Photolamp (3400 K)	ISO 100/21°	80B	ISO 32/16°
Tungsten (3200 K)	ISO 100/21°	80A	ISO 25/15°

These speeds are for shutter speeds of 1/10,000 to 1/10 second. Longer exposure times are not recommended. The speeds are for meters marked for ISO or ASA speeds.

Balance: Daylight. See table above for filtration when other sources are used. Store in a refrigerator at 55°F (13°C) or lower to minimize emulsion changes. Allow to warm up to room temperature before opening packaging.

Emulsion Characteristic: Grain—Extremely Fine

Resolving Power { High Contrast—100 lines/mm (High)
{ Low Contrast — 50 lines/mm

Process: Use Process C–41 with KODAK FLEXICOLOR Chemicals.

Characteristic Curves

DS-48

KODAK VERICOLOR Internegative Film 4114, Type 2 (ESTAR Thick Base)

This new laboratory–use film is designed for making color internegatives from color transparencies. (KODAK Internegative Films 4112 and 6011 are recommended for making reflection color copy negatives). It is balanced for 3200 K illumination with appropriate CC filtration.

Color masking in this film controls color rendition printing characteristics, while the special characteristic curve shape gives high quality tone reproduction in copy prints made from the internegatives. Contrast (density range) control is by exposure. Increased exposure results in greater density ranges, while decreased exposure results in decreased density ranges.

Detailed instructions for the use of this film are given in the text on page 110.

Color internegatives made using this film are used to make color prints on KODAK EKTACOLOR Papers, color slides on KODAK VERICOLOR Slide Film, color transparencies on KODAK VERICOLOR Print Film, display transparencies on KODAK DURATRANS Display Film, and black–and–white prints on panchromatic papers such as the various KODAK PANALURE Papers.

Form Available: Sheets

Speed: No ISO speed is given for this film because of its strictly laboratory use. The directions in the text give a method of finding starting exposures.

Balance: 3200 K. However, it is generally necessary to use color compensating filters to get an exact balance.

Emulsion Characteristic: Grain—Micro Fine

Resolving Power $\begin{cases} \text{High Contrast—100 lines/mm (High)} \\ \text{Low Contrast — 50 lines/mm} \end{cases}$

These values are for the film only. Internegatives will have the combined characteristics of the original transparency and the internegative film.

Process: Use Process C–41 with KODAK FLEXICOLOR Chemicals.

Characteristic Curves

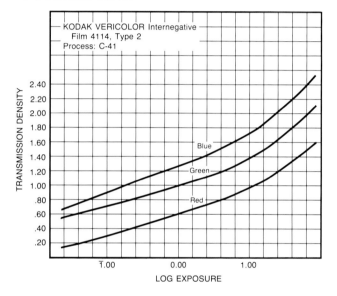

(old notch)   **(new notch)**

KODAK VERICOLOR Internegative Film 4112 (ESTAR Thick Base)
KODAK VERICOLOR Internegative Film 6011

These special laboratory–use films are designed primarily for making color copy negatives from color reflection originals such as color prints. They can also be used to make color internegatives from color transparencies. They are balanced for tungsten light (3200 K) at exposure times from 1/10 to 30 seconds. They provide color corrections by color masking, and tone–scale corrections by their special characteristic curve shape.

Contrast (density range) control is by exposure. Increased exposure gives increased density range, while decreased exposure gives decreased density range.

Detailed instructions for the use of this film are given in the text, starting on page 70.

Color copy negatives or internegatives made using these films are used to make color prints on color papers such as KODAK EKTACOLOR Papers. Color slides are made by printing color negatives on KODAK VERICOLOR Slide Film, while color transparencies are made with KODAK VERICOLOR Print Film. Black–and–white prints can be made by printing color negatives on a panchromatic paper such as one of the KODAK PANALURE Papers.

Forms Available: Sheets (4112)
Long Rolls (6011)

Speed: No ISO speed is given for these films because of their laboratory use. The directions in the text give a method of finding starting exposures; see p. 112.

Balance: Tungsten at 3200 K. However, it is generally necessary to use color compensating filters to get an exact balance. See the text on the use of these films.

Emulsion Characteristics: Grain—Micro Fine

Resolving Power { High Contrast—200 lines/mm (Very High)
{ Low Contrast — 50 lines/mm

Process: Use Process C–41 with KODAK FLEXICOLOR Chemicals.

Characteristic Curves

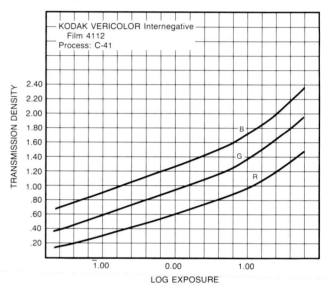

Reciprocity Curve

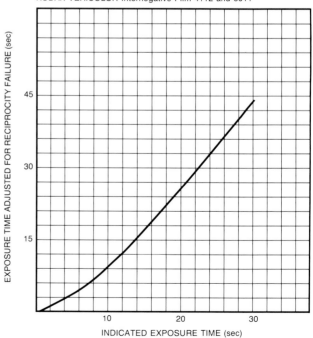

KODAK VERICOLOR Internegative Film 4112 and 6011

(old notch)   **(new notch)**

KODAK VERICOLOR II Professional Film 4108, Type L
KODAK VERICOLOR II Professional Film 6013, Type L

A moderately–fast, tungsten balanced color negative film with extremely fine grain and medium resolving power. It is designed for long exposure times of 1/50 second to 60 seconds. Exposure times shorter than 1/50 second may result in contrast differences in the color emulsion layers that prevent good color balance in printing. It is primarily designed as a studio film to be exposed with incandescent illumination.

The color negatives produced by this film can be used to make color prints using KODAK EKTACOLOR Papers, color transparencies using KODAK VERICOLOR Print Film, and display transparencies using KODAK DURATRANS Display Film. Black–and–white prints can be made from color negatives by using a panchromatic paper such as one of the KODAK PANALURE Papers.

The KODAK VERICOLOR Professional Films, Type L, can be used to copy colored reflective originals with copy set–ups using incandescent light. The contrast is likely to be too high for most reflection originals, but can be lowered by flashing. A flash exposure of a white card with the same f–number and exposure time as the main exposure but with a neutral density filtration of 1.2 is a good place to start. For calculating the main exposure, use a film speed of 50 to obtain better shadow contrast.

Forms Available: Sheets (4108), 120 roll film (6013)

Film Code Letter Designation: VPL

Speeds:

Light Source	KODAK WRATTEN Filter	Exposure Time	Speed With Filter
Tungsten (3200 K)	None	1/50	ISO 100/21°
Tungsten (3200 K)	None	1/5	ISO 100/21°
Tungsten (3200 K)	None	1	ISO 100/21°
Tungsten (3200 K)	None	5	ISO 64/19°
Tungsten (3200 K)	None	30	ISO 40/17°
Tungsten (3200 K)	None	60	ISO 32/16°
Photolamp (3400 K)	81A	1	ISO 64/19°
Daylight	85B	1/50	ISO 64/19°

These speeds are for meters marked with ASA or ISO speeds.

Balance: Tungsten. See table above for filtration for use with other light sources.

Store in a refrigerator at 55° (13°C) or lower to minimize emulsion changes. Allow to warm–up to room temperature before opening packaging.

Emulsion Characteristic: Grain—Extremely Fine

Resolving Power $\begin{cases} \text{High Contrast—80 lines/mm (Medium)} \\ \text{Low Contrast —40 lines/mm} \end{cases}$

Process: Use Process C-41 with KODAK FLEXICOLOR Chemicals.

Characteristic Curves

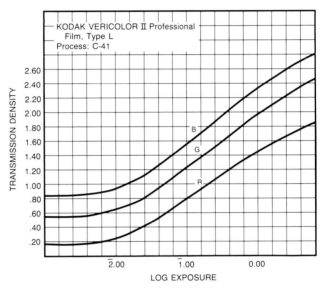

Reciprocity Curves

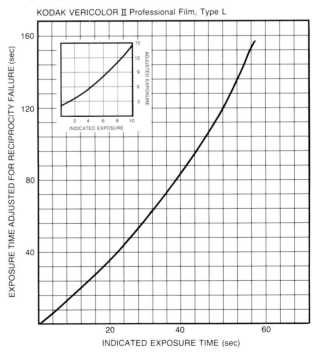

(old notch)   **(new notch)**

KODAK VERICOLOR Ⅲ Professional Film 6006, Type S
KODAK VERICOLOR Ⅲ Professional Film 5026, 2106, 4106, Type S

A fast, daylight-balanced, color negative film with extremely fine grain and high resolving power. It is designed for short exposure times of 1/10,000 to 1/l0 seconds, and is not recommended for longer exposure times. It has somewhat lower contrast and lower color saturation than many other color negative films. It can be exposed to light sources other than daylight without filtration, but special printing may be required. Proper filtration will result in negatives with consistent color balance, thus making printing easier.

This film is designed to produce color negatives that are commonly printed on color papers such as KODAK EKTACOLOR Papers. They can also be printed on KODAK VERICOLOR Slide Film to make slides, and KODAK VERICOLOR Print Film to make color transparencies. Display transparencies can be made by printing color negatives on KODAK DURATRANS Display Film. Black–and–white prints can be made by printing color negatives on a panchromatic paper such as one of the KODAK PANALURE Papers.

VERICOLOR Ⅲ Professional Film can be used as a copy film when the color of the reflection originals is fairly strong and a slight softening of the color is desired in the copy print. If copy negatives are too contrasty, flashing can be used to lower the contrast see page 79.

Forms Available: Sheets (4106)
    35-mm magazines and long rolls (5026)
    Roll Films (6006)
    Long Rolls (5026)

Film Code Letter Designation: VPS

Speeds:

Light Source	Speed Without Filtration	KODAK WRATTEN Filter	Speed with Filtration
Daylight � Electronic Flash ⎭	ISO 160/23°	None	ISO 160/23°
Photolamp (3400 K)	ISO 160/23°	80B	ISO 50/18°
Tungsten (3200 K)	ISO 160/23°	80A	ISO 50/18°

These speeds are for exposure times 1/10,000 to 1/10 second. Longer exposure times are not recommended. The speeds are for meters marked with ISO or ASA speeds.

Balance: Daylight. See table above for filtration with other light sources. Store in a refrigerator at 55°F (13°C) to minimize emulsion changes.

Emulsion Characteristics: Grain—Extremely Fine

Resolving Power ⎰ High Contrast—100 lines/mm (High)
                   ⎱ Low Contrast — 40 lines/mm

Process: Use Process C–41 with KODAK FLEXICOLOR Chemicals.

Characteristic Curves

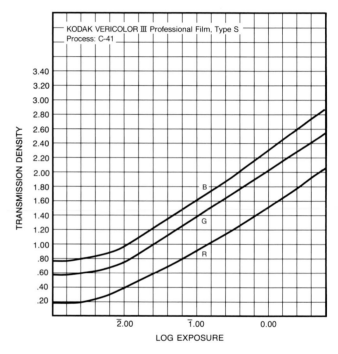

Index

Dept. 412-L
Eastman Kodak Company, 343 State Street,
Rochester, NY 14650

I have read the description of the curve-plotting method of controlling color internegatives. I find that I need the following checked publication:

☐   E-24S, *Balancing KODAK VERICOLOR Internegatives Films 4112 (ESTAR Thick Base) and 6011.*

☐   E-24T, *Balancing Procedure for KODAK VERICOLOR Internegative Film 4114, Type II.*

Name _____ Date _____

Address _____